Horsing Around

IN NEW JERSEY

THE HORSE LOVER'S GUIDE TO EVERYTHING EQUINE

ARLINE ZATZ

Photographs by the author

RUTGERS UNIVERSITY PRESS

New Brunswick, New Jersey

LIBRARY OF CONGRESS CATALOGING-IN-PUBLICATION DATA

Zatz, Arline, 1937–
   Horsing around in New Jersey : the horse lover's guide to everything equine /
Arline Zatz.
     p. cm.
   Includes bibliographical references and index.
   ISBN 0-8135-3334-1 (pbk. : alk. paper)
   1. Horsemanship—New Jersey. 2. Horsemanship—New Jersey—Safety
measures. 3. Horses—New Jersey. I. Title.
   SF309.Z28 2003
   798.2'09749—dc21

                    2003005942

British Cataloging-in-Publication information is available from the British Library.

Manufactured in the United States of America

This book is dedicated to all those
who love, value, and respect horses.

Contents

> *No animal has so inspired the creative*
> *instincts of man as the horse. No creature*
> *has been more praised and honored on*
> *canvas than the gallant, courageous,*
> *and beautiful animal—the horse.*
>
> Michael Seth-Smith

Preface

As a child growing up in Brooklyn, I didn't own a horse, but I was lucky. Nearly every day, my father would take me to a nearby stable. I was four years old the first time I saw a horse munching hay and flicking its tail, and it was love at first sight.

I still have fond memories of a horse-drawn wagon filled with vegetables parked on our corner each day. While the driver sold his produce, I fed carrots to his horse. What a thrill it was to hear the huge animal whinny as I approached.

As I grew older, my love for horses grew stronger. Rarely would I miss an opportunity to watch motion pictures starring Roy Rogers atop his handsome palomino, Trigger, or Gene Autry singing "Back in the Saddle Again" as he and his horse rode along a trail. Many enjoyable hours of my childhood were spent reading classic horse stories, such as *Black Beauty*, *National Velvet*, and *The Black Stallion*. Amazed at the great myths about horses—from the winged flying horse, Pegasus, to the half-man, half-horse Centaur in ancient Greece—I'd also thrill to tales of King Arthur and his knights, clothed in armor, riding on huge, powerful horses that were also draped with armor covering their necks and heads.

Through the years, watching and riding horses have brought me much joy. Whether you're a novice or an expert rider, or just love admiring these fascinating, graceful creatures, I can guarantee they'll bring joy to you, too.

Acknowledgments

An author writes the words, but many people play key roles in the completion of a book. My sincere thanks go to the individuals who welcomed me into their homes and barns, and took time out from their busy schedules to offer valuable information. All of you enriched this project immeasurably, including the following horse lovers, in alphabetical order:

Sue Adams, Atlantic Riding Center for the Handicapped; Janet Agresti, Readington Trail Association; Thomas Edward Allen, D.V.M.; Brian and Candace Bourne, National Trials Symposium speakers; Glen Cademartori, Meadowlands Racetrack; Kathy Cafasso, Sussex County Farm and Horse Show; Cynthia Coritz, superintendent, Bass River State Forest; Susan Data-Samtak, Paso Fino information; Craig P. Della Penna, Rails-to-Trails Conservancy; Dave Demerol, ranger, Sourland Mountain Preserve; Janice Elsishans, trails representative, New Jersey Horse Council; Janice Gray, Equestrian AIDS Foundation; Tricia Haertlein, Hunterdon County Horse and Pony Association; Susan Hammel, Cowtown Rodeo; John Hansen, naturalist, Estell Manor Park; Nancy Harding, Tennessee Walking Horse Association; Carol A. Hodes, Meadowlands Racetrack; Lucia Stout Huebner, Pony Club mother; Barbara Isaac, Riding High Farm; Pam Johnson, Lockatong Creek Adult Pony Club; Bill Knauf, Monmouth Park Racetrack; Joseph Kolicko, ranger, Wawayanda State Park; Nanci Lambert, Mercer County Equestrian Center; Vincent Lavanga, national Pony Club; Joe Lenzar, Eagle Rock Reservation; Lucia M. Malato, *Hudson Reporter*; Nancy Milne, New Jersey Trail Riders Association; Donald Mulligan, fire museum historian; Deb and Tom Parks, Desperado Farms; Joy E. Pasquariello, Bureau of Land Management; Irene Preston, Tewksbury Trail Association; Sergeant Mike Puccetti, Morristown Mounted Police; B. Reinhart, Hudson Riding Club; Steve Schwartz, Meadowlands Racetrack; JoAnna Mendl Shaw, choreographer, *Dancing with Horses*; Sara Short, U.S. Trotting Association; Samuel M. Siler, Tennessee Walking Horse Association; Charles Smith, farrier; Mary Stabile, Wild West City; Lee Treacy, Sweetbriar Farm; Liz Turrin, trail tips; U.S. Equestrian Team headquarters personnel, Gladstone; Sandy Rothschild Wolff, trails chapter checker.

Special thanks go to Dr. Karyn Malinowski and Dr. Sarah Ralston of the Rutgers University Equine Science Center, Margie Margentino, equine program associate for the New Jersey 4-H, and Janet McMillan, trails coordinator for the Morris County Park Commission, for their helpful information; to my writer friends Dr. Stevanne Auerbach, Stephanie Golden, Dr. Tina Tessina, and Betty Wiest for their words of encouragement; to Denise Mikics, one of the best editors I've ever had the pleasure of working with, who offered valuable tips, encouragement, and friendship; to Janet Savin and Maryann Simon for their company on scouting expeditions; to Darlene Jedrusiak for fun conversations and super advice; to Virginia Edwards and Lila Garfield for their faith in me; and to Dr. Lee Oliver-Smith, who encouraged me to write my first book.

Huge thanks, big hugs, and lots of love to my husband, Dr. Joel L. Zatz, for checking directions, making the trail map and horse diagram, supplying valuable computer help, offering loads of encouragement, and always being there for me on days when I needed extra comfort and love. Thanks, too, to my sons, Dr. David A. Zatz and Dr. Robert J. Zatz, for contributing interesting comments and encouragement; to Stacey Butt, for her eagerness to receive one of the first copies of this book; and to her brother, Christopher Butt, who, I hope, will eventually become as curious about horses as she is.

Special thanks to my granddaughter, Zoe Zatz—her love of horses and her drawings truly inspired me—and to my grandson, Benjamin Zatz, who I'm certain will allow me the pleasure of accompanying him on his first carousel or pony ride!

Lastly, many thanks to the Rutgers University Press team for assistance in producing this book.

Horsing Around in New Jersey

*Maryann Simon admiring one of the newborn miniature horses
at the Sweetbriar Hill Miniature Horse Farm.*

> *How the horse dominated the mind of the early races, especially of the Mediterranean! You were a lord if you had a horse. Far back, far back in our dark soul the horse prances. . . . The horse, the horse! The symbol of surging potency and power of movement, of action, in man.*
>
> Apocalypse

Introduction

Although I have been fascinated with horses since childhood, I learned many new facts while doing research for this book. I was amazed at what a vital part the horse has played in New Jersey, from colonial times to the present day.

DID YOU KNOW THAT . . .

- There are more horses in New Jersey per square acre than in Texas or Kentucky?
- New Jersey's state seal, designed in 1777, has a horse's head above the shield?
- There are numerous paintings of General George Washington atop his steed while he and his troops launched a surprise raid in Trenton; at his victory several days later over the British at Princeton; at the Battle of Monmouth; and when he set up winter headquarters in Morristown during the frigid winter of 1779?
- Tempe Wick, the nine-year-old daughter of a wealthy farmer in Morristown, protected her horse from Continental soldiers by hiding it in her house for three weeks?
- The first practical fire engine in the state was horse-drawn?
- It was in New Jersey that horses hauled ore on the first wagon road in America?
- Monmouth County is one of the top areas in the nation for breeding and training Thoroughbreds and Standardbreds?

- Cowtown Rodeo in Sharptown is one of the oldest rodeos on the East Coast?

- The annual Preakness Race, the second leg of Thoroughbred racing's Triple Crown, is named in honor of Preakness, a horse that was born in Kentucky but sold to a New Jersey resident who raised him on a farm in the town of Preakness?

- The one-hundred-foot-tall Christmas tree that stood in Rockefeller Center in 1999 was transported to New Jersey, where its trunk was cut into several pieces that are now used by the U.S. Equestrian Team in Bedminster as obstacles along the cross-country course?

THE HORSE, AN EXTRAORDINARY ANIMAL

While gathering these and other fun facts (see chapter 2), I understood why this extraordinary animal was adopted as the state's official animal in 1977, and why in 2000 Governor Christie Whitman proclaimed June as the Month of the Horse. New Jersey, even though it is the most densely populated state, boasts more horses per person than any other state. In 1996 (the most recent survey), the New Jersey Department of Agriculture found that approximately 49,000 horses, representing sixty breeds, lived on 81,000 acres devoted to equine operations. In fact, horses represent the largest livestock-based segment of the state's agricultural industry, with 7,100 equine facilities statewide. The breeding stock alone is valued at $168 million. Furthermore, equine owners and operators contribute more than $672 million annually to the state's economy.

This economic effect is felt in all corners of the state—from the farmers who grow feed to the 6 million and more people who enjoy equine racing, competitions, and entertainment. The equine industry employs over 6,000 people in a myriad of horse-related careers, not including the veterinarians, farriers, jockeys, farmers, trainers, and thousands of others employed in related service industries. Dozens of opportunities exist in New Jersey for equine-related careers (see chapter 12).

Equally important, the horse industry has helped to preserve farmland and open space, which contribute greatly to the state's air quality, scenic beauty, and wildlife habitat. If not for the horse industry, these precious acres would have become blacktop and strip malls. We derive great benefit from horses, whether it is exercise, companionship, entertainment, or the pleasure of admiring them from a distance.

*Equestrians can purchase a variety
of attractive horse-related signs.*

New Jersey's residents are fortunate, for the state actively promotes the enjoyment of horses and responsible horse ownership. For example, the not-for-profit Horse Park of New Jersey at Stone Tavern (see chapter 8), which operates under contract with the state Department of Agriculture, offers a wide range of educational, competitive, and recreational activities. When you visit the lush 147-acre grounds, consider Trustee Barbara Isaac's comment: "One acre of ground will filter toxins out of the water equal to several million gallons a year. That's the reason it's so important to have open space, because all the water, when it falls onto the park's ground, goes into the aquifer and then becomes a renewable resource."

New Jersey offers a multitude of opportunities for anyone who has a love of horses. County equine facilities present numerous educational and recreational activities, while the County Cooperative Extension Service 4-H program provides youngsters with riding instruction as well as fun nonriding challenges. Each summer, the New Jersey Museum of Agriculture invites children to Horseplay Camp, where they can discover the magic of horses while gaining practical experience by grooming and caring for their four-legged friends. New Jersey's state and county parks deserve thanks, too, for they continue to open and maintain dozens of trails for equestrians. Persons interested in riding lessons have a plethora of choices, including Lord Stirling Stables in Basking Ridge; EquiShare U.S.A. for adult riding lessons and its subsidiary, PonyShare, which caters to youngsters; and the North Jersey Equestrian Center in Pompton Plains—one of the largest riding centers in the state. (See more listings in chapter 3.)

Young and old alike can travel back in time at Howell Living History Farm or Historic Longstreet Farm, where, on special occasions, visitors are welcome to help drive a team of horses, plow a furrow with a walking plow, or enjoy a horse-drawn carriage or wagon ride.

New Jerseyans can rightfully boast that horses bred here are among the top competitors in the nation and the world. New Jersey is home to the headquarters of the U.S. Equestrian Team and to famous racetracks. Moreover, the state has some of the most advanced horse care facilities in the Northeast. Horses throughout the nation benefit from the research conducted at Rutgers, the State University and its Equine Science Center. To support the equine industry and to ensure that livestock will remain healthy, the New Jersey Department of Agriculture administers numerous disease control programs, is a leader in West Nile Virus research, and administers Breeder Reward Programs (see chapter 2).

WHAT YOU WILL LEARN FROM THIS BOOK

This book was written for anyone who loves horses—for the novice who yearns to go horseback riding, but doesn't know how or where to begin, for the experienced equestrian seeking new trails and campsites, for anyone wishing to attend an equestrian event, and for those seeking employment in the equestrian field.

Within these chapters, besides the fun facts and history of the horse, you'll learn which breeds are common in New Jersey, and how to take advantage of the state's breed incentive programs. Prospective riders can find out where to take lessons and how to judge an instructor; the proper attire and tack for safety and comfort; where to rent a horse; how to prepare for riding; and the locations of accredited therapeutic riding programs. How to be safe in the saddle and around horses is discussed, along with first aid and other tips. If you wish to ride along one of New Jersey's great equestrian trails, you'll find information on dozens of trails, how to get to each one, where to obtain necessary riding permits, and the rules and regulations that may apply.

New horse owners will find information on wise horse housing, stable management, health concerns, and disaster planning, plus ideas for adopting a horse or finding a home for one when you can no longer care for it. For those who love to play sports on horseback—or merely watch—chapter 9 is the ticket. If you just want to sit back and enjoy the vast variety of equine entertainment available in New Jersey, turn to chapter 8. To learn more about sources for equipment, recommended books, and useful websites and contacts, check the appendixes.

Be forewarned: Watching horses at work and at play can be habit forming. If you decide to take riding lessons, you may be hooked on horses forever—for once you experience nature from atop your horse, everyday stresses seem to disappear and a feeling of tremendous relaxation and joy take over.

Enjoy!

1

Through all our history, to the last,
In the hour of darkness and peril and need,
The people will waken and listen to hear
The hurrying hoof-beats of that steed,
And the midnight message of Paul Revere.

Henry Wadsworth Longfellow

History of the Horse

Where would we be if not for the noble horse? For centuries, this graceful animal has served humans in battle, plowed fields, carried goods, made travel and mail delivery possible, pulled wagons of coal out of mines, played a part in recreation and entertainment, rushed fire wagons to the rescue, and much more. Today, horses are kept as pets, ridden on trails, entered in equine sports, enjoyed during parades, and, on special occasions, employed to pull sleighs and carriages. Yet horses are also vital to the mounted police, help the disabled gain strength and confidence through therapeutic riding programs, and, above all, are simply fun to watch.

The horse has proven its value through the centuries. If not for their loyal mounts, what would Napoleon, George Washington, and Robert E. Lee have accomplished? Could Paul Revere have spread his cry of alarm through every village without his trusty steed carrying him with the utmost speed through the night? Would Roy Rogers have been as popular if not for Trigger, his beautiful palomino? Why, when automobiles can take us anywhere we want to go, and trains, planes, and trucks can deliver our supplies, is the horse still very much part of our lives? These thoughts compelled me to find out more about the origin of the horse and led to my writing this book.

ANCESTORS OF THE HORSE

From fossils found in North America, scientists believe that today's horse descended from *Eohippus*, also known as the dawn horse. Eohippus roamed the earth approximately 54 million years ago—long before humans came on the scene. Thought to have been no larger than a hare or small bear cub, with short legs and four padded toes on its front feet and three padded toes on its hind feet, it slowly made its way through swamplike forests while eating foliage. As the earth gradually changed, so did Eohippus.

Thirty-eight million years ago, this forerunner to the modern-day horse had grown to 6 hands high (4 inches to a hand), with longer legs and larger eyes that were wider apart. Referred to as *Mesohippus*, or the middle horse, it had one less toe on each foot. Its appearance changed again about 25 million years ago, when *Merychippus* stood even taller on longer legs that enabled it to outrun predators that stalked it on the open plains where it lived and grazed on thick grasses. Its weight-bearing hooves had lost another toe on each side, and flat molars allowed it to grind its food. When *Pliohippus* appeared 10 to 5 million years ago, it stood 12 hands high. Its distinguishing features included single-toed hooves, longer legs, larger teeth, a longer jaw, and eyes set farther apart.

Equus, the last major stage in the evolution of the horse approximately 1 million years ago, was capable of great speeds, had a large single toe that developed into a strong hoof, and is believed to be the forerunner of the modern horse, the donkey, and the zebra. Depending on where they lived, various types and sizes of horse are thought to have developed.

A FOOD SOURCE PROVES VALUABLE

Until about 20,000 years ago, early humans hunted horses as a source of food. When they discovered that the horse could be domesticated, they put its strength to work for transportation and other tasks. Although the archaeological record does not reveal when this transformation in the human-horse relationship occurred, it's quite possible that the nomadic tribes of central Asia were the first to domesticate horses more than 6,000 years ago. At that time, horses were about the size of small ponies, but selective breeding helped to increase this animal's size and strength.

Whether for work, recreation, or war, humans have always admired this wonderful animal. Ancient stone carvings dating to 2637 B.C.E. depict horses used to pull heavy loads; scrolls and tomb paintings from ancient Egypt show spirited horses pulling the pharaoh's chariot; and clay tablets tell us that by 1500 B.C.E. the Hittites had become great horsemen. Xenophon, a Greek general, authored a book on horse management and training as far back as the fourth century B.C.E.. During medieval times, knights depended on their mighty horses for battle, adorning both themselves and their steeds with armor.

When the Spanish conquistadors invaded Mexico in the early 1500s, their horses terrified the Indians, who had never seen these four-legged creatures before. However, it didn't take the Indians long to adopt strays and learn to ride bareback. In time, the western plains were filled with herds of wild horses roaming free. American history is filled with stories of brave horses that served their riders during intense battles, including Lexington, who died during the Battle of Monmouth in 1778, while bearing General George Washington, and Traveler King, who carried Robert E. Lee throughout the Civil War.

Early pioneers in America depended on horses for survival, transportation, and hunting. Throughout the West, they were used for herding cattle, while Pony Express riders were counted on to deliver messages from afar on lively mounts. Not too long ago, as in other states, New Jersey's travelers were carried long distances in horse-drawn stagecoaches, resting at various taverns along the way to their destinations. Interestingly, while travelers were welcome to sleep inside the tavern—and often forced to share one bed with three or four other people—the driver, thought to be covered with fleas, was forced to sleep on the kitchen floor! Thankfully, today's pleasure driver can sleep wherever he/she pleases.

Clearly, the horse has contributed immensely to our nation, and it continues to have an important role in our economy and our lives. There is no doubt that our love for the horse, and the joy it brings us, will continue forever.

2

*You cannot remain unmoved by
the gentleness and conformation
of a well-bred and well-trained
horse.*

Albert Borgmann

Horses
Across New Jersey

BREEDS COMMON IN NEW JERSEY

The term *breed* describes a group of animals recognized to have certain common characteristics as a result of having been specifically selected and bred for these characteristic over a long period of time. For example, strong, calm horses, known as coldbloods, were necessary to bear knights wearing heavy armor and to transport heavy loads. For battle, however, smaller, faster horses, called warmbloods, were preferred. Today, the warmbloods—originally bred in the Orient—are the most popular choice for riding and competition.

Through the centuries, specialization within these two types has resulted in dozens of horse breeds, ranging from small ponies to huge Clydesdales. Each breed is generally used for a specific purpose—racing, farm work, herding, and more. Horses of a particular breed may all be the same color, such as Cleveland Bays, originally bred to pull carriages in elegant teams. Members of other breeds may show a wide variety of colors and markings. A studbook or registry records the name and parentage of each purebred member of a breed. Additional registry information may refer to any white marks or patterns, called *stockings* on the feet, a *stripe* or *blaze* on the face, and a *star* on the forehead. The horse's height is measured in hands—each hand representing 4 inches, the average width of a man's hand. Of the approximately one hundred breeds found throughout the United States today, about sixty are popular in New Jersey. Below, in alphabetical order, are profiles of a few of them.

Marianne Hopke and her beautiful Appaloosa gelding, Kipper.

Appaloosa

The Appaloosa, easily identified by its spotted coat, short, strong back, and powerful hindquarters, has a rich history. Its origins, as researched by Francis Haines and published in 1937, go back to China, where it was referred to as the "heavenly" horse, and to Persia, where it was known as the "sacred" horse. Haines traced it to Spain, then Mexico and the Pacific Northwest, and finally to the Nez Percé Indian tribe of Washington, Oregon, and Idaho.

In the 1800s, the Nez Percé, as knowledgeable horsemen, bred the best of these horses, traded those that weren't strong, or gave the gentle ones to the elderly to ride. Wide heels made the Appaloosa especially surefooted, capable of galloping over the roughest terrain and charging into a group of buffalo or antelope and singling one out for the kill. When early white settlers discovered these swift animals, they quickly made friends with the Indians and were given a few as gifts. The arrival of missionaries, who encouraged the Indians to cultivate the land, led to new uses for the Appaloosa as a farm horse rather than a hunting horse. Eventually, the Indians referred to this breed as the Palousey, for its grazing land next to the Palouse River.

Conflicts with ever-increasing numbers of white farmers and ranchers over ownership of the land brought the U.S. Army on the scene. An attempt to move the Nez Percé to a reservation in Idaho led to war. Surprisingly, the tribe defeated the army three times in less than two months. However, unable to escape to Canada, the Indians were eventually forced to surrender, and their horses were taken away and sold.

The Appaloosa nearly died out. Haines, however, bred the best of the remaining animals, and he and other dedicated breeders saved these horses from extinction. Today, this very gentle horse, popular in Western events and trail riding, sports several different coat patterns: *leopard*, dark spots on a white background; *snowflake*, dark spots over a white body; *blanket*, light spots on a dark background and dark head; *white blanket*, a dark head with a white blanket over the loin and quarters without spots; *near leopard*, leopard markings at birth that disappear with age; *marble*, a dark under color that fades with age, with varnish-color marks on the face and legs; *few spot*, leopard coloration with odd spots here and there but some roan (blue or red) marks; and *frosted tip*, a dark base coat color with frost or white spots on the loin and quarters. The Appaloosa generally stands 14.2 to 15.2 hands high, often has vertically striped hooves, and bears a sparse mane and tail.

Arabian

The Arabian, the oldest pure breed in the world, is considered by many to be the most beautiful of all horses. Depictions of this fine animal, which is believed to have originated in the Arabian peninsula, can be found in ancient art dating back to 3000–2000 B.C.E. Arabs supposedly found the horses running wild and caught and tamed the foals. When the Prophet Mohammed decided to use them for his military campaigns, he devised a test to reveal the most obedient mares. One hundred thirsty mares were penned within sight and smell of a stream, then turned loose; a moment before they reached the water, a war bugle sounded. The five mares that stopped immediately were chosen for Mohammed. One in particular earned the name Of-the-Cloak. As the story goes, a rider escaping from enemies threw off his cloak. When he arrived in camp, the cloak was fluttering from his horse's arched tail. From that day on, the mare's offspring were also named Of-the-Cloak, and the high-arched tail of the Arabian is one of its chief characteristics.

Life in the harsh desert climate developed a horse of tremendous endurance. Although they are generally no more than 15 hands high,

Valerie Weil and her beautiful Arabian, Jondalar.

Arabians can easily carry a full-grown man. The Arabian has always been the preferred breed of warriors. Desert warriors rode the mares in battle because they traveled at a steady pace and warned their riders of approaching enemies by letting out a loud whinny. George Washington, who was unusually tall, rode Magnolia, a delicate Arabian charger into battle, and Napoleon's stallion, Marengo, carried him on his retreat from Moscow.

The Arabian was so valued that chieftains wisely bred their mares only to the best stallions to ensure the pedigree of the foal. They also inscribed the pedigree information on parchment, put it into a tiny bag, and tied it around the foal's neck with azure beads to ward off evil spirits. They judged their horses first by the characteristics of the head. Color—whether chestnut, bay, black, or gray—did not matter. Above all, however, the skin had to be jet black in order to afford protection against the strong rays of the sun.

Today's Arabians display the same distinctive features that characterized their ancestors—a concave face, small muzzle, flaring nostrils, large eyes, small ears, a tail carried high, and the same blackness under the hair. It still differs from other breeds by having seventeen ribs, compared with eighteen in other horses, five lumber vertebrae versus the usual six, and sixteen tail vertebrae instead of eighteen.

Belgian Draft

The Belgian Draft horse, standing 16.2–17 hands high, is as highly valued today as it was during the Middle Ages. This gentle-natured horse has a smallish head, large, powerful body, and deep barrel chest. Its coat can be red roan with black points, sorrel, chestnut, gray, dun, or bay. Belgians are capable of pulling tremendous loads because their muscular hindquarters are built for propulsion. They were brought to the United States in 1885 and recognized for their ability to accomplish unbelievable pulling feats at the tender age of eighteen months.

Used today for farm chores, exhibitions, and carriage rides, the Belgian was the all-purpose tractor of the pre-automotive age and could be found on working farms well into the mid-twentieth century. Proud farmers often competed with their teams in sled-pulling races. Sleds filled as equally as possible with stones or sacks of sand had to be pulled in a straight line. No matter which team went the farthest, there was always an argument about the winner because it was impossible to determine the sled weight exactly or to take into consideration hidden obstacles in the sled's path. When at last the dynamometer was invented—a machine with iron weights that registers how many pounds a team can pull and measures resistance—there was no longer a problem in declaring the winning team.

Clydesdale

My first sight of a Clydesdale in its stall is unforgettable, for it seemed to dwarf everything and everyone nearby. And no wonder, for this breed stands 16.3–18 hands high! First bred in Scotland, this magnificent horse, named for the Clyde River, developed its strong hooves from years of working in earth moistened by heavy ocean mists. It was crossed with larger, heavier stallions of Dutch and Flemish descent to produce a horse capable of hard work. With its muscular shoulders, back, and hindquarters, the Clydesdale is the perfect horse to pull wagons or help till the land.

This horse is recognizable by its brown or bay coat, a white stripe or blaze on its smallish face, and the white feathering on its legs. Gaining national fame as the mascot of the Anheuser-Busch Company, this breed is still used on farms, for shows, and for deliveries in rural areas.

Donkey

With origins in biblical times, the donkey, also known as a burro, has always been useful to humans. Believed to have carried Abraham on his many journeys and Jacob more than six hundred miles, this small, long-eared, surefooted animal was supposedly Jesus' choice for his long journey into Jerusalem on the first Palm Sunday. So impressed was Jesus with his patient burden bearer that he rewarded it with a dark stripe from mane to tail and a horizontal one at its withers, the symbol of the Cross, for it to carry forever.

Even today, and in all parts of the world, donkeys are used to carry heavy loads, and sometimes riders. Mature burros are capable of bearing loads up to 20 percent of their body weight! They are also kept as pets and used in driving and in exhibitions.

Miniature Horses

Miniature horses stand about 34 inches tall at the withers, weigh 100 to 350 pounds, and have the same habits, characteristics, colors, and proportions as a full-sized horse, except that their manes and tails tend to be longer and thicker. Their hooves are also tougher and require no shoes. At birth, the foals weigh about 15 to 25 pounds, are approximately 12 to 20 inches tall, and can romp energetically in about half an hour. Colors seen almost exclusively in miniature horses are silver, dapple, and perlino.

The origin of miniature horses is unknown, although theories abound. Some people attribute their small size to the misfortunes of a herd of normal-sized horses trapped in a canyon where food was scarce, resulting in smaller than normal-sized foals being born. Other theories describe how European kings and queens of the 1500s kept and bred miniature horses as pets. In the 1700s, these tiny horses were among the stars of traveling circuses, often carrying monkeys on their backs. By the late eighteenth century, these well-mannered, surefooted horses were used in the coal mines of Great Britain because they could easily fit into the narrow shafts and pull carts loaded with coal. Frequently, the miners would enter these endearing animals in country contests. In time, the miniatures became so popular that retired mine animals were adopted as family pets.

Miniatures were brought to the eastern United States in the early 1900s, and a Virginian by the name of Norman Fields put them to work in the Appalachian coal mines. He also began raising his own herd of the smallest ponies. By 1964, he had successfully raised fifty miniatures. At about the same time, realizing that the smallest horses fetched the best prices, Smith McCoy, a native of West Virginia, began raising what he called "midget ponies." After searching throughout the nation for horses under 32 inches tall and breeding the smallest of the stallions and mares, he had gathered the world's largest herd of miniature horses, which he began selling to breeders throughout the country in 1967.

Today, miniature horses are an official registered breed. The American Miniature Horse Association accepts candidates 34 inches and under, while the American Miniature Horse Registry has two classifications for registration: "A" miniatures must measure 34 inches or under; "B" miniatures can be between 34 and 38 inches.

Miniatures, highly valued as pets and companions for adults and children, are excellent for teaching small children how to ride, for they are gentle and capable of bearing up to seventy pounds. They can also be trained to pull children and grown-ups in carts and sleds; aid in therapy for the disabled and for those who suffer from mental illness; compete in halter jumping and driving events; and participate in parades.

Easy to raise, train, and keep for much less expense than a full-sized horse, miniatures seem to have only one drawback: they're irresistible, as several New Jersey equestrians have discovered. My first introduction to miniatures was at Desperado Acres, a 1.2-acre property owned by Deb and Tom Parks. As I pulled into their driveway, I thought I had

*Deb and Tom Parks admire one of their
two miniature horses on their property, Desperado Acres,
in the heart of bustling Cherry Hill.*

arrived at the wrong location—the Parks' lovely home was surrounded by other luxury houses in a neatly groomed, suburban residential neighborhood in Cherry Hill. As I sat in their living room, however, I spotted the miniatures through a huge picture window and realized they had plenty of space in the backyard corral. I also learned that this couple houses their Appaloosa and Quarter horse on the property. Their first miniature, Boomer, was originally purchased to keep the other horses happy—because whenever one was taken for a ride, the other was lonely and upset. Things didn't turn out exactly as planned, and, because the Parks had fallen in love with Boomer, they bought Scott, another miniature, to keep Boomer company. In fact, the Parks own the only four horses on the west side of the New Jersey Turnpike in Cherry Hill!

As I toured the property, I was amazed at how well the four horses got along, how much room they had, and how clean and tidy everything was. Tom filled me in on a secret . . . twice a day, he shovels up approximately eighty pounds of manure. Getting rid of it is never a problem: lots of people consider the free manure "gold" for their gardens.

While Deb and Tom take the "big" guys out daily for long rides, the miniatures are content to romp around in their fenced-in area. Occasionally they treat the neighborhood children to sleigh or cart rides. On any given weekend, it isn't unusual for dozens of families to stop by the Parks' home to feed carrots to the horses. Deb says this is an awesome experience for both children and adults who have never had the pleasure of being so close to a live horse. The Parks have also taught the miniatures to understand short phrases and love being able to see, enjoy, and play with them at any time, even though the horses require twenty-four-hour care. When they arrive home from work, no matter what kind of day it has been, these adorable members of the family are there for them.

Lee Treacy's life changed completely, and for the better, after she bought her first miniature horse. A case of Lyme disease so severe that she had to leave her job also forced her to give up her favorite hobby—riding. Soon after selling her big horses, she realized she had to have horses around her. Spotting a friend's miniature, she fell in love with this breed, immediately bought a colt and older mare, kept them together, and eventually ended up breeding them. It didn't take long for her to buy more, for she discovered that if you love horses, it doesn't matter what size they are. She also liked the pluses of owning miniatures: they don't take a lot of time, she doesn't have to ride them, they eat very little, they live longer, and she can keep eighteen of them for what it costs to keep one Thoroughbred.

Lee should know about that, because her husband, Jack Revell, keeps three Thoroughbred racehorses at Sweetbriar Hill Farm in Jackson. They bought this two-plus-acre property so that he would have room for his Thoroughbreds and Lee could raise her miniatures. Today, people come from all over the country to purchase her registered and champion miniatures.

At the time of my visit, Lee was keeping careful watch over one of the pregnant mares, explaining that miniatures often have trouble giving birth and that human assistance may be needed to pull the amniotic sac off the foal's head. Lee has the perfect solution for keeping careful tabs on a mare near her delivery date. She sets up a camera in the stall and places a television monitor in her bedroom. A transmitter attached to the mare's halter sends a message to Lee's pager when the horse lies down on its side in foaling position. Lee can then check to see whether the mare is sleeping or giving birth.

Like the Parks, Lee loves her miniatures. She points out that children are safe around them, too; even if one should step on a person's foot, it can't do much damage. The heaviest one she's owned, a big stallion, weighed about 350 pounds, whereas the smallest stallion at the farm is only 27 inches tall and weighs 125 pounds. Sweetbriar Hill is thriving, in large part because it's hard to find miniatures smaller than the ones Lee breeds. Best of all, she notes that raising these cute horses is a hobby that's been paying for itself.

Morgan

Known for its great loyalty and strength, this breed was descended from Justin Morgan, a stallion named for its owner. According to the story, a singing master by the name of Justin Morgan traveled from Vermont to Massachusetts in 1795 to collect money a farmer owed him. Instead of cash, Morgan had to accept a big colt and a small one in full payment. Morgan sold the larger colt immediately, but couldn't interest anyone in the smaller dark bay one. Desperate for money, he rented the colt out to pull stumps and drag logs for a nearby farmer. One day, he noticed something strange: this small horse succeeded in pulling a log that draft horses and oxen couldn't budge. He also proved to be a good racehorse. After the singing master died, people began calling this unbelievable work horse Justin Morgan, and the name stuck.

Just like Justin Morgan, his descendants have a round barrel chest, a full neck, and a compact appearance. Generally around 15.2 hands high, with a bay, brown, black, or chestnut coat, the Morgan is a fine horse for riding, driving, and endurance. It is the preferred horse of mounted police, as well as anyone who loves a gentle, intelligent horse.

Mule

Opinions are mixed about this strange animal, whose mother is a horse and whose father is a donkey. Some people think the mule is a stubborn creature; others believe it is smarter than a horse. Actually, the mule is smart enough not to move an inch if too heavy a load is placed on its back; it will refuse water that's not safe to drink, will move unbelievably slowly when the temperature is high, and will rest whenever it gets tired.

We have George Washington to thank for bringing mules to this country. After the Revolutionary War, he heard that the Catalonian donkeys in Spain sired mules that were inexpensive to keep and worked hard. Although the Spanish monarchy strongly forbade the export of donkeys, King Charles III was so honored by a request from Washington that he bent his own rules and sent two of his finest to America as a gift for Washington. One died en route, but the other arrived in good health. Washington announced, "I hope to secure a race of extraordinary goodness which will stock the country. He is indeed a Royal Gift, and henceforward that shall be his name." The mares that were mated to Royal Gift produced strong, tough mules that worked the land as no horse could. Before long, people throughout Virginia were scrambling to purchase these long-eared, odd-looking animals.

Mules, as sterile hybrids, cannot bear young and are bred primarily for hard labor. A few are used for show events and riding—you might be lucky enough to have a surefooted mule take you down the Bright Angel Trail to the bottom of the Grand Canyon. Color depends on the mare used in the crossing, as does height. Miniature mules stand about 9 hands high; others can be as tall as 17 hands.

New Jersey Bred Hunter

A Thoroughbred or half Thoroughbred whose sire or dam is a registered member of one of several breeds, and who was foaled in New Jersey or sired by a stallion residing in New Jersey for the full breeding season, is eligible for the New Jersey Bred Hunter classification.

Although not an official breed, this type of horse was bred to match the conditions of the countryside. The stature and stamina of the Thoroughbred provided the necessary jumping ability, while another breed might be added to the mix for its surefootedness over rough terrain. For these qualities, such horses were used during fox hunts in England, as they are today in New Jersey. The moment the horn is sounded and it's time to "tally-ho," these hunters, carrying their horsemen attired in the traditional scarlet coats, gallop across fields, into ditches, and over fences. A horse chosen as a hunter must be fit enough to keep up with the hounds, as well as give a comfortable ride and possess a calm and fearless temperament.

Paint

Also known as piebald and skewbald, this type of horse has an unusual patterned coat marking, described as either tobiano—dark patches on a white base—or overo—white patches on a dark base. Most popular in Western events, though also seen increasingly in English show rings, the paint was not accepted as a breed until 1962. Now the fastest-growing breed registry in the nation, the American Paint Horse Association requires that qualifying horses must be bred from registered American Paint horses, Thoroughbreds, or American Quarter horses, plus meet a minimum color standard.

Palomino

The palomino—known by its spectacular gold coat, white mane and tail, and hazel, brown, or black eyes—is not actually a breed, but a color. For centuries, it has been admired for its good looks and was especially prized in Spain during the fifteenth and sixteenth centuries. Horses with golden-colored coats have appeared in Asian, Japanese, and European art for ages, and are mentioned in Homer's *Iliad*.

How this golden horse came to America is a matter of speculation. One story tells of Queen Isabella giving several of these beauties to the conquistador Hernando Cortés as a gift to take to the Americas. Cortés then presented one to his friend Juan de Palomino—hence the name for the horse's color. Another theory credits Don Estaban, a cattleman in old California, with owning the first palomino in America during the early 1800s. He had promised to give a prize of silver to the person who could bring him the most beautiful horse in the country. During roundup time, when a layer of dust and mud made it difficult to see the color of the horses' coats, a small boy spotted a bit of gold, caught the golden horse, washed it, and gave it to Estaban. Yet another story tells how two Indians stole a pure white stallion and a buckskin mare from a Spanish hacienda; a year later, the mare escaped and found her way home with a small blond filly.

Regardless of how and when the first palomino arrived in the New World, this horse became legendary thanks to Roy Rogers's famous stallion. Trigger, who appeared in more than eighty-eight movies and over a hundred television shows, was taught to bow, count, nod, and blow kisses. When Trigger died at the age of thirty-three, Rogers remarked, "Trigger was my partner and my pal and part of nearly everything I did. Never did he let me down." He didn't let me down either, for I loved watching this four-legged star perform.

Today, palominos are popular in the show ring, parades, and in all horse sports. So far, there is no sure way of breeding a palomino; mating a palomino to a palomino will produce a golden foal only 50 percent of the time.

Paso Fino

Descended from Spanish horses taken to South America by the conquistadors in the sixteenth century, the Paso Fino is a gaited horse noted for its natural ability to walk at a perfect four-beat rhythm within a few hours of birth. According to equestrian and Paso Fino owner Susan Samtak, this breed is small, intelligent, and agile, and possesses a smooth gait that won't shake your body parts! People whose back or joint problems are aggravated by a normal horse's trot will often prefer the Paso Fino. In addition to the *paso fino*, a highly elevated, four-beat gait, this horse's other unique gaits are: the *paso corto*, similar to the *paso fino*, but an uncollected, four-beat gait used for traveling long distances; and the *paso largo*, a faster four-beat gait that can attain speeds of up to sixteen miles per hour. Standing approximately 15 hands high, though reaching as much as 16 hands when bred in the United States, these horses are very obedient and fast learners.

Pony

Ponies, though small, are members of the horse family, and it is size that determines whether an animal is a horse or pony. If it's no higher than 14.2 hands at the withers, it is considered a pony. Supposedly, ponies evolved in cold places where there was less grass for grazing and where they grew thick coats. Pony breeds common in America include the following ones.

Shetland. Native to the Shetland Islands north of Scotland and the smallest of the ponies at 10.2 hands high, the Shetland pony is reputed to be the strongest horse in the world for its size! Originally bred in Scotland for hauling loads of peat, it also pulled coal carts for the English and Welsh. Introduced to the United States during the nineteenth century, the Shetland pony was first used for carting heavy loads because it is capable of pulling a load twice its size. Today, this pony is popular with children, who use it to pull sleds or carts, or keep it as a gentle pet. Also valued for driving, the Shetland can easily pull an adult as well. Its coat is generally black, bay, chestnut, gray, or brown.

Welsh. This intelligent, energetic breed hailing from Wales is divided into four types based on size and shape. Section A, the Welsh Mountain pony, up to 12.2 hands high, is considered the most handsome, with its Celtic pony and Arab bloodlines. Section B, the Welsh pony, at up to 13.2 hands high, is the largest of the breed in the United States, and was originally bred by Welsh farmers for sheep herding. Section C, the Welsh pony of cob type, at up to 13.2 hands high, is stocky. Section D, the Welsh cob, is powerfully built and has been used to pull farm equipment, for trail riding, in driving, and more. Each of the types is found in a variety of solid colors.

Quarter Horse

The American Quarter horse is distinguished by its short, wide head, small muzzle, broad, deep chest, wide-set forelegs, extremely well-muscled hindquarters, strong, low-set hocks, and firm muscling on the insides of the forearms. It stands 14.3–16 hands high and bears a black, bay, sorrel, chestnut, dun, gray, palomino, or grullo coat.

The horses brought to America by the Spanish conquistadors were crossbred during the seventeenth and eighteenth centuries with horses imported horses by English settlers on the East Coast. The result was a solid work horse that could handle almost any job—tilling the land, herding cattle, and riding. Within a short time, this tough horse became indispensable. As the breed spread westward, it was particularly valued for its cattle-herding abilities, for it could follow the movements of a steer, stop and turn quickly, and maneuver the steer into a pen more quickly than any other breed.

Settlers also enjoyed racing these horses any place there was room to gallop for a few hundred yards. In fact, this horse got its name because it could run a quarter of a mile faster than any other horse in the world! When Thoroughbreds arrived from England in the 1780s, formal race courses were built and lightweight jockeys hired to ride them. It came as no surprise, when the short-legged Quarter horse and the long-legged Thoroughbred were finally matched in a race, that the Quarter horse led the first quarter mile, but that the Thoroughbred had the stamina to win.

Short racing eventually died out, but the Quarter horse did not. It was very much appreciated wherever cattlemen needed a powerful horse that could easily trot over rough land, swim across a river, pick a cow out of a huge herd, or brace against a thousand-pound steer held by a rope tied to the saddle horn. Quarter horses are still popular, for they are good-natured, possess smooth gaits, and adapt to a wide variety of disciplines and uses.

Saddlebred

Bred originally in the southern part of the United States during the nineteenth century by plantation owners who needed a versatile horse, this fine-boned animal—a mixture of various breeds, including the Thoroughbred—is one of the best known in North America. Standing 15–16 hands high, with a bay, gray, roan, pinto, palomino, or chestnut coat, it is one of the world's greatest show horses and is capable of performing two artificial gaits in addition to the normal walk, trot, and canter. With its small, shapely head, muscular neck, and strong body, the Saddlebred is also a favorite for jumping, trail riding, and driving.

Standardbred

Known as the fastest harness-racing breed in the world, the Standardbred is descended primarily from Thoroughbreds imported in the late 1700s. The crossing of Messenger, an imported English Thoroughbred, with the Narragansett Pacer produced offspring with a highly developed trotting ability. Between 1851 and 1875, Hambletonian, one of Messenger's descendants, sired more than a thousand offspring with the extremely strong legs needed to withstand the strains of harness racing. Standardbreds are trained either as trotters, that is, for races where the horses' legs move on a diagonal pattern in unison (right front and left hind; left front and right hind), or as pacers in races where the horses' right-side and left-side legs work in tandem in a lateral pattern. Standing 14–16 hands high, Standardbreds usually have a coat in the bay, black, and brown range.

Harness racing dates back to the horse-and-wagon days, when settlers raced from one place to another. Standardbred is a term for a time standard adopted in 1879 to measure the qualities of the horse. To be eligible for the U.S. Trotting Association registry, a horse must be able to trot or pace one mile in 2½ minutes or less.

Tennessee Walker

The Tennessee Walker is fast, has the stamina to travel at a constant pace for several hours, and is reputed to be the most comfortable riding horse in the world. Early in the nineteenth century, Tennessee's plantation owners bred sturdy saddle stock for the good characteristics of the Thoroughbred and Standardbred until one stallion was selected as the foundation sire. He was Black Allan (born in 1886), a great-great-grandson of Rysdyk's Hambletonian; his mother was a great-great-granddaughter of Justin Morgan himself. The result of careful breeding was a horse that could be ridden forty to fifty miles, day after day, in comfort—for this gaited horse possesses a four-beat running walk in addition to the walk, trot, and canter. Traveling preachers and doctors favored the Tennessee Walker because its ride was so smooth. A rider will sometimes demonstrate his horse's smoothness by holding a glass of bubbly and not spilling one drop!

The Tennessee Walker stands 15–16 hands high, has an arched neck and large hooves, and is commonly found in a chestnut, black, or bay coat. Watching it walk is almost mesmerizing: the left front hoof hits the ground just a bit earlier than the right hind, followed by the left hind foot reaching forward beyond the right front hoofprint.

Thoroughbred

The Thoroughbred, a spirited horse that can bear a wide variety of colors, stands from 14.2 to 17.2 hands high. Known as the fastest breed in the world, these horses are capable of reaching speeds up to forty miles per hour. In addition to racing, Thoroughbreds are also used for jumping, dressage, pleasure riding, and driving.

The origins of the Thoroughbred go back to the seventeenth century and the reign of England's King Charles II. Wishing to improve the quality of his racehorses, Charles imported Oriental stock and bred them with some of England's finest horses. The Thoroughbred eventually resulted from three sires: Byerley Turk, a tough charger ridden during wartime; Darley Arabian, a swift horse imported from Syria to Yorkshire in 1704; and the Godolphin Barb, a small stallion purchased from the king of France.

The breeding of champions slowly took hold in America. As early as 1775, Daniel Boone suggested that the Kentucky legislature pass a bill for improving horse breeds. In 1900 a jockey by the name of Tod Sloan changed the style of riding racehorses forever by shortening his stirrups, moving high on his horse's back, and crouching close to its ears. The position, soon copied by other jockeys, allowed the horse to attain greater speeds and spared its back.

All Thoroughbred racehorses have the same birthday, January 1; a foal born in March will celebrate its first birthday the following January 1.

BREEDER INCENTIVE PROGRAMS

To support the state's ever-growing pleasure horse industry, the New Jersey Department of Agriculture, along with the New Jersey Equine Advisory Board, sponsors various incentive programs.

The *Youth and Educator Program* consists of clinics on horse care and management, various events, Boy and Girl Scout badge programs, and a multitude of equine-related activities for children. In addition, educators can take advantage of video presentations on equine careers and farm safety.

The *New Jersey Junior Breeder Program* is a revolving loan program created through private endowment funds in 1921. Its sole purpose is to lend students the necessary funds to acquire livestock for educational projects. It serves as a source of capital for 4-H members and students in agricultural education classes.

The *Horse Breeding and Development Program* distributes funds to owners and breeders of pleasure horses within the state through the New Jersey Bred All Breed Horse Show and the Non-Racing Breeder Awards program. Funding for this program comes from a portion of the pari-mutuel monies waged on horse races in New Jersey.

The *New Jersey Sire Stakes Program*, established by law in 1971, encourages the breeding of Standardbred horses—the trotters and pacers familiar to harness-racing fans. To be eligible for this program, an owner must purchase or breed a foal sired by a stallion that is registered with the Standardbred Breeders and Owners Association of

New Jersey and conforms to the rules of the New Jersey Sire Stakes. Through a series of races each year for two- and three-year-old colts and fillies registered in the program, stallion owners are eligible to win hefty purses as an incentive to locate their stallions and horse farms within New Jersey. The program can be credited with preserving more than 100,000 acres of open space. Just under one percent of the pari-mutuel earnings at the harness tracks is used to fund the program, along with payments made by Standardbred owners.

The New Jersey Department of Agriculture also has established *Individual Breed Incentive Awards* for owners who have a purebred horse bred in New Jersey. The animal must be certified as New Jersey–bred by the appropriate breed association.

For more information on all of these programs, contact the Department of Agriculture Equine Programs at 609-292-8830 or visit the website www.state.nj.us/agriculture/markets/equine.htm#sire.

MORE HORSE FACTS

Did you know that . . .

- 2002 was the Chinese Year of the Horse, the character for the horse appears in ancient Chinese writing, and the Chinese invented the breast-strap harness, the horse collar, and the stirrup?

- George Washington thought mules could be used not only for their labor but also as good mounts, and today mules participate in amateur pleasure driving, trail rides, backpacking trips, endurance riding?

- President Ulysses S. Grant's children traveled to school via a pony cart, and almost one hundred years later President John F. Kennedy's daughter, Caroline, had a pony named Macaroni?

- "Charley horse" is a term that refers to a cramp or muscle spasm usually caused by overexertion, and may have originated to describe the discomfort experienced by people who do not ride regularly?

- Horses mate during the spring, and it takes a year for a foal to be born?

- A mare must teach her foal which plants are edible, and the foal learns by imitating, including how to clean its coat?

- A rambunctious foal reprimanded by other horses will clap its teeth to show that it is giving up the bad behavior?

- Horses can turn their ears 180 degrees, and they rely on hearing and smell to sense danger?

- The horse's eye is nearly twice as large as the human eye, the horse can see much better than humans in dim or bright light, and it can see about 340 degrees, but, because its eyes are set on either side of its head, it cannot see objects in depth with binocular vision and objects appear flat instead?

- A horse's cerebellum is larger than a human's, but the same portion of the brain that in horses controls large muscle coordination is in humans devoted to association, interpretation, and memory?

- Socializing is essential to horses?

- Horses kept in enclosed stables can develop serious digestive problems?

- Horses make decisions based on learned experiences?

- Horses sleep about four hours each day, about half an hour at a time, and can sleep standing up because the joints and ligaments in a horse's elbows prop it up on its forelegs to keep it upright?

- A horse carries 60 percent of its weight on its front legs?

- A horse's natural forward movements are known as gaits: the four-beat walk at approximately four miles per hour; the two-beat trot at about nine miles per hour; the three-beat canter at approximately ten miles per hour; and the fast run, or gallop, at thirty-five miles per hour or more?

- An adult horse has forty teeth, eats about twenty to thirty pounds of hay a day, needs approximately twenty minutes to chew one pound of hay or dried grass, and expels nearly 40 percent of what it eats unprocessed?

- Horse manure, aged about three to six months, is great for gardens?

- New vaccines and medicines make it possible for horses to live as long as thirty-two years?

- The Smithsonian Institution has a horse's halter and a vial of botulism antitoxin in its medical collection? Both came from First Flight, a Thoroughbred who, after retirement from racing in 1978 at age ten, served first as a ceremonial caisson horse and then was selected for a new botulism antitoxin program. His blood was drawn over and over again, and then reinjected after scientists produced small quantities of each toxin type and changed them slightly so that First Flight would not become ill but would respond by producing the necessary antibodies to neutralize the toxin. In 1990 First Flight became the world's only known source of antitoxins used against all seven known types of the neurotoxin that causes botulism. He died of natural causes at the age of thirty-one in 1999; his ashes are buried at Fort Detrick, North Carolina, with a small marker that commemorates his value to medical research.

- Horseshoes are nailed to a doorway with the points upward so that none of the good luck will fall out? Horseshoes have been considered a symbol of good fortune as far back as the tenth century. According to legend, Saint Dunstan, a blacksmith later named Archbishop of Canterbury, was asked to attach horseshoes to a man's feet. Noticing that the feet were cloven, Dunstan surmised this person must be Satan and proceeded to beat him mercilessly. Dunstan agreed to stop only when the Devil swore never to enter a house where a horseshoe was placed above the door.

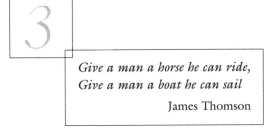

Give a man a horse he can ride,
Give a man a boat he can sail

James Thomson

Learning to Ride

TIPS FOR THE NOVICE

No matter how old you are, whether you're rich or poor, whether you live in a city or suburb, if you want to learn to ride, you can! Not only is horseback riding fun; it also improves balance and self-confidence, and is an excellent form of exercise because it requires the use of all your muscles. Working in sync with an animal weighing hundreds of pounds can be exhilarating and, as a stress reliever, it can't be beat—for who can resist the pure joy of being outdoors surrounded by nature's grandeur?

Where to start is the big question. Your local library has numerous books for basic information. The easy-to-read guides in the children's section generally have informative illustrations and concise definitions. Books in the adult section can be consulted for more detailed information on all aspects of riding. I've also recommended a few books, ranging from riding basics to advanced disciplines, in appendix C.

YOUR CHOICE: ENGLISH
OR WESTERN SADDLE

Before taking lessons, plan on arranging for a short guided ride with an outfitter that uses either English- or Western-style saddles, or both, so you can decide which is more comfortable. Your choice may depend on your long-term goals. Are you interested only in an occasional guided trail ride, or are you hoping eventually to jump, compete in barrel racing, or participate in another equine sport? New riders often feel more secure with the larger, deep-seated Western saddle, which features a large horn in the front, as compared with the smaller, hornless English-style saddle.

Even if you do not own a horse, once you've gotten hooked on riding lessons, you may decide to buy a saddle. The stirrup leathers will always be adjusted to the correct length for you, and the saddle will eventually mold to your shape. The type of saddle you buy will depend upon the type of riding you wish to pursue. Saddles are designed specifically for various levels and disciplines, such as general purpose, dressage, endurance, show jumping, and gaited pleasure riding.

If you wish to own a saddle, the fit is important for both your safety and your comfort. Moreover, a saddle may fit one horse, but not another. Before purchasing a used or new saddle, read various catalogs to learn which features are available and check online websites and local tack shops for information and policies on saddle fitting and test rides. When you're ready to be measured at a tack store, go with an experienced rider and ask for a money-back guarantee in case the saddle proves uncomfortable after a few rides (a restocking fee may be charged). Additional necessary items, such as stirrup irons, bridle, and clothing, are described below.

CHOOSING AN INSTRUCTOR

Whatever your ambitions as a rider, it is important to acquire a good foundation in horsemanship. In addition to learning how to mount, sit on a horse, and guide it properly, a basic knowledge of horse safety and equipment care is essential. An instructor can help you achieve your goals, but because New Jersey has not yet established standards for evaluating and certifying instructors, it's wise to scout around to find an experienced one. The American Riding Instructors Association (ARIA) can help. Since 1984, it has sponsored the American Riding Instructor Certification Program (ARICP), which "is meant for the serious, above-average instructor who teaches safety in a professional, competent manner, with high standards of honesty and integrity." To become certified, candidates are evaluated through written and oral testing for up to three levels of experience and in fourteen teaching specialties (including hunt seat, dressage, and Western pleasure). To ensure that a certified instructor's standards remain high, re-certification is required every five years. Check the ARIA website (www.riding-instructor.com) for a list of certified instructors in New Jersey.

WHERE TO TAKE LESSONS OR RENT

Recommendations from friends and relatives who ride can help you to choose among the numerous academies listed in the Yellow Pages.

Tack shop proprietors are generally knowledgeable about reliable stables offering lessons. You can also check with a 4-H club, Pony Club, equine veterinarian, or the Rutgers Cooperative Extension Service. A sampling of stables across the state appears at the end of this section.

If a particular stable interests you, call and ask to observe a beginner lesson. Take note of the surroundings. Is the stable clean and in good repair? Do the horses look bright-eyed and healthy, or do they have to be urged on with whips and spurs? Do students learn how to groom the horse and care for equipment? Is the tack clean and in good shape? Are beginners required to take private lessons until they learn to control a horse and are allowed to ride with others? If most of the students are children, an adult may find the level of instruction too simplistic and the size of the saddles too small for comfort. Find out how long your prospective instructor has been teaching at the stable; a constantly changing staff will frustrate you with inconsistent teaching. Is the instructor certified?

While observing lessons, take note of the proper way to mount— basically standing on the horse's left side, putting your left foot into the stirrup, standing up, and swinging your right foot over the top of the saddle. Does the student have to adjust the stirrups, or does the instructor do it? How are students dressed? Is everyone wearing a helmet?

Lessons are expensive, but are excellent for developing the confidence and skills needed to feel comfortable—and safe—on any mount. Expect to pay $40–50 for group lessons and quite a bit more for private ones. Some stables and instructors offer only private lessons, but the individual attention is well worth the price. Packages of lessons at a reduced rate are often available.

Many stables, such as Overpeck Stables in Leonia, offer summer or year-round riding programs for all ages in a safe, structured environment with instructional videos, demonstrations, and talks on equipment, feeding, anatomy, horse ownership, and more. The Watchung Stable in Watchung, part of the Union County Department of Parks and Recreation, has offered lessons since 1935 to thousands of people, from age eight on up, and the North Jersey Equestrian Center in Pompton Plains is one of the largest riding centers in the state. Many counties offer similar programs. For example, in Middlesex County the New Jersey Museum of Agriculture invites children from the ages of nine to thirteen to participate in Horseplay Camp, a week-long equine adventure that includes two riding sessions and practical experience at a horse farm. EquiShare U.S.A. offers riding lessons to adults, and its subsidiary, PonyShare, caters to youngsters (visit www. ponyshare.com).

No matter where you choose to take lessons, usually one level at a time will be mastered, beginning with properly leading and turning a horse, basic grooming, mounting and dismounting without help, and the correct position in the saddle at the walk and trot. Further training includes the sitting trot, the canter, and simple circular and turning patterns. Advanced lessons may involve learning how to jump over small fences, how to stop a runaway horse, and how to ride safely in groups and along trails. Don't be afraid to switch instructors and stables if you feel you are not receiving instruction that is safety-oriented and fits your goals.

A few stables in New Jersey rent horses for guided and unguided trail rides; others may allow you to rent their school horses for additional practice after you've taken lessons and have proven your ability to ride safely. Most rental trail horses are chosen for their even temperament and willingness to follow the horse in front of them in a single file. Riding next to your child or friend is not allowed, nor is galloping. If you have never ridden before, or if you are going on a ride with other novices, be sure that everyone in your group understands basic safety around horses and is in fit shape for the length of ride you plan to undertake. It's important to be honest when asked for the level of your riding skills. You wouldn't want to mount a frisky horse that will quickly sense you're afraid of it and may decide to take off at a gallop. *Always remember: Horses can be dangerous—even when standing still! Use caution, know your skills, and get the best horse you can for your capability.* For detailed information on safety on and off your mount, consult chapter 4.

Listed below are a few of the many stables that offer lessons. Those that also rent horses are indicated by an asterisk. Stables are always opening, closing, or changing their policies. Call ahead to confirm hours, condition of the trail, duration, and difficulty of the ride. *Note: The mention of individual businesses does not imply endorsement.*

BERGEN COUNTY

Knockeen Farm, 24 Piermont Road, Rockleigh; 201-768-9745.

Overpeck Riding Center, 40 Fort Lee Road, Leonia; 201-944-7111.

*Saddle Ridge Horseback Riding Center, 900 Saddle Ridge Road, Franklin Lakes; 201-848-0844 (disabled accessible).

Top of the Line, 294 Red School House Road, Chestnut Ridge, N.Y. (along the Bergen County border); 201-930-0606.

CAPE MAY COUNTY

Hidden Valley Ranch, 4070 Bayshore Drive, Cape May; 609-884-8205.

Triple R Ranch, 210 Stagecoach Road, Cape May Court House; 609-465-4673.

ESSEX COUNTY

*Essex Equestrian Center, 12-22 Woodland Avenue, West Orange; 973-731-4182.

HUNTERDON COUNTY

Center Line Farm, 245 Route 517, Tewksbury; 908-832-9448.

Creekside Farm, 397 Mechlin Corner Road, Pittstown; 908-735-6847.

Flying Change Farm, Inc., 60 Sutton Road, Lebanon; 908-832-5279.

Revelation Farms, 45 Fitcer Road, Frenchtown; 908-996-2123.

Silver Bit and Spur Farm, 631 Country Road 523, Whitehouse Station; 908-534-4010.

Smoke Hollow Farm, 247-249 Pittstown Road, Pittstown; 908-730-8389.

*Upper Creek Farm, 33 Upper Creek Road, Stockton; 908-996-3625.

Whiskey Lane Eventing Center, 40 Whiskey Lane, Flemington; 908-581-5135.

MERCER COUNTY

*Mercer County Equestrian Center, 431B Federal City Road, Pennington; 609-730-9059.

Royal Crest Farm, 238 Pleasant Valley Road, Titusville; 609-737-3209.

Weidel's Boxwood Farm, 1429 Trenton Harbourton Road, Pennington; 609-737-1036.

MIDDLESEX COUNTY

Farrington Farms, 28 Davidson Mill Road, South Brunswick; 908-821-9844.

Jay Heatherwood Farm, 55 Gravel Hill Spotswood Road, Monroe Township; 732-656-0750.

*Royal Farms Horse Center, 271 Englishtown Road, Old Bridge; 908-251-9810.

Sann Hill Farm, 91 Major Road, South Brunswick; 908-329-6259.

*Washington Riding Stables, 1707 Washington Avenue, Piscataway; 732-249-2471.

MONMOUTH COUNTY

Astor Place Riding Club, 169 Robertsville Road, Freehold; 908-294-7798.

Capitol Crossing Farm, Box 132, Route 537, Colts Neck; 908-542-9010.

Circle A Riding Academy, 116 Herbertsville Road, Howell; 732-938-2004.

High Hopes Farm, 338 Adelphia Road, Farmingdale; 732-919-3080.

Huber Woods Park, Browns Dock Road, Middletown; 609-872-2928.

Hunter's Run Farm, 4111 Belmar Boulevard, Neptune; 732-280-1432.

Park Place at the Equestrian Center, 982 Route 33, Freehold; 908-409-4911.

Tall Oaks Farm, 151 Oak Glen Road, Howell; 732-938-5445.

Winner's Circle Horse Farm, 71 Larchwood Avenue, Oakhurst; 732-870-1796.

MORRIS COUNTY

EquiShare USA/PonyShare (Catch a Breeze Farm), 28 Fox Hill Road, Califon; 908-439-3901.

North Jersey Equestrian Center, 1 Carlson Place, Pompton Plains; 973-839-0077; www.njequestrian.com.

Seaton Hackney Stables, 440 South Street, Morristown; 973-267-1372.

Snowbird Acres Farm, 204 Schooley's Mountain Road, Long Valley; 908-876-4200.

OCEAN COUNTY

Lakewood Riding Center, 436 Cross Street, Lakewood; 732-367-6222.

*Plumsted Equestrian Center, 102 Jacobstown Road, New Egypt; 609-758-1547.

PASSAIC COUNTY

*Echo Lake Stables, 50 Blakely Lane, Newfoundland; 973-697-1257.

*Farmstead Estates, 600 West Brook Road, Ringwood; 973-831-7879.

Garret Mountain Reservation, 317 Pennsylvania Avenue, Paterson;
    973-881-4832.

Rocky Top Stables, 885 Macopin Road, West Milford; 201-697-6927.

West Milford Equestrian Center, 367 Union Valley Road,
    Newfoundland; 201-697-2020.

SOMERSET COUNTY

Black Horse, 656 South Branch River Road, Somerville;
    908-369-5477.

*Lord Stirling Stables, 256 S. Maple Avenue, Basking Ridge;
    908-766-5955 (rentals for experienced English riders only).

Pine Hill Farm, 104 Harlan School Road, Somerville; 908-722-7087.

Somerset Stables, 425 Demott Lane, Somerset; 908-873-9885.

SUSSEX COUNTY

*Spring Valley Equestrian Center, 56 Paulinskill Lake Road, Newton;
    973-383-3766.

UNION COUNTY

*Watchung Stables, 1160 Summit Lane, Mountainside; 908-789-3685.

WARREN COUNTY

Double D Guest Ranch, 81 Mount Hermon Road, Blairstown;
    908-459-9044.

North Wind Stables, Ltd., 6 Meadow Cliff Lane, Blairstown;
    908-362-7858; www.northwindstables.com.

ATTIRE AND TACK
FOR SAFETY AND COMFORT

There is always a risk of injury when riding and working around horses.
When you begin lessons, your instructor will ask you to sign a liability
waiver, and you will be required to wear certain clothing. Some riding
apparel may look fashionably stylish, but all of it is designed for safety.
The necessary riding equipment is known as *tack*.

At the top of the list is the *helmet*. We are born with only one
head—a fragile and irreplaceable one. A fall from a horse can cause
paralysis, brain damage, a concussion, or even death. According to the
Consumer Products Safety Commission, eight thousand head injuries

resulted from horseback riding activities throughout the United States in 1988 (the most recent survey period). It is imperative always to wear a well-fitted helmet when riding. In fact, USA Equestrian, the national governing body for equestrian sports, requires that anyone seventeen years of age and younger wear a helmet in hunter and jumper classes at sanctioned shows.

Some stables supply helmets to new riders; call ahead to see if one will be provided. However, it's best to buy your own. If you haven't bought one in the past twenty years, the good news is that they've changed tremendously. Not only are they more comfortable and available in many more styles, but the polystyrene liner will help keep you cooler and better absorb the impact in case of a fall. They're also cut higher over the back of the neck area to prevent injury to the spinal column in a bad fall. Choose a helmet that has been approved by the Safety Equipment Institute (SEI), doesn't wobble on your head after adjustments have been made, has a removable visor or one that will snap off on impact, and includes a chin cup or adjustable strap that fits under your jaw. Always keep the helmet buckled when riding.

Footwear is also essential to safety. Whether you choose boots or riding shoes, they should have at least a half-inch heel to prevent your foot from sliding forward through the stirrup. High riding boots provide good ankle support; shorter paddock boots are another good bet. If you're riding in hot weather, you might prefer riding sneakers. Made with a half-inch heel, they breathe well and are easy to put on.

Long pants are necessary to protect your legs. Blue jeans are usually acceptable, although, if they are not made specifically for riding, the seams can cause chafing. A *long-sleeved shirt* will protect your arms from scratches when riding close to brush.

Eventually, it makes good sense to buy *riding tights, gloves, chaps*, and other apparel that will help to make you more comfortable in the saddle. In recent years, there have been vast improvements in fabrics, such as polarfleece, which conserves body heat during winter riding while wicking away moisture. For summer riding, microfiber fabrics wick away moisture and provide a cool, comfortable feeling during hot, humid weather. Clothing is available in everything from earth tones and animal prints, to bright colors and a wide selection of solid or bold patterns.

Rainwear is readily available, ranging from the Australian drover's coat, with straps to hold it around the legs and a gusset to fit over the saddle, to the quiet and breathable Western slicker, to rain pants for keeping legs dry. Inexpensive plastic ponchos should be avoided because they're noisy and can frighten your horse.

Western attire, the only equine fashion created in the United States, ranges from turn-of-the-century styles and tapestry vests, to yoked shirts and close-fitting clothing for women. Men usually don a tailored suit, Western shirt, highly polished cowboy boots, and a sharp-looking hat.

English-style riding demands a totally different look. For hunt-seat riding, the norm is still tall leather boots; high-collared, pin-striped or white shirts for women, and a regular collar for men; buttoned, tight-fitting jackets; breeches; and a velvet cap. For dressage, white shirts are worn with a tie, breeches, hunting jacket, highly polished dress boots, and a top hat.

Everything you need can be found at local tack shops (check the phone book under "Riding Apparel"), in catalogs, or on the Internet (see appendix B). Tack shops abound in New Jersey, and browsing through their stocks of amazing items while sniffing the pleasant aroma of leather goods is lots of fun as well as educational. Frequently, these shops offer apparel packages for youngsters going off to riding camp, and they may accept quality boots and clothing on trade or consignment. These used items can save you a lot of money, especially if you're the parent of a growing young rider.

What you purchase depends on the type of riding you'll be doing. If you hope eventually to compete or desire to join a particular breed association, find out what the customary and legal attire rules are before making your choices. This information is readily available from the association or show event judge. Once you decide, visit several tack shops, devote lots of time to examining what's available, listen to what the sales people have to say, and join an equestrian club where you'll receive reliable suggestions and information that can help you make an informed decision. Buy the best equipment and clothing you can afford. The investment for pleasure, comfort, and safety will pay dividends in the years to come.

The instant made eternity—
And heaven just prove that I and she
Ride, ride together, forever ride.

Robert Browning

Safety and First Aid on the Trail

SAFETY IN THE SADDLE
AND AROUND HORSES

Novice riders are usually schooled in an enclosed area. Once the basics are mastered, you'll be free to experience the tremendous joy that comes with riding along a trail in open country or dense woods. However, whenever working around horses or starting out on a trail, always review the following tips gathered from the National Institute for Occupational Safety and Health and the New Jersey Horse Council. Heeding this advice will help to ensure a safe and pleasant ride.

- Always approach the horse from the side.
- Talk calmly and gently to your horse so it feels secure.
- When leading, keep the horse on your right side. If using a long lead rope, fold it accordion-style in your left hand. Never wrap the rope or reins around your wrist, hand, or body. Always turn the horse to the right and walk around it.
- Always leave an escape path away from the horse. It may be especially stressed by moving, loading, or saddling.
- Check your equipment before mounting to be certain everything is in good shape.
- Keep children at a safe distance.
- Stay on the trail, whether it's a marked track in a state park or a pathway between privately owned fields.
- Always wear your helmet when riding—and keep it buckled.

On the trail, wise and considerate riders will abide by the *Leave No Trace* guidelines:

- *Know before You Go.* Be prepared. Don't forget clothes to protect you from cold, heat, or rain. Study maps to be familiar with where you're going and take them along so you won't get lost. Learn about the areas you plan to visit. Read books and talk to people before you go. The more you know, the more fun you'll have.

- *Choose the Right Path.* Stay on the main trail and don't wander off by yourself. Steer clear of flowers and small trees; once trampled, they may not grow back. Use existing camp areas. Camp at least 100 big steps from roads, trails, and water.

- *Trash Your Trash.* Pack it in; pack it out. Put litter, even crumbs, in trash cans or carry it home. Use bathrooms or outhouses when available. If you must leave body waste, bury it in a small hole 4–8 inches deep and 100 big steps from water. Place your toilet paper in a plastic bag and put the bag in a garbage can back home. Keep water clean. Do not put soap, food, or waste in lakes or streams.

- *Leave What You Find.* Leave plants, rocks, and historical items as you find them so the next person can enjoy them. Treat living plants with respect. Good campsites are found, not made. Don't dig trenches or build structures at your campsite.

- *Be Careful with Fire.* If feasible, use a camp stove rather than a fire for cooking; it's easier to cook on and clean up. Be sure campfires are allowed in the area you're visiting. Use an existing fire ring to protect the ground from heat. Keep your fire small. Do not snap off branches from live, dead, or downed trees; instead, collect loose sticks from the ground. Remember, campfires aren't for disposing of trash or food. Burn all wood to ash and be sure that the fire is completely out and cold before you leave.

- *Respect Wildlife.* Observe animals from a distance and never approach, feed, or follow them. Human food is unhealthy for all animals, and feeding them encourages bad habits. Protect wildlife and your food by storing your meals and trash.

- *Be Kind to Other Visitors.* Make sure the fun you have in the outdoors does not interfere with anyone else's enjoyment. Listen to nature. Avoid making loud noises or yelling. You will see more animals if you are quiet.

For more information on the Leave No Trace program, contact 1-800-332-4100 or www.lnt.org.

PLANNING AHEAD

When planning a trail ride, it is essential to know and be honest about your physical condition and your horse's. I learned this important lesson while on vacation. Believing myself to be in great shape, I opted for a three-hour ride—without realizing there would be no break to dismount, stretch, and rest. I subsequently experienced leg pain that lasted for three days! When renting, you won't know the physical condition of the horse you're assigned to. If you're taking your own mount, however, ask yourself whether it can endure long rides on extremely hot or cold days. Or, for that matter, can you? To keep your horse and yourself in excellent shape, plan on riding at least two or three times weekly.

Choose a trail appropriate in length and difficulty for your ability and that of your horse. Introduce new terrain to your horse slowly, study typographic maps beforehand, and/or talk to riders who have taken the same route. If you're going to be on rocky trails, be sure to check your horse's hooves and shoes.

Know when the sun will set, allow ample time to return, and *always* tell a friend or family member your route and approximate return time. A global-positioning satellite receiver (GPS) is an excellent way to keep track of where you've been and have to go. Bear in mind, however, that an exact GPS reading may not be possible in dense woods, so learning how to use a compass in conjunction with a good map is essential.

Prepare any papers (identification; health insurance card; current health and Coggins test papers for your horse; facility permits) that should be carried whenever you're riding, together with phone numbers to call in case of an emergency.

For the Trailer

A bucket of fresh water should be placed inside the trailer to refresh your horse if none is available on the trail. Many horses dislike drinking unfamiliar water, so it's always best to bring some from home. If the bucket doesn't have a lid, splashing can be avoided by placing a plastic garbage bag in the bucket, filling the bag with water, and then tying the bag with a rubber band or piece of wire. Check the end of this chapter for a list of first aid items to keep in your trailer.

The Well-Stocked Saddlebag

No matter how long you plan to be out on the trail, it's prudent to pack your saddlebag with basic supplies both for yourself and for your horse. (The saddlebag, also known as a pannier, is made of leather or lightweight fabric and fitted to and positioned behind the saddle and hung over one or both sides of the horse.) See the end of this chapter for a list of first aid items that should also be part of your kit.

For you:

- Cellular phone, or a two-way radio if you're with a companion.
- Compass, map, and whistle (GPS receiver optional). Be sure to note the direction you start out from. If you get lost, blow the whistle three times, rest, and repeat.
- Flashlight.
- Insect repellent. Avoid applying perfume during warmer months.
- Knife. A Swiss Army knife or a Leatherman® tool can make all the difference.

Tack is available for almost every purpose, including these saddlebags, used on the trail to carry belongings, and the seat saver for long hours in the saddle.

- Matches. Carry waterproof matches or place a book of matches in a film canister (available from camera stores) in case you're stuck somewhere after dark and need a small fire to keep you warm.
- Rain gear and extra clothing. Always be prepared for inclement weather. Dress in layers so you can take off or add clothing. A rain slicker helps, too, for that sudden downpour, and a thermal space blanket for emergency purposes is a good bet.
- Sun gear. Bring a hat, sunglasses (with a neck strap), lip balm, and sunscreen. Use a waterproof sunscreen with an SPF of 15 or more, applied generously at least half an hour before going outside.
- Toilet tissue. Have a shovel as well if burying your body waste.
- Trash bag. Take out everything you've brought in.
- Water, lots of it, and some trail mix. Carry a spray bottle filled with water. If you've been riding on a hot day, spray your horse with it when returning to the trailer.

For your horse:

- One or more Easyboots, in case your horse throws a shoe or if you're riding in the rain or in muddy areas. Make certain it fits correctly before starting out.
- Halter and lead line, or some other means to tie or secure your horse. Hobbles should be used only for horses that have been trained to accept them.
- Mesh face mask if the insects are annoying.
- Hoof pick.
- String or a synthetic shoelace, for a temporary tack repair.

GETTING YOUR HORSE TO THE TRAIL

Loading a horse into a trailer for the first time may be difficult, and unless done properly, the exercise will not only be exasperating every time but may prove dangerous to both you and your horse. Think about how your horse feels when faced with going into dark, small quarters. Naturally, it will be frightened. However, with patience, a positive attitude, and the common-sense approach endorsed by the American Association of Equine Practitioners, it's possible to teach your horse to load willingly and stand quietly. The association suggests using a halter, soft lead rope, and a stiff, six- to seven-foot fishing rod with a plastic bag taped to its end to coax the horse. According to the association, "The rod with attached bag shouldn't be used to cause pain, but to direct [the horse] into the trailer. Once inside, reward him. If he tries to back out, simply use the rod and bag to aggravate him until he walks forward again." Never use brute force or pull or push the horse. He's bigger than you, and when he wins, he'll know he's the boss!

New Jersey law requires that your horse be transported in a humane manner to minimize injury, disease, and transportation stress. The New Jersey Equine Advisory Board has the following recommendations for trailer features and use:

- The floors should be sturdy and covered with a non-skid material, such as sand or a rubber mat to provide traction and prevent injuries.
- Interior walls should be smooth and free of protuberances.
- The interior height should allow your horse adequate room to hold its head at a normal, relaxed level.
- Horses should be housed individually in the trailer, with the exception that a mare may share a compartment with her foal.
- Restrain trailered horses with a quick-release safety knot or device.
- On long trips, horses should be watered, fed, and off-loaded at least every eight hours.

The Back Country Horsemen of America (Box 1367, Graham, Wash. 98338) further recommend that an inexperienced horse practice loading with a calm, experienced animal and that transported horses "be tied short and lower than is usual to prevent them from rearing or getting a foot over the rope." A horse must always have good footing when loading or unloading; never leave a crack that a horse can get its foot stuck in. Be mindful of your precious cargo and take corners slowly and avoid quick starts and sudden stops.

Remember that a valid Coggins test certificate, current within two years of the date of travel, must be on hand for any horse transported on a roadway within New Jersey.

ENJOYING THE RIDE

At the Trailhead

When you saddle up, be sure your girth or cinch is snug, but don't ride with an extremely tight cinch. Use a breast collar and, if necessary, a crupper to help keep the saddle in place. When it's cold out, use a rump rug under the saddle to keep your horse's haunches warm.

On the Trail

Before starting out, take a few moments to check your girth or cinch. Sit up straight in the saddle, with your weight evenly distributed to avoid strain or sores to your horse's back. However, when going down a steep grade, be easy on your mount by leaning way back in the saddle to take some of your weight off the horse's front legs so that it can maintain its balance—but apply the proper pressure on the bit so it will descend slowly. If you have to dismount on a grade that is particularly steep, turn your horse so that you can dismount and mount on the upside. Because you may not have room to maneuver on a narrow hillside trail, it's wise to practice mounting and dismounting from either side at home before the ride. When ascending a hill, raise yourself a little with the aid of the stirrups and lean forward while, at the same time, applying a loose rein, which will enable your horse to breathe properly.

If you are exploring a new trail, ride slowly so you have time to spot holes or ditches, and so you and your horse can become familiar with the terrain.

The courtesy and respect you show for the farmers and landowners who allow riders to cross their property will maintain good will and open trails for those who come after you. If you encounter livestock as you ride through a pasture, pass them quietly. Close any gates you open, but open gates should be left open. They could be the only access to water that stock in the area may have.

At the 2002 National Trails Symposium, speakers Candace and Brian Bourne made these suggestions for practicing good equestrian trail conservation:

- Respect the land on which you ride.

- Be aware of your impact based on the experience of others and respect that experience.

- Be willing to accept the guidance and input of land managers.

- Use common sense in determining acceptable conditions for competition and realize the benefits, direct and indirect, of volunteering to help maintain trails (see chapter 5).

Riding with a Group

Riding with others can bring added enjoyment, but companionship also entails additional responsibilities.

Riders enjoying one of New Jersey's great trails.

A horse that kicks is an undesirable choice for trail use. If you know or suspect that your horse will kick, but insist on riding it in a group, you will be held responsible for any damage or injuries it causes. Tie a red ribbon in its tail as a warning and be alert to the distance between you and other horses. Equestrian Janice Elsishans suggests "placing a yellow bow on your horse's tail if it's a stallion. Horses, like dogs, behave or misbehave depending upon the training received from the owners/trainers. Some have impeccable manners; others are borderline safe." By remembering to use these ribbons, you will help the riders and horses in your group to be safer on the trail.

Good trail manners require that you be mounted and ready to leave at the designated starting time. Maintain a safe distance between your horse and the one ahead. You don't want to be responsible for your horse pulling off another's shoe; worse, you or your horse could be kicked. (You should be able to see the feet of the horse in front of you between your horse's ears.)

Stay behind the trail boss unless told otherwise. You may think you know where the ride is going, but you will annoy others if they have to wait for you to return to the group after taking a wrong turn. On the other hand, you should not lag behind the rest of your group. Most rides have a drag or security rider. Your slow pace could force that person to lose sight of the riders ahead.

Be considerate when passing. Pass only on sections of the trail that are safe to do so, and pass quietly. You could cause a serious accident by speeding around inexperienced riders and/or horses.

When crossing a road, be alert to the trail boss's signal and cross quickly.

Remember, all the comforts of home will not be available on the trail. Don't make the ride unpleasant for others by complaining about inconveniences.

MEETING BEARS

From a distance, spotting one of New Jersey's black bears is a memorable experience. However, approaching one can prove deadly. Attaching bells to your saddle, saddlebags, or person may alert bears that you are nearby and cause them to scamper away before you even spot them. It's wise to use extra caution in areas where bears are likely to roam, such as berry patches. Should you spot one at close range, do not ride toward it, but make it aware of your presence by clapping, talking, singing, or jingling those bells! If you come upon one suddenly, avoid direct eye contact. If mounted, or if you're on the ground walking your horse, back up slowly, and speak in a calm, assertive, and assuring voice.

Bears learn quickly, and the New Jersey Division of Fish and Wildlife warns that a bear that associates food with people may become aggressive and dangerous. Such a bear may cause personal injury and property damage, and force authorities to euthanize it. Because bears have an extraordinarily keen sense of smell, it is imperative that you keep any food you may have in your saddlebags in double-wrapped aluminum foil, enclosed in a double layer of zip-lock bags.

Be especially cautious when camping or picnicking. Cook only as much food as you will eat to minimize the amount of food garbage. Keep a clean camp or picnic site. Food and all items that come in contact with food carry odors that bears can smell. Immediately store food articles after every use in airtight containers. Coolers are not airtight, and bears often associate them with food. Secure the containers in a locked trunk or truck cab concealed from view. Clean all utensils thoroughly and immediately after use.

Never deposit food residues, such as grease, into campfires or into barrels that are not closed with a heavy lid. Place garbage where bears cannot smell or gain access to it, either in bear-proof containers or in dumpsters. Do not burn your garbage or bury it—bears will dig it up.

Never eat or cook in your tent. Avoid storing food or even non-food items that will attract bears—such as gum, soap, or deodorant—in tents, sleeping bags, backpacks, or saddlebags.

Should a bear come into your camp or picnic area, remain calm and do not try to bribe it away with food. Stay at least fifteen feet away from the bear and make certain it has an escape route. Yell, bang pots and pans, or use an air horn to scare the bear away. Most bears are easily frightened into leaving. A bear that stands on its hind legs is merely trying to get a better view rather than acting in a threatening way. Should the bear utter a series of huffs, snap its jaws, and swat the ground, you are too close. Slowly back away. The black bears common in New Jersey will sometimes "bluff charge" when cornered, threatened, or caught stealing food. Stand your ground and slowly back away. If the bear will not leave the campsite, move to your trailer or a building, if available, and take necessary measures to protect your horse.

AT REST AND CAMPING OVERNIGHT WITH YOUR HORSE

Be as considerate of your horse as you are of yourself. For example, on a hot day, at lunch or rest stops, find shade for your horse. Upon arrival at a good picnic spot or campsite, refrain from giving your horse water or food immediately, especially if he is hot, and do not unsaddle him. If the horse is hot and tired, too many demands upon his system may cause colic. After he's had an opportunity to cool down, you can offer him small amounts of water until he's satisfied, followed by a small amount of hay. After he's rested for about fifteen to thirty minutes, unsaddle him. This delay will reduce the likelihood of "heat bumps," which are caused by the sudden release of pressure when you dismount and remove the saddle.

When trail camping, do not feed your horse more than he is accustomed to receiving at home; if anything, feed him slightly less to reduce the chance of colic. The major feeding should come in the evening, rather than in the morning just before the day's work.

Camping overnight is a great way to spend more time with your horse. Imagine relaxing, gazing up at the stars, cooking over a fire or grill, and awakening to the chirping of birds and tiny critters in lush woods. Now that's heaven! Unfortunately, there are only two places in New Jersey that I know of where it's allowed at the present time— Allaire State Park and Wharton State Forest (see chapter 5, trails 1 and 20). For information on private campgrounds in New Jersey, ask for a free copy of the annual *Campground and RV Park Guide* from the New Jersey Campground Association, 29 Cook's Beach Road, Cape May Court House 08210; 1-800-222-6765.

No matter where you camp, consider purchasing a lightweight portable pen, either the portable panel or the electric pen type, that you can easily transport in your trailer. After setting up either type at a campsite, you can relax because your horse will be safe while you snooze. If you purchase the electric pen kit, it will contain the necessary poles, electric line, and battery holder. Be sure to take along extra batteries. For the portable type, you'll need ready-made panels and fasteners. To save money, consider making your own pen, as suggested by equestrian John Samtak: "Using PVC pipe, take a ten-foot length, cut a foot off each end; this becomes the vertical spacer to attach the next length of PVC pipe. Using three PVC lengths for each panel, and making about four panels, is enough to create an eight foot enclosure." Each type of enclosure has its advantages and disadvantages. To decide which is best for your needs, investigate the products offered on the Internet and in catalogs, and talk to your local tack shop owner and fellow horse people.

As an alternative, Janice Elsishans of the New Jersey Horse Council suggests "simply tying the horse to your trailer and filling the hay net with enough feed for the evening. Or, if you wish to high tie, use a long heavy rope with either a loop knot every 10–12 feet (if you have more than one horse), and use the knot to attach each horse." Elsishans suggests investing in "tree savers," the equivalent of a long seat belt with a "D" ring at each end to wrap around the tree, with the rope tied to the "D" rings to prevent any damage to the tree.

If you've never spent a night outdoors with your horse, it's wise to accustom him to being confined in a small area by setting up the same conditions at home that you would experience while camping. Also, you will want to get the advice of experienced horse campers. Their tips may include taking along a large tarp to protect your gear in case of rain; freeze-dried food in case of an emergency; a topographic map of the area; and many of the items suggested above for the well-stocked saddlebag and trailer.

Should you capture an unknown horse during the night, secure him apart from your horse and the horses in your group. He may have pulled down a picket line elsewhere, and you don't want him to do the same thing to yours.

FIRST AID KITS FOR TRAILER AND TRAIL

Consult your veterinarian about which first aid supplies to carry in your trailer and on the trail. Items for the trailer kit can be placed in a clean bucket clearly labeled "First Aid." Depleted supplies should be replaced as soon as possible. Among the items to include are:

- Cleaning materials, including Betadine scrub, dilute Betadine solution, cotton for cleaning wounds, gloves, and a clean bucket designated solely for use in cleaning wounds.
- Wound ointments, such as Neosporin, triple antibiotic, or biozide gel.
- Bandages, gauze, and pads in various sizes; thick quilted fabric leg rolls or disposable ones; polyester or cotton bandages for standing wraps; and even disposable diapers, which can be used for wounds or hot/cold compresses.
- Scissors.
- Thermometer.
- Extra halter.
- Dose syringe.
- Clean paper and cloth towels.
- Nonsteroid eye ointment.

Items to have on hand in case of accident or injury to you or a companion on the trail include:

- Antibiotic ointment.
- Sterile dressing.
- Gauze.
- Self-adhesive elastic wrap.
- Butterfly closure strips.
- Triangular bandage; elastic bandage; adhesive tape; bandage scissors.
- Cotton-tipped applicators.
- Antiseptic towelettes or baby wipes.
- Moleskin.
- Aspirin or Tylenol®.
- Tweezers; tick remover forceps.
- Wire cutters.
- A bandanna or other device to stop bleeding.

Taking a first-aid and cardiopulmonary resuscitation (CPR) course offered by the American Red Cross or local hospital is an excellent way to ensure that you will be prepared, on or off the trail, to save a life—perhaps your own! Remember, too, that a sprained or broken limb can be immobilized by using almost anything at hand—a branch, bandanna, or rolled-up jacket—and wrapping it with adhesive tape. If bleeding occurs, apply direct pressure to the wound area but do not make a tourniquet (it may lead to a blood clot). Do not move a seriously injured person, but use your cell phone or send a buddy to get help. It's important to recognize the signs of shock: breaking out in a sweat, feeling dizzy or nauseous, or exhibiting a weak pulse. An injured person experiencing these symptoms should be laid flat on the ground with legs elevated (using a jacket, saddlebag, or other available item). Make certain to keep the victim as warm as possible using saddle blankets, clothing, or even piles of leaves or pine needles. Always have your health insurance card with you, just in case.

Now that you know how to take care of yourself and your horse on the trail, check out some of New Jersey's great places to ride in the next chapter.

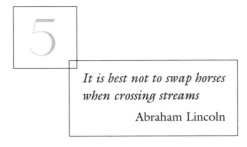

*It is best not to swap horses
when crossing streams*

Abraham Lincoln

Saddle Up
and Let's Go Riding!

New Jersey's state parks, forests, county parks, recreation areas, wildlife management areas, municipal lands, club trails, private lands, and converted railroad lines (part of the national Rails-to-Trails system) offer equestrians approximately 800 miles of riding trails. For descriptions of some of the trail riders' organizations in the state, see chapter 10. This chapter will help you to choose a trail appropriate to your horse's experience and fitness. First, however, be sure to apply for the necessary permits, and familiarize yourself with park rules and regulations.

FEES, PERMITS, AND REGULATIONS

State Parks and Forests

New Jersey residents age sixty-two or over, or those who are disabled, may apply for a permanent pass entitling them to free admission and free parking at state parks and forests upon proof of their status. In addition, the pass offers a reduction in nightly campsite rates, with the exception of group campsites. For those under age sixty-two, an annual New Jersey State Park Pass is available for a low fee. It provides free entrance for one calendar year to state parks and forests that charge daily walk-in or parking fees. It does not cover camping fees or special events; nor does it guarantee entry when facilities are filled to capacity. Applications for both types of passes are available from the New Jersey Division of Parks and Forestry, Box 404, Trenton 08625; 1-800-843-6420 or 609-984-0370. A complete guide to New Jersey's state parks and forests can be purchased by mail; call for current cost.

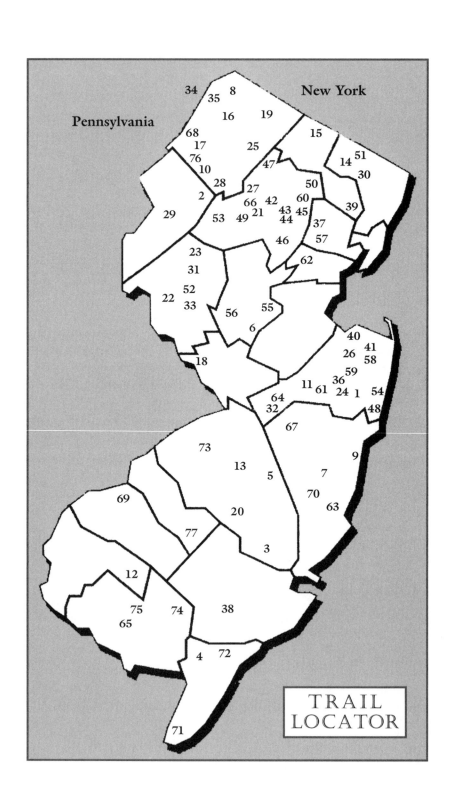

Pennsylvania

New York

34   8
35
16   19
68   15
17   25
76   47   14 51
10   28   50   30
27
2   66 42 60 39
29   53 49 21 43 45 37
44   57
46
23   62
31
52   55
22   33   56 6
18   40
26 41
58
36 59
11 61 24 1 54
64   67   48
32   9
73   7
13   70
5   63
69   77   20
3
12
75 74 38
65
4 72
71

TRAIL
LOCATOR

State Parks and Forests

1 Allaire State Park
2 Allamuchy Mountain State Park
3 Bass River State Forest
4 Belleplain State Forest
5 Brendon T. Bryne State Forest
  (formerly Lebanon State Forest)
6 Delaware and Raritan Canal State
  Park
7 Double Trouble State Park
8 High Point State Park
9 Island Beach State Park
10 Kittatinny Valley State Park
11 Monmouth Battlefield State Park
12 Parvin State Park
13 Penn State Forest
14 Ramapo Mountain State Forest
15 Ringwood State Park
16 Stokes State Forest
17 Swartswood State Forest
18 Washington Crossing State Park
19 Wawayanda State Park
20 Wharton State Forest

Rail-Trails

21 Black River Rail-Trail
22 Capoolong Rail-Trail
23 Columbia Rail-Trail
24 Freehold and Jamesburg Rail-Trail
25 Hamburg Mountain Rail-Trail
26 Henry Hudson Rail-Trail
27 Ogden Mine Railroad Path Rail-Trail
28 Paulinskill Valley Rail-Trail
29 Pequest Rail-Trail

More Great Trails

30 Campgaw Mountain County
  Reservation
31 Christie Hoffman Farm Park
32 Clayton Park
33 Deer Path Park
34 Delaware Water Gap National
  Recreation Area/Conashaugh View
  Equestrian Trail
35 Delaware Water Gap National
  Recreation Area/Upper Ridge
36 Dorbrook Recreation Area
37 Eagle Rock Reservation
38 Estell Manor Park
39 Garret Mountain Reservation
40 Hartshorne Woods Park
41 Huber Woods Park
42 James Andrews Memorial Park
43 Jockey Hollow/Morristown
  National Historical Park
44 Lewis Morris County Park
45 Loantaka Brook County Park
46 Lord Stirling Stable Trails
47 Mahlon Dickerson Reservation
48 Manasquan Reservoir Recreation
  Area
49 Patriots' Path
50 Pequannock Watershed
51 Ramapo Valley County Reservation
52 Round Valley Recreation Area
53 Schooley's Mountain County Park
54 Shark River Park
55 Six Mile Run Reservoir
56 Sourland Mountain Preserve
57 South Mountain Reservation
58 Tatum Park
59 Thompson Park
60 Tourne County Park
61 Turkey Swamp Park
62 Watchung Reservation
63 Wells Mills County Park

Wildlife Management Areas

64 Assunpink Wildlife Management
  Area
65 Bevan (Edward G.) Wildlife
  Management Area
66 Black River Wildlife Management
  Area
67 Colliers Mills Wildlife Management
  Area
68 Flatbrook Wildlife Management Area
69 Glassboro Wildlife Management Area
70 Greenwood Wildlife Management
  Area
71 Higbee Beach Wildlife Management
  Area
72 MacNamara (Lester G.) Wildlife
  Management Area
73 Medford Wildlife Management Area
74 Peaslee Wildlife Management Area
75 Union Lake Wildlife Management
  Area
76 Whittingham Wildlife Management
  Area
77 Winslow Wildlife Management Area

State parks and forests have implemented a carry in/carry out program, which means that visitors must take their trash home for proper disposal. Bags are usually available at the entrances to parks, forests, and recreation sites. However, because access to horse trails is often located elsewhere than at the main park entrance, it's wise to carry a trash bag with you at all times.

Wildlife Management Areas

An annual application and fee are required for an individual permit to use New Jersey's wildlife management areas (WMAs). Equestrians may ride on horseback anywhere in designated areas within the WMAs, except on dams, fire lines, or cultivated or planted fields. Horse-drawn carriages are restricted to main and secondary roads and may not drive off-road, through fields, or on any established horseback riding trails.

Note that WMAs are passive recreation areas reserved primarily for hunting, fishing, and hiking. Most do not have drinking water or toilet facilities; nor do they offer established trailheads or markers (except for Assunpink WMA). Be aware that, except on Sundays, hunting is permitted in season. In addition to the possibility that gunshots will upset your horse, you could find yourself in a dangerous situation. A bright orange vest is strongly advised. (Note that the jumps along the trails within the Assunpink WMA belong to the Monmouth County Hunt Club, and nonmembers are not allowed to use them.)

Your permit must be carried with you at all times while riding in the WMAs. For a hunting schedule, directions, regulations, and further details, contact the Division of Fish and Wildlife, Central Region Office, One Eldridge Road, Robbinsville 08691; 609-259-2132. When applying by mail, include your phone and license plate numbers.

Motor Vehicle Regulations

Equestrians are afforded the same rights as motor vehicle operators when using a public road or highway. Motor vehicle operators approaching horseback riders may not use their horns and are prohibited from driving more than twenty-five miles per hour.

A horse-drawn vehicle traveling on New Jersey roads thirty minutes after sunset, thirty minutes before sunrise, or when fog makes it impossible to see a long distance must have lighted lamps front and back. In front, at least one lighted lamp must show a white light and be displayed so that it can be seen by an approaching vehicle from at least 500 feet away. The rear of the carriage must have two lighted lamps, each displaying a red light visible for a distance of at least 500 feet behind.

Remember: for any horse transported on a roadway within New Jersey, a valid Coggins test certificate, current within two years of the date of travel, must be on hand.

TRAIL SAFETY AND COURTESY

When entering a public park area, equestrians should be especially aware of safety. In addition to familiarizing yourself with individual parks' rules and regulations, review the precautions and tips in chapter 4. The following common-sense measures also apply:

- Alcohol is not permitted on publicly owned lands without permission.
- Check all tack and mounts before and after your trip.
- Carry saddlebags with a first aid kit and other items recommended in chapter 4.
- Stay on designated trails.
- Never gallop around bends or downhill.
- Approach strange horses carefully.
- Move carefully and quickly when crossing roadways.
- Learn how to recognize poison ivy. Remember: leaves of three, let it be.

Trails designated as *multiuse* are intended to accommodate hikers and bicyclists as well as equestrians. Therefore, it is of utmost importance to be aware of what is happening all around you and your horse at all times. You may encounter hikers who are paying more attention to the scenery than to an approaching horse, unleashed dogs, fast-pedaling cyclists, individuals in motorized wheelchairs, or excited children who want to run up to your horse and pet it. Before setting out on any trail, make certain your mount is accustomed to the sounds of tractors, motorcycles, airplanes, and other potentially frightening or startling objects. When near water, be aware of anglers—your horse may associate a rod being cast with a whip being raised. If a cyclist is ahead of you, call out a warning. Be on the lookout especially for mountain bikers; they frequently seem to appear from nowhere without warning.

NEW JERSEY'S GREAT TRAILS

Trail routes may change or close, so it's best to call in advance before starting out. Periodic inquiries to your county parks department may turn up new trails in your area.

Listed below are dozens of great trails within New Jersey. The numbers correspond to those on the trail locator map, and trail length is round-trip unless otherwise noted. So, saddle up, and let's go riding! Enjoy!

State Parks and Forests

1. ALLAIRE STATE PARK

County:	Monmouth
Admission:	Free; parking fee from Memorial Day to Labor Day
Hours:	Sunrise to sunset
Water:	Horse, streams; rider, main office and rest room
Rest room:	Yes
Trail length:	Approximately 17 miles
Trailer parking:	Where designated; check with park office
Terrain:	Mostly level, some hills; sand and dirt

Location: Farmingdale. Take exit 98 off the Garden State Parkway or exit 31B off I-195.

This delightful park offers several miles of level terrain and small hills along marked and unmarked trails that are a combination of sandy, paved, and unimproved roads. Thanks to the Allaire Trail Users Group (ATUG; see chapter 10), a new trail has recently been blazed past the Hospital Road parking area toward the Manasquan River. This particular trail, according to equestrian Liz Turrin, starts out as a narrow path skirting the river and winds up with some challenging climbs up the side of a hill, from which you'll be rewarded with a glimpse of the river through the treetops below.

Along many of the other trails, you'll pass through lush woods beside tiny streams where dozens of varieties of wildflowers can be seen each spring. Many species of birds, including the blue-winged warbler and the ruby-throated hummingbird, will provide you with sweet melodies. You might even spot a woodcock or white-tailed deer. Before or after your ride, be sure to explore Allaire Village, where well-preserved nineteenth-century buildings include a general store, blacksmith shop, carpenter's shop, and more, with docents in period dress demonstrating crafts of yesteryear.

This historic village was once a self-contained industrial community centered on one of the finest bog ironworks in the country. When anthracite and iron were discovered in Pennsylvania in 1846, however, the demand for bog iron products declined, and the ironworks and the more than four hundred workers and their families eventually left. In the state park, you'll not only learn about this part of American history, but you can also ride the Pine Creek Railroad, an antique narrow-gauge steam train, spend the night or longer camping beneath the pines, fish, and much more.

Note: Allaire State Park is one of the few places to allow overnight horse camping, at the Allaire Group Campsite on Squankum Road. Permits are available for 75 cents per camper (minimum seven people) and a $7 reservation fee. Turrin reports that, although primitive, the campsites are very good. She notes that those who wish to camp overnight with their horses should bring their own water; do all cooking and necessary toilet breaks at the adjacent campsite; and, if riding here for the first time, plan on coming during the cooler months to avoid the pine and deer flies that are so abundant in hot weather.

The main trail starts from the Hospital Road parking lot (marked with plastic markers stuck in the ground—orange in one direction, blue in the other). The trailhead leads to an approximately five-mile loop trail that branches onto mostly unmarked side trails for exciting exploration opportunities (see trail 24, the Freehold and Jamesburg Rail-Trail).

Contact: Allaire State Park, Box 220, Farmingdale 07727; 732-938-2371; www.state.nj.us/dep/parksandforests/parks/allaire.html.

2. ALLAMUCHY MOUNTAIN STATE PARK

Counties: Sussex and Warren
Admission: Free
Hours: Sunrise to sunset
Water: Horse, pond; rider, none
Rest room: Yes
Trail length: 27.5 miles
Trailer parking: In any of three lots
Terrain: Hilly; rocky

Location: Three miles north of Hackettstown, between Route 604 (Willow Grove–Waterloo Road) on the east, Route 517 on the west, and Route 206 on the north. Drive south on Route 517 from exit 19 on I-80 (toward Hackettstown) and make the first left turn at a post next to a brick house after passing a restaurant. Proceed 2.3 miles to the parking lots.

Gorgeous scenery awaits in this area, where you'll encounter some ups and downs as well as a level area that circles Deer Park Lake. Around the north shore of the lake you may spot the broad-tailed beaver, the largest rodent in North America. Its cone-shaped house and the dozens of gnawed tree stumps are evidence of its presence. A canopy of beech, oak, and tulip trees provides shade. After crossing the concrete dam on the eastern shore, you'll arrive at a green oasis of evergreens, red maples, and sassafras—a perfect place to rest and take in the charming lake setting in the serene wilderness.

Contact: Allamuchy Mountain State Park, c/o Stephens State Park, 800 Willow Grove Street, Hackettstown 07840; 908-852-3790; www.state.nj.us/dep/parksandforests/parks/allamuch.html.

3. BASS RIVER STATE FOREST

County: Burlington
Admission: Free; parking fee from Memorial Day to Labor Day
Hours: Sunrise to sunset
Water: Horse, none; rider, yes, in rest room
Rest room: Yes
Trail length: Approximately 100–150 miles, including secondary roads
Trailer parking: Anywhere on the side of the dirt road, depending on where you start. Be sure to place a note on your dashboard stating that you are horseback riding.
Terrain: Level; a mix of sandy and paved roads

Location: About 25 miles north of Atlantic City and 6 miles west of Tuckerton. From the Garden State Parkway heading south, take exit 52; heading north, take exit 50.

Although horses are not allowed on the hiking trails in this state forest, you're welcome to ride anywhere along the secondary roads. Terrain is flat and sandy, with loops leading through dense stands of pitch pine (a three-needled cone-bearer that is the dominant tree here) and scrub oak (a common shrub found on drier ground). As you ride, you'll probably wonder why this particular area is part of the famous Pine Barrens. Theories abound. Some believe that most of this area of the state was once covered with pines. Another theory arose from colonial days, when settlers discovered that the acid soil was unsuitable for most traditional crops. However, the land does support an abundance of plant communities, including false heather, which blooms with a yellow flower in May; pixie moss, a light green plant that hugs the ground and produces white and pink blossoms in spring; and foxtail club moss, a ground runner.

On a hot summer's day, cool off by taking a swim at the bathing beach on the east shore of Lake Absegami within Bass River State Park. The entrance fee from Memorial Day to Labor day is worth it.

Contact: Bass River State Forest, 762 Stage Road, Box 118, New Gretna 08224; 609-296-1114; www.state.nj.us/dep/parksandforests/ parks/bass.html.

4. BELLEPLAIN STATE FOREST

Counties:	Cape May and Cumberland
Admission:	Free; parking fee from Memorial Day to Labor Day if you enter the park with a trailer
Hours:	Sunrise to sunset
Water:	None for horse or rider
Rest room:	Yes, at park office
Trail length:	27 miles
Trailer parking:	Anywhere on the side of the road before entering the park
Terrain:	Mostly level; a mix of sand and pavement

Location: Reachable via Routes 9 and 550. From the Garden State Parkway southbound, use exit 17 for Route 550; northbound, use exit 13 for Routes 9, 83, and 47.

The easy, level trail through this magnificent forest follows old roads and abandoned railroad rights-of-way. If you're lucky, you'll catch sight of white-tailed deer, red foxes, and ruffed grouse. If not, you'll still be a winner, because Lake Nummy, named for an Indian chief, is lovely—as is a quick dip in its refreshing waters. You'll be riding through trees typical of the coastal plain, such as pitch pine, black and white oak, and American holly. In the low swamp areas, feast your eyes on huge stands of Atlantic white cedar. Here you might spot a red-bellied turtle or hear a frog. Riding in this area during fall or winter is preferred because summer draws mosquitoes and ticks. Long sleeves are excellent protection year-round against overgrown shrubs.

Contact: Belleplain State Forest, County Road 550, Box 450, Woodbine 08270; 609-861-2404; www.state.nj.us/dep/parksand-forests/parks/belle.html.

5. BRENDAN T. BYRNE STATE FOREST (FORMERLY LEBANON STATE FOREST)

Counties:	Burlington and Ocean
Admission:	Free
Hours:	Sunrise to sunset
Water:	Available for horse and rider
Rest room:	Yes
Trail length:	Approximately 11 miles

Trailer parking: Available by the fire tower on Route 72, New Lisbon, and at the intersection with campsites near the park office

Terrain: Mostly level; sand or gravel roads

Location: From the junction of routes 72 and 70 at Four Mile circle, take Buddtown Road north about 1.7 miles to Ong's Hat; turn right onto a small road marked by pink blazes and follow it to the parking lot.

A local group has been blazing a new trail here; until it's finished, you can enjoy any of the sand or gravel roads in the forest (though not the Batona Trail or the Cranberry Trail). Riding trails have color-coded blazes and are labeled with signs graphically depicting allowed uses. The Garden State Horse and Carriage Society arranges many drives along these trails. Consult the park ranger on the best routes and ask for a map.

Among the interesting sights you'll encounter are the tall, thin pitch pines. Many have been charred by repeated fires, but this particular type of tree is very hearty and always springs back to life. The woods in this, New Jersey's second largest forest (more than 34,000 acres), abound with species of wildlife that depend upon the luscious blueberries and huckleberries.

The area is also steeped in history. In 1851 the Lebanon Glass Works was established here because the necessary sand, wood for charcoal, and other natural resources were available. This industry devoured the trees for miles around, however, and the operation was abandoned by 1867, when the supply of wood had run out. In 1908 the state acquired the land that eventually became Lebanon State Forest, and tree plantings carried out by the Civilian Conservation Corp in the 1930s helped to bring back the pine, oak, maple, and Atlantic white cedars we enjoy today.

Camping is also available if you want to stay overnight or longer.

Contact: Brendan T. Byrne State Forest, Box 215, New Lisbon 08064; 609-726-1191; www.state.nj.us/dep/parksandforests/parks/byrne.html.

6. DELAWARE AND RARITAN CANAL STATE PARK

Counties: Somerset and Mercer

Admission: Free

Hours: Sunrise to sunset

Water: Horse, none; rider, at park headquarters

Rest room: Yes, at park headquarters

Trail length: 25 miles

Trailer parking: At park headquarters: Blackwells Mills Road and
                    Canal Road, Franklin Township
        Terrain: Level; cinder and asphalt

Location: From the junction of Routes 206 and 514 in Hillsborough,
take Route 514 east (Amwell Road) to Route 533 south (Millstone River
Road). After 2.1 miles, turn left across the bridge onto Blackwells Mills
Road, then turn right on Canal Road to the second house on the left.

This linear park is seventy miles in length, but horseback riding is
restricted to the twenty-five-mile section between East Millstone and
Kingston. No need for disappointment, however. The ride is sheer joy
in the early morning hours, when it's almost deserted, except for an
occasional bicyclist, jogger, or hiker. At East Millstone, the brid-
getender's house, wooden bridge, and mill site are reminders of days
long gone. More than 150 years ago, laborers dug the long, deep
trench using only picks and shovels. Many died on the job from exer-
tion, poor hygiene, and a cholera epidemic. Yet they completed the
canal, which opened in 1834 and allowed coal and other goods to
move between Philadelphia and New York City. The canal closed in
1933, after trains and trucks made shipping faster and cheaper.

Today the canal serves as a major source of drinking water for
people in twenty-two towns. Since becoming a state park in 1974, it is
also used by canoeists, anglers, hikers, bicyclists, and those who love
horseback riding. Trees line both sides of the trail where mules once
pulled barges. Watch for thick beds of pickerelweed, identifiable by
elongated, heart-shaped leaves and, from May through October, showy
blue-flowered spikes. But be aware of the poison ivy on either side of
the trail; remember, "leaves of three, let it be." The sight of turtles
basking on the bank or on a log on a sunny day is common, as are the
beautiful melodies of some of the more than 150 species of birds that
frequent this area.

Contact: Superintendent, D & R Canal State Park, 625 Canal
Road, Somerset 08502; 732-873-3050; www.dandrcanal.com.

7. DOUBLE TROUBLE STATE PARK

         County: Ocean
      Admission: Free
           Hours: Sunrise to sunset
           Water: None for horse or rider
       Rest room: Yes, at park entrance
    Trail length: Approximately 5 miles
Trailer parking: Available at the park entrance
         Terrain: Level; sandy

Location: From the Garden State Parkway south, take exit 80, turn left (south) onto Double Trouble Road, and travel about 4 miles to the stop sign. The park entrance is straight ahead across the road. From the Garden State Parkway north, take exit 74, and turn east onto Lacey Road; make a left onto Manchester Boulevard, left again onto Western Boulevard, and, at the stop sign, turn left onto Route 618 (Veterans Boulevard) and continue west under the Garden State Parkway bridge. The park entrance is on the left.

No matter which flat, sandy trail you decide to take—the two-mile loop; the half mile to the reservoir; or the three miles to Lacey Road—the ride will be interesting. This park of more than 5,000 acres offers lots of history, too. Village buildings at the entrance date to the early 1900s, and an 1883 machine in the sawmill is capable of cutting a thousand shingles an hour! At the height of the village's prosperity, millworkers produced high-quality lumber for shipbuilding and home construction. Cranberries were also grown here for commercial purposes. During your ride, you'll see lots of cottonweed and a stand of huge Atlantic white cedars. If you come during September and October, you'll probably see workers harvesting the cranberries.

Contact: Double Trouble State Park, Box 175, Bayville 08721; 732-341-6662; www.state.nj.us/dep/parksandforests/parks/double. html.

8. HIGH POINT STATE PARK

County: Sussex
Admission: Free; parking fee from Memorial Day to Labor Day
Hours: Sunrise to sunset
Water: Available for horse and rider
Rest room: Yes
Trail length: 14 miles
Trailer parking: Stop at the ranger station near the park entrance for directions to the parking areas
Terrain: Fairly level; rocky

Location: Follow Route 23 about 7 miles north of the town of Sussex.

This fairly level riding trail basically goes to and around the campground, where, from some campsites, you can view the High Point Monument. At 1,803 feet above sea level, the monument site offers spectacular panoramas of surrounding farmland and forest in three states. After your ride, stretch your legs by hiking through this beautiful park, or take a swim in the spring-fed twenty-acre natural Lake Marcia.

Contact: High Point State Park, 1480 Route 23, Sussex 07461; 973-875-4800; www.state.nj.us/dep/parksandforests/parks/high-point.html.

9. ISLAND BEACH STATE PARK

County:	Ocean
Admission:	Fee for parking
Hours:	Sunrise to sunset
Water:	Available for horse and rider
Rest room:	Yes
Trail length:	6 miles along the ocean
Trailer parking:	At the south end of the first bathing area
Terrain:	Level; sandy

Location: Take Route 37 east to Route 35 south to the park entrance

Note: Riding is allowed only from October 1 through April 30. Reservations for riding must be made in advance.

From the starting point at Beach House 1, feel the ocean breeze and salt spray on your face, and enjoy the sound of the waves hitting the beach and the sight of the open sky and vast expanse of sand. The seven-month period when riding is allowed is actually the best time to be at the park, because all the sun worshipers have disappeared!

Before the ride, stop at the nature center, about a mile or so past the entrance gate, to learn more about the plants and animals found in the park. Bring binoculars so you can spot a few of the 240 species of birds that frequent this area, including some on the endangered species list—the black skimmer, least tern, and piping plover. When you can turn your eyes away from the ocean, check the sand for casts left by horseshoe crabs, dunes created by the never-ending wind carrying sand, beach grass that flutters with pretty yellow flowers in early spring, and many other treasures.

Until the 1950s Island Beach was known as Cranberry Inlet and was part of an island created when the sea opened a sliver between the ocean and Barnegat Bay (near the northern end of the park). Shipping was a big industry here in the 1780s. During the American Revolution, bands of privateers made Barnegat Bay their base for preying on boats supplying the British forces in New York City. Their plan was simple. The pirates would tie a lantern to an animal's back and lead it along the dunes parallel to the coast. An unsuspecting captain would turn his vessel toward the light, thinking it was another vessel. Once the vessel ran aground, the pirates would grab its valuables. Fortunately, the pirates are gone and the riding here is a treat!

Contact: Island Beach State Park, Box 37, Seaside Park 08752; 732-793-0506; www.state.nj.us/dep/parksandforests/parks/island. html.

10. KITTATINNY VALLEY STATE PARK

County:	Sussex
Admission:	Free
Hours:	Sunrise to sunset
Water:	Horse, at stream crossings and along paths to the river and creeks; rider, at rest room
Rest room:	Yes, at parking lot
Trail length:	Approximately 8 miles within the park; access is available to the adjacent Paulinskill Valley Trail/Sussex Branch Trail (see trail 28)
Trailer parking:	Depends on trail preference. For riding inside the park, go to the large hayfield on Gooddale Road in Andover Township or the grassy field opposite the Twin Lakes Park area. For the Paulinskill Valley Trail, park in Lafayette (see trail 28).
Terrain:	Trails within the park are single track, made by mountain bikers; they are hilly and rocky. The rail-trails are mostly flat gravel beds.

Location: From I-80, take Route 206 north approximately 7 miles to Andover Borough and turn right onto Route 669 (Limecrest Road). The park entrance is 1.1 miles ahead on the left.

Note: This park oversees two rail-trails, the Sussex Branch Trail, which goes through the park, and the Paulinskill Valley Trail (see trail 28 for both). Before going, contact the park office for current trail conditions.

Acquired in 1994, and thus one of New Jersey's newest state parks, Kittatinny Valley embraces the 117-acre Lake Aeroflex—one of the deepest lakes in the state—and the 39-acre Gardner's Pond. This very scenic park is home to white-tailed deer, wild turkeys, chipmunks, and other wildlife. The mostly undeveloped cinder-based Sussex Branch Trail, which skirts swamps, lakes, fields, and several small communities, and crosses through Allamuchy Mountain State Park (see trail 2), makes this park a great place for a ride.

Contact: Kittatinny Valley State Park, Box 621, Andover 07821; 973-786-6445; www.state.nj.us/dep/parksandforests/parks/kittval. html.

11. MONMOUTH BATTLEFIELD STATE PARK

County:	Monmouth
Admission:	Free

Hours:	Sunrise to sunset
Water:	Horse, none; rider, yes
Rest room:	Yes, at park headquarters
Trail length:	10 miles
Trailer parking:	Available at park headquarters, on Route 522, Manalapan
Terrain:	Mostly flat, with wet areas

Location: From the Garden State Parkway, take exit 123 to Route 9 south; travel 15 miles to business Route 33 west. The park is located 1.5 miles on the right.

One of the most important battles of the American Revolution took place here on June 28, 1778. If you arrive during the last weekend in June, you'll be treated to a reenactment, complete with authentically dressed troops firing muskets and women and children in eighteenth-century dress cooking over campfires. Nearby, watch the "soldiers" drill and march off to battle. The flat, surfaced trail, four to six feet wide, follows along a heavily shaded swampy area where deer, turkey, and red foxes have been spotted.

    Contact: Monmouth Battlefield State Park, 347 Freehold-Englishtown Road, Manalapan 07726; 732-462-9616; www.state.nj.us/dep/parksandforests/parks/monbat.html.

12. PARVIN STATE PARK

County:	Salem
Admission:	None; there is a charge for the beach if you want to swim or sunbathe after your ride
Hours:	Sunrise to sunset
Water:	Horse, none; rider, yes
Rest room:	Yes
Trail length:	Approximately 10 miles; ask ranger for a map
Trailer parking:	Across from the beach area
Terrain:	Nice cleared dirt trails

Location: From Route 55 north or south, take exit 35 and follow signs to the park, which is located between Centerton and Vineland on Route 540.

In the 1930s, young men enrolled in the Civilian Conservation Corps (CCC) built these trails while living in army-style barracks in the middle of the woods. The work was strenuous and the hours long, but the project gave the men an opportunity to earn a few dollars during the Great Depression. Later, the barracks they built within the park were used to house German prisoners of war during World War II.

Today, the 1,125-acre park provides solitude on trails leading through a variety of habitats, including cedar swamps, pine forests, holly groves, and vast patches of lush mountain laurel. Even if you don't spot any of the 123 species of birds that visit and nest here, you're bound to hear their sweet melodies.

Contact: Parvin State Park, 701 Almond Road, Pittsgrove 08318; 609-358-8616; www.state.nj.us/dep/parksandforests/parks/parvin. html.

13. PENN STATE FOREST

County:	Burlington
Admission:	Free
Hours:	Sunrise to sunset
Water:	Horse, yes; rider, in recreation area
Rest room:	Pit toilets in recreation area
Trail length:	Approximately 20–25 miles, unmarked
Trailer parking:	At entrance
Terrain:	Level; sandy

Location: Off Route 563, south of Chatsworth. Take Lake Oswego Road for about 4 miles. Parking is on the right, immediately after crossing a bridge.

This 3,366-acre forest is a year-round delight. Here, along sandy roads, you'll find portions of the state's pygmy pine forest community, Lake Oswego (the result of an upstream dam constructed to create a reservoir for a downstream cranberry operation), plus an abundance of trees—red maple, Atlantic white cedar, pitch pine, and blackjack oak, among others. The variety of shrubs is astounding, including pepper bush, huckleberry, American holly, mountain laurel, and swamp azalea, to mention only a few examples.

Contact: Bass River State Forest, 762 Stage Road, Box 118, New Gretna 08224; 609-296-1114; www.state.nj.us/dep/parksandforests/ parks/penn.html.

14. RAMAPO MOUNTAIN STATE FOREST

County:	Bergen
Admission:	Free
Hours:	Sunrise to sunset
Water:	Available for horse and rider
Rest room:	Yes
Trail length:	Approximately 26 miles
Trailer parking:	Available at the upper- and lower-level parking areas, but a bit tight at the entrance to the park on Skyline Drive in Oakland

Terrain: Hilly; rocky

Location: Take I-287 to exit 57 and follow Skyline Drive to the parking lot.

Note: Come on weekdays; it's too crowded on weekends.

The lovely trail through this forest has many ups and downs but affords the possibility of seeing abundant wildlife, including muskrats. You'll probably spot one because the trail goes along the perimeter of Ramapo Lake, a good place to see turtles and water plants as well. Along part of the historic Cannonball Trail—a secret route through the Ramapo Mountains that was used during the Revolutionary War to transport cannonballs that had been cast in local furnaces—you'll also see huge boulders, rich in iron ore. The strange-looking circular stone tower with antennas is a radio tower on private property.

    Contact: Ringwood State Park, 1304 Sloatsburg Road, Ringwood 07456; 973-962-7031; www.state.nj.us/dep/parksandforests/parks/ringwood.html.

15. RINGWOOD STATE PARK

    Counties: Passaic and Bergen
    Admission: Free; parking fee from Memorial Day to Labor Day
    Hours: Sunrise to sunset
    Water: None for horse or rider
    Rest room: Yes, at Skylands entrance
    Trail length: 22 miles
    Trailer parking: At lot C; see directions below
    Terrain: Hilly; rough, rocky dirt roads

Location: Off I-287, exit 57 (Skyline Drive/Ringwood exit); follow signs for Ringwood State Park into the town of Ringwood. At the second stop sign, bear right; turn onto Route 511; turn right onto Sloatsburg Road; turn right onto Morris Road. Go through entrance to Skylands Manor; at stop sign, bear left. Pass parking lot B; turn left and park at lot C.

During the Revolutionary War, General George Washington was a frequent visitor to Ringwood Manor, home of John Erskine, whose furnaces and forges supplied the Continental Army with cannon and munitions. Although the blacksmith's shop where the general's horses were shod is gone, this 5,237-acre park in the heart of the Ramapo Mountains offers great scenery and history. Skylands is the state's official botanical garden, and the park boasts a swimming beach, several lakes, and good hiking and riding trails.

Equestrians here are especially fortunate, for the riding trails are located far from hikers and mountain bikers. For the most part, you'll be riding on old fire roads; these are rough and rocky in places, but take you through dense woods and past several lakes. The wildflowers during spring and the abundant wildlife all year are well worth the trip.

A bulletin board in lot C outlines the trail directions. Bear in mind that there are often fallen trees across the trail; and, although you'll be passing lakes, it's often too muddy to lead your horse to them for a drink.

Contact: Ringwood State Park, 1304 Sloatsburg Road, Ringwood 07456; 973-962-7031; www.state.nj.us/dep/parksandforests/parks/ringwood.html.

16. STOKES STATE FOREST

County:	Sussex
Admission:	Free; parking fee from Memorial Day to Labor Day
Hours:	Sunrise to sunset
Water:	None for horse or rider
Rest room:	Yes
Trail length:	Approximately 31 miles
Trailer parking:	Available at the main entrance to the park or at Culver's Gap on Sunrise Mountain Road
Terrain:	Hilly; rocky (shoes recommended)

Location: Entrance to the park is 4 miles north of Branchville on Route 206.

The rangers here are very helpful about recommending the best places to ride. Although the going sometimes gets tough, the trails are well worth the effort. Here, amid 15,735 acres, you'll find thousands of odd-shaped rocks adorned with lush, green moss, magnificent vistas of Pennsylvania and the Delaware Water Gap from the mountain ridge, a great variety of trees, and wildflowers during spring. If you arrive during fall, bring binoculars to scan the bird migration route.

Contact: Stokes State Forest, 1 Coursen Road, Branchville 07826; 973-948-3820; www.state.nj.us/dep/parksandforests/parks/stokes.html.

17. SWARTSWOOD STATE PARK

County:	Sussex
Admission:	Free for equestrian trails; fee for the park from Memorial Day to Labor Day
Hours:	Sunrise to sunset
Water:	Available for horse and rider

Rest room: Yes

Trail length: 3 miles

Trailer parking: From Route 619, look for the sign for Swartswood State Park; turn right onto Ridge Road, and at the next road (Dove Island Road), turn right and continue about a mile. Turn right at the sign marked "Equestrian Trail Lot" and the start of the trail.

Terrain: Hilly; dirt trail with some rocky areas

Location: Off Route 619 in Stillwater Township

Although the ride here is short in length, it's long on scenery, and you'll immediately gain an appreciation for the outdoors. Today, the dirt trail with gentle ups and downs is very safe, but around 1756, during the French and Indian War, you would have been risking your life to ride here even for a few minutes. At that time, an Indian war party burned down a home owned by Captain Anthony Swartwout, a British officer, near Swartswood Lake, scalped Swartwout, killed four of his children, and kidnapped two others. As the story goes, after this terrible incident, the royal governor offered a bounty to anyone brave enough to capture or kill male Indians over fifteen years of age. The practice ended by 1758, when a new governor took over and appointed patrols to guard the area until a peace pact was made with the Indians.

In the early 1800s, visitors came to this gorgeous area to rest, swim, fish, and hunt. Swartswood State Park, encompassing 1,304 acres and a grist mill at the southwestern tip of Swartswood Lake, was named for the Swartwout family. Its campground, open from April through October, boasts huge, wooded sites.

The equestrian trail follows alongside stone fences, fields, ponds, wetlands, forest, and hemlock groves. It offers great opportunities to spot wildlife. You'll also hear lots of songbirds, and you may spot a red-tailed hawk or a turkey vulture. During warm weather, you might want to cool off by taking a dip in the lovely lake.

Contact: Swartswood State Park, Box 123, Swartswood 07877; 973-383-5230; www.state.nj.us/dep/parksandforests/parks/swartswood.html.

18. WASHINGTON CROSSING STATE PARK

County: Mercer

Admission: Fee for main section of the park from Memorial Day through Labor Day; free at trailer parking area (see below)

Hours: Sunrise to sunset

     Water: None for horse or rider
   Rest room: At park headquarters, nature center, and campsite
       area
  Trail length: Approximately 5 miles
Trailer parking: Available at the Philp's Farm day use area off
       Route 579
    Terrain: Unimproved trail; rocky, narrow

Location: On Route 546 in Titusville

This trail is not maintained, so it's wise to check with park staff before bringing your horse. The trail passes through fields, a wooded area, and the back end of the park's natural area.

  The park itself is a delight, with an abundance of deer and a variety of trees, shrubs, and wildflowers, plus a great deal of history.

  Contact: Washington Crossing State Park, 355 Washington Crossing–Pennington Road, Titusville 08560; 609-737-0623; www.state.nj.us/dep/parksandforests/parks/washcros.html.

19. WAWAYANDA STATE PARK

    County: Sussex
  Admission: Free; parking fee from Memorial Day through
       Labor Day
     Hours: 5 a.m. to 9 p.m.
     Water: Horse, from numerous creeks; rider, yes, but
       bringing your own is more convenient
   Rest room: Yes
  Trail length: Approximately 21 miles
Trailer parking: Obtain a free trail map at the park entrance
       after the entry gate. Continue approximately
       1.5 miles past the office, turn left into the
       beach/picnic area, and look for the grass parking
       lot on the left (marked "horse trailer parking").
    Terrain: Hilly; partially rocky (shoes recommended)

Location: Enter the park from the northern section of Warwick Turnpike, from the north on N.Y. Route 94 (which becomes Warwick Turnpike) and from the south on Clinton Road. The park entrance is on the west side of Warwick Turnpike, about 1.25 miles north of Upper Greenwood Lake.

Note: Horses are not permitted on the Appalachian, Cedar Swamp, and Pump House Trails. To negotiate the trails in this park, your horse should be willing to cross or walk in water. Be aware that hunting is conducted here during the fall and winter—and this is bear country.

Ellen and Diane Fox are ready to explore one of the fabulous trails within Wawayanda State Park— but they've forgotten their helmets!

This park is one of my favorites. It offers the equestrian approximately twenty-one miles of sheer riding pleasure through dense forests, as well as spectacular views of Wawayanda Lake, a crystal-clear body of water covering 255 acres. Parts of the trails, which can be extremely rocky with ups and downs, go past stands of hemlock and rhododendron, adding a touch of welcome color to the huge rock formations on either side.

The blue-blazed William Hoeferlein Trail, although rocky, is terrific for balance and agility. For trotting, try the long trail along the Wawayanda service road to the ranger station and then cross the road to the Hoeferlein Trail, which leads leads to Double Pond. For a good two- to three-hour loop, start from the parking lot, follow Double Pond Trail (right) to Cherry Ridge Road (right) and return on the Laurel Pond Trail. You'll come to a washed-out bridge on Cherry Ridge Road, but with care you can get around this section. These are quiet roads with little traffic.

From the parking lot, another two- to three-hour loop follows the Laurel Pond Trail to Cherry Ridge Road to the Cabin Trail to Turkey Ridge Trail to Old Coal Trail, which leads back to Cherry Ridge Road and Laurel Pond. Another section, good for trotting for longer periods and worth exploring along old dirt roads that aren't too hilly, runs from the Iron Mountain Trail to Crossover Road and back onto Wawayanda Road.

    Contact: Wawayanda State Park, 885 Warwick Turnpike, Hewitt 07421; 973-853-4462; www.state.nj.us/dep/parksandforests/parks/ wawayanda.html.

20. WHARTON STATE FOREST

Counties:	Atlantic and Burlington
Admission:	Weekend fee from Memorial Day to Labor Day; fee for camping
Hours:	24 hours
Water:	Horse, limited along the trail; rider, hand pump at camping area
Rest room:	At camping area
Trail length:	At least 150 miles. Riding is allowed on any unimproved sand trail.
Trailer parking:	Call park headquarters for the best locations in addition to the Atsion Ranger Station on Route 206 and the Carranza Memorial on Carranza Road
Terrain:	Mostly flat; soft to hard-packed sand, with large puddles/small ponds across some trails

Location: This huge state forest can be reached from the Garden State Parkway, Route 9, and Route 542. Call the park office for directions from your area.

Note: Horses are not allowed on the Batona Trail. According to park rangers, horse camping (with trailer) is allowed at the Goshen Pond, Batona, and Bodine Field Campgrounds. Check with the park before going.

Wharton, the largest single tract of land within New Jersey's state park system, offers one of the longest trail systems. With approximately 150 miles of unimproved multiuse sand trails to choose from, you can ride from sunrise to sunset and still have lots of room to roam. You'll also have lots of opportunity to spot wildlife, including red-tailed hawks, great blue herons, turkeys, beavers, river otters, and deer. Wharton State Forest is also the site of Batsto Village, a bog iron and glassmaking center that thrived from 1766 to 1867. A self-guided walking tour through the working village will introduce you to this era. Wharton's main office is at Batsto.

    Contact: Wharton State Forest, 4110 Nesco Road, Hammonton 08037; 609-561-0024; www.state.nj.us/dep/parksandforests/parks/ wharton.html.

Riding Opportunities on New Jersey's Rail-Trails

In New Jersey, as well as all over the country, numerous rail lines were abandoned during the twentieth century. Thanks to the efforts of the Rails-to-Trails Conservancy, a nonprofit organization based in Washington, D.C., many of these old railroad rights-of-way have been converted to multiuse paths. The conservancy's mission, "to enrich America's communities and countryside by creating a nationwide network of public trails from former rail-lines and connecting corridors," has certainly proven successful in New Jersey with hikers, bicyclists, cross-country skiers, bird watchers, and equestrians. In *24 Great Rail-Trails of New Jersey*, Craig P. Della Penna notes that the transformation of abandoned rail lines to multiuse paths "gives the same sense of spiritual or kindred journey that the nation used to experience on the great 'name-trains' of the 1940s."

Today, these rail-trails offer excellent recreational opportunities with few road crossings, steep climbs, or sharp turns. They are generally surfaced with crushed stone known as quarry dust. Each linear path affords a new opportunity to stop and gaze at ducks on a pond, watch deer in the surrounding woods, listen to the melody of a flowing river, and discover insights into our transportation history. Building the train lines was no easy task. Tunnels had to be blasted through rock, and gullies filled to create the necessary flat bed. To get the most enjoyment from each rail-trail, read Della Penna's book before starting out and keep it in your saddlebag so that you can check out fishing spots, historic sites, towns, and memorabilia that you'll encounter on the trails.

At this writing, there are twenty-four rail-trails in New Jersey, but only the few listed below permit horseback riding. If you enjoy these lovely trails, get involved in the effort to gain permission to use others. Contact the New Jersey RailTrails (NJRT, Box 23, Pluckemin 07978; 215-340-9974), the New Jersey Horse Council (25 Beth Drive, Moorestown 98957; 856-234-1081), or your local trail riding group.

Note: The trails indicated by an asterisk require a permit for horseback riding. Apply to the New Jersey Division of Fish and Wildlife, Central Region Office, One Eldridge Road, Robbinsville 08691; 609-259-2132.

21. *BLACK RIVER RAIL-TRAIL

County: Morris
Admission: Permit required
Hours: Sunrise to sunset
Water: None for horse or rider

      Rest room: No
     Trail length: Various lengths
  Trailer parking: Pleasant Hill Road, Chester; or at Hacklebarney
               State Park, Hacklebarney Road, in Chester
       Terrain: Fairly level; gravel and dirt, depending on area

Location: Contact the WMA for exact location

A portion of the Patriots' Path rail-trail (see trail 49) passes through the Black River WMA in Chester Township from Chestnut Hill Road to Ironia Road in Chester, covering four miles along a gravel and dirt trail beside the former Chester Branch of the Lackawanna Railroad. Originally, this line—built in 1868 to transport iron ore from area mines—ran for ten miles. The section that is open travels along the end of the line between Ironia Road and where the Chester Depot used to be on Oakdale Road.

     Competition from higher-grade ore discovered in Minnesota led the Lackawanna to switch to passenger service by 1933. When the state bought the right-of-way from Ironia to Chester in 1965, the section became part of the Black River Wildlife Management Area. Highlights include a hardwood forest, the ground pine (a protected plant), and sightings of the Black River.

     Trails, which vary in length, include the blue-blazed Black River Trail (2.3 miles) and the red-blazed Conifer Pass Trail, plus Patriots' Path loops.

     Contact: Black River Wildlife Management Area, 275 North Road, Chester 07930; 908-879-6252.

22. *CAPOOLONG RAIL-TRAIL

        County: Hunterdon
     Admission: Permit required
         Hours: Sunrise to sunset
         Water: Horse, streams; rider, none
     Rest room: No
     Trail length: Approximately 5–8 miles one way
  Trailer parking: Local side street
       Terrain: Mostly level; cinder and gravel, with some steep
               spots around former bridges

Location: From I-78, take exit 15 (Clinton/Pittstown/Route 173 east); from the exit ramp, turn left onto County 513 south. Go about 4 miles and turn left on Quakerton Road.

Passing through Pittstown and Landsdown, this rail-trail covers a 3.7-mile section of the former Pittstown Branch of the Lehigh Valley Railroad. Protected by the Division of Fish and Wildlife as a wildlife management area, this is a pleasant place for a short ride. The trail, next to Capoolong Creek, is composed of cinder and gravel. Starting from the southern terminus at the MCI Electric Company, you will pass an abandoned railroad station behind a shop off Route 513 south and an iron bridge with its ties still in place. At about 2.3 miles, you'll come to a tie bridge across a drainage gully. Lead your horse to the right along the path going up a hill and back onto the trail. There are lots of bird-watching possibilities along this trail, as well as opportunities to observe other wildlife.

Contact: Division of Fish and Wildlife; 609-259-2132.

23. COLUMBIA RAIL-TRAIL

Counties:	Morris and Hunterdon
Admission:	Free
Hours:	Sunrise to sunset
Water:	Horse, occasional streams; rider, none
Rest room:	No
Trail length:	Approximately 16.2 miles
Trailer parking:	Junction of Vernoy and Valley Brook Road, Califon; also at a lot on Main Street north of the center of High Bridge
Terrain:	Mostly level

Location: Various; contact the agencies below for exact details

Note: As of this writing, there is a short break in the trail in downtown Long Valley. The Morris County Park Commission has plans to complete this portion and accommodate trailer parking in downtown Long Valley.

Passing through Flanders, Long Valley, Califon, and High Bridge, this rail-trail follows a section of the former High Bridge Branch of the Central Railroad of New Jersey. Built in the 1860s, the single track of thirty-three miles connected the main line at High Bridge to small branches for access to numerous iron mines. Until operations ended in the 1970s, the line carried iron ore, milk, passengers, items for the nearby federal arsenal, and ice from Lake Hopatcong.

Depending on where you start from, you'll see a few reminders of rail days long past including a set of railcar wheels; a thirty-foot bridge over Drake's Brook, complete with former railroad abutments and solid decking; an exact duplicate of this bridge crossing the Raritan River; two horse farms at a busy grade crossing; and many more bridges, including an old girder bridge. At one spot, a stand of trees seems to grow out from crevices in the rockface; shortly thereafter, you'll come to a waterfall. At the town of High Bridge, a dedication sign marking the end of this trail can be seen at the grade crossing for Main Street.

Use caution when riding Bartley Road in Long Valley; sight is limited at the mid-point of an S curve. The South Branch of the Raritan River will immediately appear on your right, and will stay beside you to High Bridge.

Contact: Morris County Park Commission, 53 East Hanover Avenue, Morristown 07960, 973-326-7600, www.morrisparks.net; Hunterdon County Parks and Recreation Department, 1020 Highway 31, Lebanon 08833, 908-782-1158.

24. FREEHOLD AND JAMESBURG RAIL-TRAIL

County: Monmouth
Admission: Free
Hours: Sunrise to sunset
Water: None for horse or rider
Rest room: In Allaire State Park
Trail length: 4.5 miles
Trailer parking: Various places; call Allaire State Park
Terrain: Flat; gravel and dirt

Location: Various; see below

This gravel and dirt rail-trail passes through Wall Township and Farmingdale. In the 1800s, the Freehold and Jamesburg Agricultural Railroad ran from Monmouth Junction, through Jamesburg, Freehold, Farmingdale, Allenwood, and Manasquan, to the New York and Long Branch Line. Later, the Penn Central Railroad took it over. Although the line still runs from Monmouth Junction to Farmingdale, the section east of Farmingdale was abandoned and sold to Jersey Central Power and Light. The right-of-way was then sold to Wall Township, which wisely developed this portion from Hospital Road to Main Street in Manasquan as the Freehold and Jamesburg Trail.

Part of this very scenic trail goes through Allaire State Park. At its start, at the Hospital Road end heading west, bear right of the golf course and toward the trees. Turn right at the trees, follow the trail along the right side, and then head left into the woods following the Red Trail. When you reach Spring Meadow Golf Course, cross the entrance and, after entering the Allaire Road parking lot, ride toward the left to the opposite side, go between the wood barriers, and take the straight trail. At one mile, turn right; here you'll be back on the railroad right-of-way before turning left on Allaire Road. You'll hear the Pine Creek Railroad before seeing it. After entering Allaire State Park, turn right onto the Red Trail. At the four-way trail crossing, turn right; at the abandonment go left and continue straight where a road bears left. Continue straight when you come to another road bearing right; cross Hurley Pond Road. At about four miles, continue straight when the trail turns right and end at Route 547.

Contact: Allaire State Park, Box 220, Farmingdale 07727; 732-938-2371.

25. *HAMBURG MOUNTAIN RAIL-TRAIL

County:	Sussex
Admission:	Permit required
Hours:	Sunrise to sunset
Water:	None for horse or rider
Rest room:	No
Trail length:	2.7 miles
Trailer parking:	Various places; see below
Terrain:	Mostly level

Location: See below

This short rail-trail passes through the townships of Ogdensburg and Franklin. The Hanford Branch of the New York, Susquehanna and Western Railroad operated here during the peak years of the New Jersey Zinc Company mines in Ogdensburg and Franklin. Zinc and iron ores were transported to the main line and then to refineries.

The scenic trail is ideal for hiking, bicycling, and horseback riding. At the beginning, north of Ogden Way, the trail climbs uphill, where remnants of a rail bed are visible. In a short time, you'll come to a deep cut through bedrock and evidence of the construction of this branch. A huge piece of quarried rock exhibits drill marks, and a drill bit still sticks out of one of the holes!

On a clear day, you may be lucky enough to see the High Point Monument to the north. At approximately two miles, you'll come upon large stone piers to the right that once supported elevated, open tracks. The trail ends next to the main line west of Beaver Lake Road.

Contact: Division of Fish and Wildlife, Central Region Office, One Eldridge Road, Robbinsville 08691; 609-259-2132.

26. HENRY HUDSON RAIL-TRAIL

County:	Monmouth
Admission:	Free
Hours:	Sunrise to sunset
Water:	Horse, none; rider, in activity center

Rest room: In activity center
Trail length: 9 miles one way
Trailer parking: Near the intersection of Gerard Avenue/Clark Street and Lloyd Road/Broadway at the border of Aberdeen and Hazlet; off Spruce Street in Union Beach; in McMahon Park, off Atlantic Avenue in North Middletown; at the Bayshore Development Office, 945 State Highway 345 westbound, near Avenue D; and at the Atlantic Highlands/ Middletown border.
Terrain: Paved

Location: Various; see below

This rail-trail named in honor of the first European to land in Monmouth County starts at the intersection of Gerard Avenue/Clark Street and Lloyd Road/Broadway at the border of the towns of Aberdeen and Hazlet. The eight-foot-wide paved trail leads over man-made and natural environments, with an elevated rail bed and bridge crossings that provide open views of stream corridors, tidal wetlands, and Raritan Bay.

Contact: Monmouth County Park System, 805 Newman Springs Road, Lincroft 07738; 732-842-4000; www.monmouthcountyparks. com.

27. OGDEN MINE RAILROAD PATH RAIL-TRAIL

Counties: Morris and Sussex
Admission: Free
Hours: Sunrise to sunset
Water: Horse, none; rider, in rest rooms when open
Rest room: Portajons and rest rooms in Mahlon Dickerson Reservation
Trail length: 2.5 miles, plus additional trails within Mahlon Dickerson Reservation
Trailer parking: At Saffins Pond on Weldon Road; Hedley Overlook; Rock Rill in Jefferson Township
Terrain: Mostly level; rocky on many of the trails (shoes advisable)

Location: Various; see below

Passing through Hardtown and Sparta, this rail-trail continues for 2.4 miles along the former Edison Branch of the Central New Jersey Railroad. Originally built in 1864 as the Ogden Mine Railroad to transport iron and other minerals, the line led to boats along the Morris Canal that took the ore to neighboring blast furnaces. Other lines closed down in 1890, when higher-quality ore was discovered near the Great

Lakes and the New Jersey mines were no longer in demand; but this branch continued to operate until 1935.

The rail-trail crosses into Mahlon Dickerson Reservation, a wonderful 3,200-acre park with picnic facilities, rest rooms, tent camping, sites for recreational vehicles, and lots of equestrian trails (see trail 47). While riding the Ogden Mine rail-trail, you'll see Saffins Pond on the left, swamp and wetlands, a hardwood forest, and a stone retaining wall built to carry the roadbed above the wet area. A variety of birds frequent the area. The trail ends at Hayward Road.

Contact: Morris County Park Commission, 53 East Hanover Avenue, Morristown 07960; 973-326-7600; www.morrisparks.net.

28. PAULINSKILL VALLEY RAIL-TRAIL

Counties:	Sussex and Warren
Admission:	Free
Water:	Available for horse and rider
Rest room:	Yes
Trail length:	27 miles
Trailer parking:	Various locations; see below and call Kittatinny Valley State Park
Terrain:	Gentle grades; cinder and gravel

Location: Varies; see below

This very scenic trail passes through Kittatinny Valley State Park (see trail 10) and connects with the Columbia Lakes Wildlife Management Area in Knowlton; the Delaware Water Gap National Recreation Area and the Appalachian Trail; the Lackawanna Cut-Off and the Lehigh and New England right-of-way; and the Sussex Branch Trail (twenty miles), which follows the abandoned Sussex Branch of the Erie Lackawanna Railroad. Abandoned in 1962 by the New York, Susquehanna and Western Railroad, the right-of-way was purchased by the city of Newark. According to Len Frank, in *Paulinskill Valley: Before & After*, the city foresaw the need "for a possible future water conduit to connect the proposed Tocks Island Dam reservoir with the Pequannock Watershed."

Thanks to the Paulinskill Valley Trail Committee, the rail-trail was purchased with New Jersey Green Acres funds. Today, according to Frank, "The cinder base trail traverses two counties for twenty-seven miles." It has an average width of eight to ten feet and covers a total area of 102 acres. Along this multiuse trail, which travels through rural landscapes, northern deciduous forests, wetlands, and numerous towns, equestrians can view many artifacts, including remnants of creameries and ice houses that serviced the railroad, cattle passes, railroad bridges, whistle markers, mileage markers, battery boxes, and station foundations. If you have a fishing rod, take it along; there's lots of fishing access where the river bridges cross the trail. You'll be riding parallel to the Paulinskill River, frequented by anglers and canoeists. You may even spot beaver, deer, otter, and a variety of birds.

Sections of the trail can be accessed from Limecrest Road at the railroad crossing in Sparta; Swartswood Lake Road (Route 622); Paulinskill Lake Road (Route 614); Stillwater Road (Route 610); Cedar Ridge–Dixon Road; Marksboro Road (Route 659); Footbridge Park (off Route 94) in Blairstown; and Kittatinny Valley State Park.

Caution: The Sussex Branch Rail-Trail has missing bridges and is dangerous in places. It is being worked on and lengthened.

Contact: Kittatinny Valley State Park, Box 621, Andover 07821, 973-786-6445; Paulinskill Valley Trail Committee, Box 175, Andover 07821, 908-852-0597.

29. *PEQUEST RAIL-TRAIL

County:	Warren
Admission:	Permit required
Hours:	Sunrise to sunset
Water:	Horse, none; rider, yes
Rest room:	Yes
Trail length:	4.1 miles
Trailer parking:	Various areas
Terrain:	Mostly level; cinder, gravel, original ballast, and ties

Location: Varies; see below

Note: Fallen trees may block the trail in some places, and the area is managed for hunting and fishing.

This section of rail-trail, which runs parallel to the Pequest River and Route 46 in the Pequest Valley near Oxford, is the former rail bed of the Lehigh and Hudson River Railroad (L&HR). Completed in 1862, the line chiefly carried coal. During World War I, it transported supplies destined for Europe, as well as troop trains bound for New England. Passenger service ceased during the 1930s, except for occasional excursion trains run by large connecting carriers that were partners with the L&HR. The railroad continued to thrive as a freight hauler until the 1960s. The right-of-way was eventually sold to Conrail in the mid-1980s. Although the line is now abandoned, bridges, telegraph poles, mile markers, and signal posts have remained intact and can be seen along the rail-trail.

Leave some time for a side trip to the Pequest Trout Hatchery and Natural Resource Education Center in Oxford (call 908-637-4125 for hours). It's free and fantastic. Here you can stretch your legs on a variety of easy, short trails; learn how approximately 600,000 brown, rainbow, and brook trout are raised annually to stock the state's waterways; watch a short video describing the trout production process; take a self-guided tour to an observation deck overlooking concrete raceways where trout are kept until they're large enough to be released; and, inside the center, enjoy the hands-on exhibits.

Contact: Division of Fish and Wildlife, Central Region Office, One Eldridge Road, Robbinsville 08691; 609-259-2132.

More Great Trails

Many of the following trails are the result of initiatives by local officials and residents to preserve open space for multiple uses.

30. CAMPGAW MOUNTAIN COUNTY RESERVATION

           County: Bergen
        Admission: Fee from Memorial Day to Labor Day
            Hours: Sunrise to sunset
            Water: Horses, streams depending on weather; rider, faucet in rest rooms (open April to November)
        Rest room: Indoor flush, April to November; portajon, November to April
     Trail length: Approximately 5 miles
   Trailer parking: Designated area (see below) or at Saddle Ridge Stable
          Terrain: Hilly; rocky (shoes recommended)

Location: Take I-287 north to Route 202 north (exit 58); pass Ramapo Reservation and take the next right onto Darlington Avenue. Bear right at the fork. Pass the ski lift area and park at the maintenance building on the left.

This trail starts across the road from the maintenance building and power lines. Alternatively, you can ride along the road to the end, where there's another rest room, and continue through the grassy area onto the well-worn horse trail. Head up to the power line, where Saddle Ridge Stable is located.

When last explored, the trails here were wide but in need of maintenance and trail markers. However, the reservation is a nice place to ride year-round, with numerous clear streams and muddy areas, depending on weather conditions. Hunting is not allowed here at any time.

Contact: Campgaw Mountain County Reservation, 200 Campgaw Road, Mahwah 07430; 301-327-3500; www.co.bergen.nj. usparks/parks/campgaw.htm.

31. CHRISTIE HOFFMAN FARM PARK

County:	Hunterdon
Admission:	Free
Hours:	Sunrise to sunset
Water:	Horse and rider, at both a gravity-fed pump and a water fountain
Rest room:	At the park office (when open)
Trail length:	Over 4 miles
Trailer parking:	To the immediate left of the driveway entrance
Terrain:	Low rolling fields, slight hills; wood chips along wet areas

Location: From I-78, take exit 24 to Fairmount Road west

Note: Riders must clean up any horse droppings in the parking area. Dogs are not allowed with riders. Groups may not exceed six riders.

Riding is easy and pleasurable at this former 150-acre farm, and wildlife abounds in the beautiful open green meadows. The trails traverse the edges of cornfields and lush evergreen forests. You will find streams to cross and a wonderful combination of natural jumps with go-arounds. Many trails connect with others, so it could take a rider from one to two hours or longer to make all the loops.

Contact: Tewksbury Trail Association, Box 173, Oldwick 08858; 908-236-9339.

32. CLAYTON PARK

County:	Monmouth
Admission:	Free
Hours:	Sunrise to sunset
Water:	Horse, pond; rider, none
Rest room:	Portajon
Trail length:	6 miles
Trailer parking:	The parking lot is small; it's empty during the early morning hours
Terrain:	Gentle, with some uphill climbs; dirt trail, bridges to cross

Location: From Route 9 in Freehold, take Route 537 west; turn right onto Route 526; turn left at Davis Station Road, and left again at Emley's Hill Road; follow the sign to the park. From I-195, take exit 11 east (Imlaystown/Cox's Corner); turn right and follow to end, west-bound; turn left and follow to end; turn left onto Route 526 and make an immediate right onto Imlaystown–Davis Station Road; follow to Emley's Hill Road; turn left and follow to park on left.

This hidden oasis is fine for a nice ride. The 409-acre county park offers farm fields, meadows, wooded areas, and Imlaystown Lake. It's been quiet each time I've visited, except for the occasional mountain biker.

Contact: Clayton Park, Emley's Hill Road, Upper Freehold 07728; 609-259-5794.

33. DEER PATH PARK

County:	Hunterdon
Admission:	Free
Hours:	Open, 8 a.m.; closing varies, depending on season
Water:	Horse, none; rider, yes
Rest room:	Yes
Trail length:	Approximately 5 miles
Trailer parking:	At the Deer Path Park soccer lot
Terrain:	Hilly; sometimes muddy

Location: From the Flemington area, take Route 31 north approximately 4 miles; turn right onto From the Clinton area, take Route 31 south approximately 6.5 miles; turn left onto West Woodchurch Road and follow signs to the park.

Note: There is a half-mile section of railroad tracks, where you should employ extreme *caution.* Stop, look, and listen for freight trains.

Depending on how far you wish to ride, pleasant trails await you both inside Deer Path Park and alongside the South Branch of the Raritan River. You'll find peaceful open fields, hills, wide sections of power line easements, patches crossing private property, lovely pine woods, streams, and river crossings. The river trail can be challenging, owing to the many water crossings and obstacles, as well as some tree branches to duck under.

Both the park and the river trails were created by the Readington Trail Association (RTA), whose members continue their hard work to maintain and preserve these and other trails in Readington Township. At first, the trail within the park was shared with hikers, bikers, and dog walkers. Conflicts with these users eventually led the RTA, with the park's blessing, to establish a new trail solely for equestrians. It is clearly marked with horseshoes to avoid misunderstandings. Members are currently working on a new trail leading from Deer Path Park to Round Valley Recreation Area.

Contact: Hunterdon County Department of Parks and Recreation, 1020 Highway 31, Lebanon 08833, 908-782-1158; Readington Trail Association, c/o Janet Agresti, 908-788-3075.

34. DELAWARE WATER GAP NATIONAL RECREATION AREA/ CONASHAUGH VIEW EQUESTRIAN TRAIL

County:	Pike (Pennsylvania)
Admission:	Free
Hours:	Sunrise to sunset
Water:	None for horse or rider
Rest room:	At Kittatinny Point and Bushkill visitor centers
Trail length:	Approximately 9 miles, including a 5.25-mile loop
Trailer parking:	On Conashaugh Road, about 5 miles south of Milford, Pennsylvania
Terrain:	Hilly; dirt trail with some bridges

Location: From U.S. Route 209, take Pennsylvania Route 739 west approximately 3 miles. Turn right onto Milford Road. Drive 1 mile and turn right onto Long Meadow Road (a church is on the corner). Drive 1.5–1.75 miles to the parking lot on the right.

This trail, although located in Pennsylvania, is only a couple of minutes from the New Jersey border and worth the drive across the Delaware River. The trail proceeds mostly through dense woods, with a couple of opportunities to see the river in the distance. Only hikers and equestrians are allowed on this trail.

Contact: Delaware Water Gap National Recreation Area, Kittatinny Point Visitor Center, Columbia 07832, 908-496-4458; Bushkill Visitor Center, 570-588-7044 or 570-588-2451.

35. DELAWARE WATER GAP NATIONAL RECREATION AREA/ UPPER RIDGE EQUESTRIAN TRAIL

County:	Sussex
Admission:	Free
Hours:	Sunrise to sunset
Water:	None for horse or rider
Rest room:	At Kittatinny Point visitor center
Trail length:	5 miles
Trailer parking:	In the field
Terrain:	Wide dirt trails, which can also accommodate horse-drawn carriages

Location: From the intersection of Routes 206 and 15 north of Newton, take 206 north 11.8 miles. Turn left onto Route 675. At the stop sign, turn right onto Route 645. Go 0.2 mile and turn left onto Route 646 (Jager Road). Go approximately 0.8 mile to a field on the left, just beyond an overgrown road across from a one-story house. A gate to the trail is at the back of the field.

Note: If you have a horse-drawn carriage, call 717-588-2435 to get the latest combination for the gate lock.

This lovely trail traverses dense forest, open fields, and isolated ponds.

   Contact: Delaware Water Gap National Recreation Area, Kittatinny Point Visitor Center, Columbia 07832; 908-496-4458.

36. DORBROOK RECREATION AREA

       County: Monmouth
   Admission: Free
       Hours: 8 a.m. to dusk
       Water: Horse, none; rider, fountains (but taste isn't good)
   Rest room: Near the shelter building
 Trail length: 2.2 miles
Trailer parking: In the furthest lot, near the hockey field
     Terrain: Gentle paved and grass multiuse trail

Location: On Route 537 in Colts Neck. From the Garden State Parkway, take exit 109; from the southbound direction, turn right onto Route 520 (Newman Springs Road); northbound, turn left onto Route 520. Follow Route 520 for 1.5 miles to Swimming River Road. Turn left and proceed to the intersection with Route 537; turn right (west). Follow about 1.5 miles to the park entrance.

It doesn't matter that hikers, runners, bicyclists, and in-line skaters use this trail, because you'll be focusing on the features of this 534-acre park. Previously the estate of Murray Rosenberg of Miles Shoe Stores fame, the park was acquired by the county in 1985. Lying within the Navesink Area Watershed, the recreation area offers rolling open fields and inconspicuous playing courts, while retaining a rural atmosphere.

   In 1994 more property was acquired from the Nathan Family Association of Festoon Farm, the former estate of Allison L. S. Stern. Today, the houses of the former owners are used for indoor activities from Tai Chi to arts and crafts workshops.

   Contact: Dorbrook Recreation Area, Route 537, Colts Neck, 732-542-1642; Monmouth County Park System, 805 Newman Springs Road, Lincroft 07738, 732-842-4000, www.monmouthcountyparks.com.

37. EAGLE ROCK RESERVATION

     County: Essex
 Admission: Free
     Hours: Sunrise to sunset

> *Water:* None for horse or rider
> *Rest room:* At picnic area
> *Trail length:* 6.7 miles
> *Trailer parking:* In main parking area off Eagle Rock Avenue
> *Terrain:* Hilly; gravel

Location: From I-280, take exit 8B at Prospect Avenue going south. Continue to the light, and at the sign for Eagle Rock Reservation, turn right. The entrance is on the left.

This is a good place to get away from suburban sprawl. The area got its name in the early nineteenth century for the bald eagles that nested in the rocky cliffs on its eastern edge. The first acres were purchased for the reservation in 1895, and the final portions were assembled in 1907, creating a tract of 408.3 acres. The famous firm of Frederick Law Olmsted designed open spaces, lush plantings, and paths there in the early 1900s.

Mostly undeveloped today, the reservation offers many bridle paths and hiking trails through predominately red oak forest. A spectacular view of New York City's skyline can be had from atop Lookout Point—once a famous destination for visitors who would travel by trolley from New York City, transfer in Newark, take another trolley to Harrison Avenue, and then walk up the mountain or be transferred via the Eagle Rock line.

The Essex Equestrian Center (formerly the Montclair Riding Club)—a 22,000-square-foot indoor facility—is located within the park.

Contact: Essex County Park Commission; 973-268-3500 ext. 238.

38. ESTELL MANOR PARK

> *County:* Atlantic
> *Admission:* Free
> *Hours:* Park, 7:30 a.m. to dusk; Fox Nature Center, 8 a.m.–4 p.m. Monday–Friday, and 10 a.m.–4 p.m. weekends and holidays
> *Water:* Horse and rider, an artesian well at the end of the entrance road
> *Rest room:* At the Fox Nature Center at the north end of the park
> *Trail length:* A minimum of 28 miles one way
> *Trailer parking:* At the north end of the park (see below)
> *Terrain:* Elevated and flat; cinder, gravel, and some sandy sections

Location: 3.5 miles south of Mays Landing on Route 50. The main entrance to the park is south of where the horse trails begin. Go to the Fox Nature Center and get a map of the riding trails; then go about a mile toward the north entrance to the park, following the sign for trailer parking.

This fantastic park offers good riding trails over the remains of old railroad sidings that were used by a munitions factory. According to naturalist John Hansen, the trail takes riders through a variety of ecological zones in the south Jersey Pinelands and Cape May peninsula area. From elevated areas you can look down upon ponds and interconnected fingers of habitat areas where deer, foxes, and even a river otter may sometimes be spotted. Pine Barrens tree frogs, salamanders, owls, and red-tailed hawks thrive here. When you come upon the ruins of the Bethlehem Loading Company, a World War I munitions plant, note how nature has reclaimed much of the land.

Contact: Estell Manor Park, 109 State Highway 50, Mays Landing 08330; 609-645-5960.

39. GARRET MOUNTAIN RESERVATION

County: Passaic
Admission: Free
Hours: Sunrise to sunset
Water: None for horse or rider
Rest room: No
Trail length: Over 3 miles
Trailer parking: See directions below
Terrain: Groomed dirt trails

Location: From I-80, take exit 56 (Squirrelwood Road). Go south (uphill), and where the road splits, go left. Parking is about 300 yards down the road on the right.

This 569-acre facility includes a lake for fishing and the Garret Mountain Equestrian Center, which offers summer riding camps, plus trail rides for families and groups. Along the trail, there are views of northern New Jersey from Passaic County to the New York City skyline.

Contact: Passaic Parks Department, 973-881-4832; Garret Mountain Equestrian Center, Garret Mountain Reservation, West Paterson, 973-279-2974, www.garretequestrian.com.

40. HARTSHORNE WOODS PARK

County: Monmouth
Admission: Free
Hours: Sunrise to sunset

Water: None for horse or rider
Rest room: No
Trail length: Approximately 15 miles
Trailer parking: Yes, very limited
Terrain: Hilly; rocky

Location: Drive east past Keyport on Route 36 to a sign for Red Bank Scenic Road and turn right onto Navesink Avenue. Parking, which is very limited, is on the left side of the road.

Note: It's best to arrive early because parking is limited. To avoid mountain bikers, come during the week. Trail maps are available at the kiosk adjacent to the parking area, or contact the Monmouth County Park System in advance of your trip.

Hartshorne Woods Park encompasses 736 acres overlooking the Navesink River, but you won't spot the river unless you come during the fall or winter, after the trees have shed their leaves. The Rocky Point Trail, a challenging 4.1-mile section meandering over the hills and valleys, provided a natural fortress for the Highlands Army Air Defense Site (H.A.A.D.S.) from 1940 until the mid-1970s. It was in this area, during World War II, that Battery Lewis—the largest and one of three remaining army facilities—housed two sixty-six-foot-long guns. According to a park brochure, "H.A.A.D.S. and nearby Fort Hancock, at Sandy Hook, were part of the Atlantic Coast Defense System. By 1950, the coastal battery guns were phased out and Rocky Point became a Nike-Hercules Missile Control Center. When H.A.A.D.S. was declared surplus property by the federal government, Monmouth County acquired the 224-acre site as an addition to Hartshorne Woods Park."

In addition to the beautiful Rocky Point Trail, the Rocky Point section of the park offers the 0.3-mile Black Fish Cove Trail from the Battery Loop Trail down to the pier on the Navesink River (with a very steep return). In this section, you'll also find the Command Loop, a 0.4-mile paved trail to the site of the old H.A.A.D.S. Command Center, and the Bunker Loop, a 0.3-mile trail along a paved surface into the wooded hollow and to the site of one of the two remaining bunkers. You can also try the Buttermilk Valley section of the park, where the Laurel Ridge Trail affords a moderate ride of 2.5 miles. In the Monmouth Hills section, the Cuesta Ridge Trail is a moderate 1.6-mile one-way route along the backbone ridge of the park, with access to the Rocky Point section.

Contact: Monmouth County Park System, 805 Newman Springs Road, Lincroft 07738; 732-842-4000; www.monmouthcountyparks.com.

41. HUBER WOODS PARK

     County: Monmouth
    Admission: Free
      Hours: Sunrise to sunset
      Water: Horse, none; rider, at rest room fountain
    Rest room: At the environmental center
   Trail length: 6 miles
 Trailer parking: At main parking area
     Terrain: Slightly hilly; one section of step-over logs

Location: Take Route 35 to Navesink River Road, Monmouth; go east for 2.8 miles to Brown's Dock Road; turn left. The park entrance is at the top of the hill.

The wooded trails in this park are designed for walkers, hikers, bikers, and, best of all, equestrians. Here you can enjoy a grove of tulip trees, an oak-hickory forest, and a meadow that's alive each spring with partridgeberry, trailing arbutus, and pink lady's slipper. Among the local wildlife are chipmunks, foxes, great horned owls, and woodpeckers. Maps of the marked trails are available at the information station between the parking lot and the environmental center.

  Nestled on a hill overlooking the Navesink River, the park was established in 1974 with a 118-acre gift of land from the Huber family and the J. M. Huber Corporation. Today the park has grown to 255 acres, thanks to donations and the efforts of the Monmouth Conservation Foundation. The environmental center occupies the former Huber home, which was built in 1927. Nearby is the Monmouth park system's Sunnyside Equestrian Center, which serves people with physical and mental disabilities, as well as able riders. Special People United to Ride (SPUR), a nonprofit organization, provides support for this riding program. The facility has a large, covered, heated arena in Middletown so that SPUR can continue its activities year-round.

  Contact: Huber Woods Park, 25 Brown's Dock Road, Middletown 07748, 732-872-2670; Monmouth County Park System, 805 Newman Springs Road, Lincroft 07738, 732-842-4000, www.monmouthcountyparks.com.; SPUR, Middletown-Lincroft Road, Middletown, 732-224-1367.

42. JAMES ANDREWS MEMORIAL PARK

     County: Morris
    Admission: Free
      Hours: Sunrise to sunset
      Water: None for horse or rider

Rest room: No
Trail length: Approximately 10 miles
Trailer parking: Possibly behind the municipal building at Millbrook Avenue; see below
Terrain: Crushed gravel

Location: From I-80 west, take I-287 south to the exit for Route 10 south. Turn left at the intersection with Route 513 (Dover-Chester Road), and turn left again at Sussex Turnpike and then West Hanover Avenue. Proceed 0.7 mile to a small pull-off.

Opened in 2000 for hikers and bicyclists, this very pleasant trail is being considered for equestrian use at the time of this writing. Contact Randolph Township (973-989-7073) to confirm that the trail is open to equestrians and where the best trailer parking is located.

43. JOCKEY HOLLOW/MORRISTOWN NATIONAL HISTORICAL PARK

County: Morris
Admission: Fee; weekly and annual passes are available; the National Parks Pass and Golden Pass (Age, Eagle, Access) are accepted (call 973-539-2085 or 973-543-4030). Groups of six or more riders and commercial riding activities must call park headquarters (973-539-2016) to obtain a permit.
Hours: Subject to change; they are posted at road entrances, on bulletin boards, and in the visitor center
Water: Horse, streams (these sometimes dry up); rider, in the visitor center
Rest room: Yes
Trail length: Approximately 20 miles, plus extra miles on side roads
Trailer parking: In far parking lot near the visitor center; for best access to the trail system, park at the New York Brigade area
Terrain: Gradual ups and downs; rocky

Location: From Route 202 north of Basking Ridge, take Tempe Wick Road west and follow signs to parking for the visitor center

Note: Use *caution.* Some parts of the trail are narrow, steep with loose rocks, and dotted with numerous woodchuck holes. Be careful when crossing fields and intersecting trails. Riding is not permitted adjacent to the Wick House; near the visitor center; or on the Aqueduct, Primrose Brook, and Soldier Hut Trails.

Equestrians can enjoy most of the trails open to hikers in this 1,500-acre setting—the first national historical park created in the country—where George Washington and his troops spent the bitter winter of 1779–1780. Today, you'll appreciate the solitude, the flora and fauna, the historic sights, and, if there's been a lot of rain, the sound of a meandering stream. On a hot summer's day, the canopy of oak, birch, and ash leaves will provide shade and beauty, too.

Contact: Morristown National Historical Park, Washington Place, Morristown 07960; 973-539-2085; www.nps.gov/morr/.

44. LEWIS MORRIS COUNTY PARK

County:	Morris
Admission:	Free
Hours:	Sunrise to sunset
Water:	Horse, limited in streams; rider, none
Rest room:	Yes
Trail length:	Over 4 miles, plus many more in the adjacent Jockey Hollow (fee) portion of Morristown National Historical Park
Trailer parking:	At the Old Army and Sunrise Lake parking lots within Lewis Morris County Park, and off Tempe Wick Road in the Jockey Hollow portion of Morristown National Historical Park
Terrain:	Hilly, with some flat areas; rocky

*Susan and John Samtak enjoy riding
in Lewis Morris County Park.*

Location: From I-287 north, take exit 35; turn left at traffic light onto South Street. Take Route 124 west through Morristown, around the Green, and continue for about 3.5 miles. Park entrance is on the left; take the first left to the large parking area.

This park is named for Lewis Morris, the first royal governor appointed to oversee New Jersey as a colony separate from New York. Since opening in 1958, it has grown to 1,154 acres. Lewis Morris County Park boasts a boat and floating dock, a beach area, lake, and snack bar, in addition to playgrounds and summer programs (which you might enjoy after your ride).

Although short, the blue-blazed trail, part of the Patriots' Path linear park system (see trail 49), will give you the feeling that you're away from it all. As you listen to the birds singing overhead, stress is bound to disappear. This trail also leads into the gorgeous Jockey Hollow portion of Morristown National Historical Park, which has additional miles of trails to explore (see trail 43).

Contact: Morris County Park Commission, 53 East Hanover Avenue, Morristown 07960; 973-326-7600; www.morrisparks.net.

45. LOANTAKA BROOK COUNTY PARK

County:	Morris
Admission:	Free
Hours:	Sunrise to sunset
Water:	Horses, lake and stream; rider, yes
Rest room:	Yes
Trail length:	8 miles
Trailer parking:	At Seaton Hackney Stables
Terrain:	Level; dirt

Location: Kitchell Road and South Street, Morris Township. From Route 124 east or west, proceed to South Street and follow signs.

Loantaka Brook, often referred to as "the place of the cold winter," became part of the Morris County park system in 1957 through donations of land by local residents. The nearby Seaton Hackney Stables was a gathering place for the "horsey set" in the 1900s. Today, the more than 570 acres of Loantaka Brook Park include the Seaton Hackney Stables, the South Street recreation area, and the Loantaka Way trail access area.

The riding is easy and relaxed here on the blue-blazed equestrian trail. There's much to admire, including the skunk cabbage, which pops up as early as February in the wet areas. Shagbark hickory and lots of wildflowers add to the beauty of the area.

Contact: Morris County Park Commission, 53 East Hanover Avenue, Morristown 07960; 973-326-7600; www.morrisparks.net.

46. LORD STIRLING STABLE TRAILS

      County: Morris
   Admission: Fee; permit required
       Hours: Vary; call first
       Water: Available for horse and rider
   Rest room: Yes
 Trail length: Approximately 10 miles
 Trailer parking: At stable parking lot
     Terrain: Mostly level

Location: 256 South Maple Avenue, Basking Ridge

Managed by the Somerset County Park Commission, these ten miles of well-groomed trails traverse a historic area. To qualify for a trail card to ride here, you must demonstrate your ability to ride with a balanced seat and control your horse at the walk, trot, and canter.

Contact: Lord Stirling Stable, 908-766-5955.

47. MAHLON DICKERSON RESERVATION

      County: Morris
   Admission: Free
       Hours: Sunrise to sunset
       Water: Horses only
   Rest room: Yes
 Trail length: Approximately 8 miles, with additional loops affording 3 to 4 hours of riding
 Trailer parking: Follow signs to Saffins Pond. Trailer parking is at the far end of the pond.
     Terrain: Hilly; unpaved and rocky (shoes recommended)

Location: From I-80 take Route 15 north (exit 33 westbound; exit 34B eastbound). Proceed on Route 15 north approximately 4 miles to the Weldon Road exit. Follow Weldon Road east approximately 1 mile to the beginning of the reservation, which is on both sides of the road.

With more than 3,000 acres, this park—named in honor of a governor who also served as a justice of the New Jersey Supreme Court in the 1880s—is the largest in the Morris County park system. Riding in these surroundings is a wilderness experience and offers a feast for the eyes. Before visiting this park, it's a good idea to obtain a trail map and learn which trails are multiuse and which are reserved exclusively for equestrians.

From the parking area, you can go either north or south on the yellow-blazed trail. Going north, you'll reach the highest point in Morris County at 1,395 feet. Continuing in an easterly direction, you'll pass wetlands and Pine Swamp, and then connect with the white- and green-blazed Boulder Trail, in addition to riding along the perimeter of a camping area before looping back to the yellow-blazed trail you started on. If you've chosen to head south from the parking area, you'll pass Saffins Pond, the visitor center, and a loop that will return you to the parking area.

Contact: Morris County Park Commission, 53 East Hanover Avenue, Morristown 07960; 973-326-7600; www.morrisparks.net.

48. MANASQUAN RESERVOIR RECREATION AREA
           County: Monmouth
        Admission: Free
            Hours: Sunrise to sunset
            Water: Horses, yes; riders, yes (when visitor center is open)
        Rest room: Yes
      Trail length: 5 miles
  Trailer parking: At the main entrance at Windeler Road (see below)
          Terrain: Fairly level; varying grass, gravel, and dirt path

Location: In Howell Township. From the Garden State Parkway, take exit 98 to I-195 west. Proceed to exit 28B, Route 9 north (Freehold), and stay to the right when entering the highway. At the first traffic light, turn right onto Georgia Tavern Road and continue 0.3 mile to Windeler Road. Turn right and proceed 1.5 miles to the reservoir entrance on the left.

Note: Please respect and do not enter the wetland areas; these have been designated as wildlife habitats.

While hikers explore the perimeter of this beautiful 770-acre reservoir and fisherman try for a tasty morsel as kayakers glide by, equestrians can view the wetlands, grassy plains, and hemlock grove that encircle the water.

Facing the reservoir, start from the right side of the parking lot. Go between two wooden posts and, with the water to your left, bear right into the wide, grassy area; cross over the dike and, at the T junction, turn left onto the gravel road heading toward the water. Soon you'll be on a wide dirt path flanked by junipers, mountain laurel, and hollies. Along the way, you'll encounter wet areas, deep woods, and lovely spots to admire the ducks, geese, and a variety of wildlife. After your ride, you may want to enjoy a great view of the reservoir from the new visitor center's second-level observation deck, complete with lounge area, fireplace, and rest rooms.

Contact: Monmouth County Park System, 805 Newman Springs Road, Lincroft 07738; 732-842-4000; www.monmouthcountyparks. com.

49. PATRIOTS' PATH

County:	Morris
Admission:	Free
Hours:	Sunrise to sunset
Water:	Available for horse and rider, depending on area
Rest room:	At some areas
Trail length:	Various; see below
Trailer parking:	Main parking at Fosterfields Living Historical Farm in Morristown (see below); call for other locations
Terrain:	Mostly level; gravel and cinder

Location: From I-287 north, take exit 35 (Madison Avenue) and turn left onto South Street. Continue west to the center of Morristown. At the Green, take Route 510 west (Washington Street) and go 1 mile. Turn right onto Kahdena Road. The entrance to Fosterfields is on the left.

Note: The main Patriots' Path, going east to west, is blazed in white; the spurs off the main trail are blazed in blue; and a spur off a spur is blazed in red.

According to the Morris County Park Commission, the Patriots' Path is "a gradually developing network of hiking, biking, and equestrian trails and green open spaces linking several dozen federal, state, county and municipal parks, watershed lands, historic sites and other points of interest across southern Morris County." Eventually, more than seventy miles of trails will be joined together. Already, the completed white-blazed trail system, running from east to west, has dozens of miles of trail in place. Surfaces vary: wide paved or crushed stone and gravel trails; narrow paths of earth and rock; and cinder and gravel beds of old railroad lines in Morris and Chester Townships. Many spurs branch off the main white-blazed trail, including ones that go through Lewis Morris County Park to Jockey Hollow (see trails 43 and 44), to Cooper Mill at the Black River County Park in Chester, to the Kay Environmental Center in Chester, and to the Bamboo Brook Outdoor Education Center in Chester Township.

Approximately twenty miles of continuous, dedicated Patriots' Path lie between Speedwell Avenue in Morristown and Ralston Corners on Route 24 in Mendham Township. A connecting branch travels between Sunrise Lake in Mendham Township and the New Jersey Brigade hut sites in Bernardsville. Another branch goes through

Stephens State Park, Historic Speedwell, Lewis Morris County Park (see trail 44), Scherman Hoffman Wildlife Sanctuaries, the Black River Wildlife Management Area (see trails 21 and 66), and Fosterfields; it will eventually go along the mountain trails at Schooley's Mountain County Park (see trail 53).

A rail-trail passes through Morristown for 5.1 miles over an asphalt, gravel, and cinder path on part of the former Rockaway Valley Railroad (RVRR) bed. This rail line, built in 1888, brought passengers and cargo into Morristown's downtown area on special days at no charge in an effort to draw business to local merchants. It also transported thousands of bushels of peaches. In 1904 the RVRR made plans to expand, but when an intercity trolley began operation in 1910, the free shuttle service was discontinued. Shortly thereafter, the RVRR began work to extend its track beyond the terminus at Watnong, but the area was too hilly, and the effort was abandoned. A fire destroyed the bulk of the RVRR infrastructure in Watnong in 1913, forcing the unlucky line to cease operations. It was ultimately sold at auction and then dismantled in 1917, when the buyer realized he couldn't reopen the line.

Contact: Morris County Park Commission, 53 East Hanover Avenue, Morristown 07960; 973-326-7600; www.morrisparks.net.

50. PEQUANNOCK WATERSHED

Counties:	Morris and Passaic
Admission:	Fee; permit required
Hours:	Sunrise to sunset
Water:	None for horse or rider
Rest room:	No
Trail length:	Approximately 18 miles; most trails are one way
Trailer parking:	Anywhere along the road
Terrain:	Hilly; rocky

Location: Headquarters are based at the Echo Lake area, 1.5 miles south of Newfoundland. From I-287, take Route 23 north for 7.6 miles.

This area is steeped in history. In 1826 William Jackson of Rockaway began an ironworks operation after purchasing nearly a thousand acres here and building a furnace, forge, sawmill, and gristmill. Buck and Cedar Ponds provided the necessary water. By 1837, however, the furnace was closed down for lack of timber to provide charcoal. Despite an attempt to revive the ironworks in 1850, it closed permanently in 1852. In 1900 the area became part of the Pequannock Watershed Supply System, and today its trails are used by both hikers and equestrians.

The yellow-blazed Bearfort Waters Clinton Trail, off Old Coal Road, is a major north-south trail that heads south through a laurel patch and grassy slopes to an old pipe line, travels along the west bank of Buckabear Pond, crosses a log bridge and then ends at the junction with a white-blazed trail for a total ride of 8.5 miles one way. The yellow-blazed Fire Tower West Trail, at 1.9 miles one way, offers a good view of Cedar Pond and the valley below. The Fire Tower Ridge Trail, blazed both red and white, starts 0.4 mile off Clinton Road and runs north for 2.0 miles to the Bearfort Fire Tower. The blue- and white-blazed Hank's West Trail starts on the west side of Hanks Pond and is mostly level for 2.6 miles north, one way, to the junction with Stephens Road. The white-blazed Hank's East Trail is 3.0 miles one way, and the white-blazed Twin Brooks Trail is 0.8 mile one way.

Contact: Newark Watershed Conservation and Development Corporation, 223 Echo Lake Road, West Milford 07480; 973-697-2850.

51. RAMAPO VALLEY COUNTY RESERVATION

County:	Bergen
Admission:	Free
Hours:	Sunrise to sunset
Water:	Horse, in streams and lake; rider, at fountain before bridge
Rest room:	In back of the office
Trail length:	11.5 miles
Trailer parking:	At the entrance, limited
Terrain:	Hilly and rocky on one trail; almost level on another

Location: From Oakland, take Route 202 north about 5 miles; entrance is on the left.

This reservation was once known as the "horse park," but if you come on a weekend, you'll have to contend with dozens of dogs, many of which are unleashed and bound to startle your horse. On weekdays, however, the riding is very pleasant, particularly during the summer months, when the woods provide shade and cooler temperatures. As you climb into the hilly areas, the trail gets rocky; trails in the lower areas are fairly level.

Contact: Ramapo Valley County Reservation, 584 Valley Road, Mahwah 07430; 201-825-1388; www.co.bergen.nj.us/parks/parks/ramapo.htm.

52. ROUND VALLEY RECREATION AREA

County:	Hunterdon
Admission:	Parking fee from Memorial Day to Labor Day

> *Hours:* Sunrise to sunset
> *Water:* Horse, at campground; rider, yes
> *Rest room:* Yes
> *Trail length:* 9 miles one way
> *Trailer parking:* At the south lot within the park
> *Terrain:* Hilly; rocky

Location: From I-78, take exit 20 to Route 22 west and Route 31. Follow signs to the park office, ask for a map, and drive to the No. 1 parking area.

You couldn't ride here before 1958. That's because Round Valley Recreation Area didn't exist. Since the natural horseshoe-shaped valley was filled with 55 billion gallons of water, the seventy-foot-deep, 4,000-acre reservoir has provided not only drinking water for the surrounding area but also recreational opportunities for fishermen, hikers, swimmers, boaters, and equestrians.

For a lovely ride, head to the Cushetunk Trail, which begins at the bulletin board at the No. 1 parking lot. As you ride toward the wilderness campground, you'll have stunning views of the reservoir, farmland, and houses so far in the distance that they resemble toys. No doubt you'll also spot deer, raccoons, opossums, and perhaps a striped skunk. The rufous-sided towhee and the mockingbird are among the many birds that frequent the area.

Contact Round Valley Recreation Area, 1220 Lebanon-Stanton Road, Lebanon 08833; 908-236-6355; www.state.nj.us/dep/parks-andforests/parks/round.html.

53. SCHOOLEY'S MOUNTAIN COUNTY PARK

> *County:* Morris
> *Admission:* Free
> *Hours:* Sunrise to sunset
> *Water:* Horse, streams; rider, none
> *Rest room:* Yes
> *Trail length:* Approximately 5 miles one way, plus another 5 miles one way on the Columbia Rail-Trail
> *Trailer parking:* Designated area near the park entrance, reachable off East Springtown Road
> *Terrain:* Hilly; rocky

Location: From the junction of Routes 24 and 206 in Chester, take Route 24 west. Proceed up Schooley's Mountain and past the municipal building. Turn right on Camp Washington Road and continue about 1.5 miles. Bear right onto Springtown Road. The park entrance is on the right.

Named for the Schooley family, who owned land in this area in the 1790s, this park largely consists of lands used from the 1920s through the 1950s as a YMCA camp. Purchased by the Morris County Park Commission in 1968 and opened to the public in 1974, the 782-acre, heavily forested facility is now a haven for hikers, picnickers, boaters, and equestrians.

This is a delightful place to ride, either on the park's multipurpose trail or on the additional five miles (one way) of the Columbia Rail-Trail (see trail 23), which goes along the South Branch of the Raritan River. You'll have beautiful views and can spot many birds. The white-blazed Patriots' Path also traverses the park (see trail 49). The mowed meadow area is always a nice section to trot the horses.

Contact: Morris County Park Commission, 53 East Hanover Avenue, Morristown 07960; 973-326-7600; www.morrisparks.net.

54. SHARK RIVER PARK

County:	Monmouth
Admission:	Free
Hours:	Sunrise to sunset
Water:	Available for horse and rider
Rest room:	Yes
Trail length:	2 miles
Trailer parking:	At the main entrance; pull into the back
Terrain:	Ranges from flat to hilly, depending on trail

Location: From Route 33 east of the Garden State Parkway (exit 100), turn south onto Schoolhouse Road. Turn right at the park entrance to the parking area.

The short rides on both the easy, level Cedar Trail (1.4 miles round trip) and the hilly River Edge Trail (a 0.75-mile loop) are worth the effort. The Cedar Trail intersects a short loop shared by the fitness trail, while the River Edge Trail follows along the Shark River and through a wild section that's deeply wooded. Unfortunately, parts of the Hidden Creek Trail cannot support the weight of horses; it's best not to ride there.

As you pass through a coastal river and floodplain, sandy hills, a cedar swamp, and several sphagnum bogs, you can see a variety of wildflowers dotting the forest floor during spring, as well as pitch pine and a thick understory filled with bracken fern, pepper bush, blueberry, and catbrier.

Contact: Monmouth County Park System, 805 Newman Springs Road, Lincroft 07738; 732-842-4000; www.monmouthcountyparks.com.

55. SIX MILE RUN RESERVOIR

County: Somerset
Admission: Free
Hours: Sunrise to sunset
Water: Horse, streams; rider, at the visitor center
Rest room: At the visitor center
Trail length: Approximately 4 miles
Trailer parking: At Delaware and Raritan Canal State Park headquarters, Blackwells Mills Road and Canal Road, Franklin Township
Terrain: Varies from flat to hilly

Location: See Delaware and Raritan Canal State Park (trail 6)

Approximately four miles of trails in this 3,037-acre reservoir site are open to equestrians. The first two miles of the Blue Blaze Trail, which runs along field edges and some wooded areas on the north side of the reservoir, are normally dry, but then you'll be in a low, wet area. The trail connects with the Red and Yellow Blaze Trails, but these are restricted to hikers and bicyclists.

This stretch of gently rolling lowland along the Millstone River was settled in the early eighteenth century by Dutch farmers from Long Island. They subdivided their properties into long lots running east/west from the Millstone River to an Indian path we know today as Route 27, with a longitudinal "Middle Line" that shaped land ownership patterns here for generations. The reservoir has been under the supervision of the New Jersey Division of Parks and Forestry since 1989.

Contact: Division of Parks and Forestry, c/o Six Mile Run Reservoir Site, D & R Canal State Park, 625 Canal Road, Somerset 08873; 732-873-3050; www.state.nj.us/dep/parksandforests/parks/drcanal.html.

56. SOURLAND MOUNTAIN PRESERVE

County: Somerset
Admission: Free
Hours: Sunrise to sunset
Water: Horse, pond; rider, none
Rest room: Portajon
Trail length: 8 miles
Trailer parking: At the park entrance on East Mountain Road
Terrain: Hilly; rocky

Location: Situated in Hillsborough and Montgomery Townships. From the north, take Route 206 south to Hillsborough; turn right at Route

514 (Amwell Road) and go 2 miles to East Mountain Road; turn left and continue about 1 mile to the park entrance on the right. From the south, take Route 206 north to Rocky Hill; turn left onto Route 518 west and continue to the stoplight in Blawenburg; turn right on Route 601 and proceed to East Mountain Road, which is on the left just before the Carrier Foundation Clinic; the park entrance is about 1 mile on the right.

Note: This is black bear country; don't carry food.

This county-owned preserve, administered by the Somerset County Park Commission, covers 2,835 acres and offers trails that are marked at intersection posts. Maps are available inside the small white building adjacent to the parking lot. Trails meander gradually uphill and pass over numerous wooden bridges and streams. Magnificent oak, hickory, and tulip trees offer a delightful canopy of shade. Phragmites are found in the wetter areas. Slow down when nearing the stream; the gurgling water sounds like a Japanese garden and is quite soothing. Among the many roads with interesting names in the Sourland Mountain area is Featherbed Lane. According to legend, Revolutionary War suppliers wrapped their horses' hooves in torn quilts to muffle their sounds as they traveled to Washington's troops.

   Contact: Somerset County Park Commission, Box 5327, North Branch 08876; 908-722-1200 or 908-369-1458.

57. SOUTH MOUNTAIN RESERVATION

County:	Essex
Admission:	Free
Hours:	Sunrise to sunset
Water:	None for horse or rider
Rest room:	No
Trail length:	20 miles
Trailer parking:	At the Locust Grove parking area opposite the Millburn Railroad Station. Arrive early; parking is tight and limited.
Terrain:	Hilly; rocky

Location: From I-78, take exit 50B into Millburn; in Millburn, turn right off Glen Avenue–Lackawanna Place behind and across the street from the railroad station. Or, from Route 24, take the exit for Route 124 east (Springfield Avenue) and continue to Millburn Avenue; turn left and proceed to the train station.

You'll be riding on old carriage roads in this 2,048-acre park, which features hardwood trees, streams, creeks, and ponds. Land purchases for this park, the largest of Essex County's reservations, began in 1895. It was designed by Frederick Law Olmsted, of Central Park fame, who admired the exceptional terrain. Construction of many of the trails, footbridges, and shelters was carried out by the Civilian Conservation Corps in the 1930s.

The yellow-blazed Lenape Trail leads to Crest Drive, overlooking Interstate 78 where the Passaic River once flowed. From this point you can see Millburn, Springfield, and the ridge where the Watchung Reservation is located. You'll also pass Washington Rock, which bears a plaque that relates how the British attempted to sneak up on Washington's encampment near Morristown. *Use caution* as you approach Maple Falls Cascade; it has a twenty-five-foot drop. Eventually you'll come to Hemlock Falls, which is heavily used by picnickers. When the trail turns right, follow the white-blazed Rahway Trail, which parallels the Rahway River; go south along the east bank to return to the parking area.

Contact: Essex County Department of Parks, 115 Clifton Avenue, Newark 07101; 973-268-3500.

58. TATUM PARK

County:	Monmouth
Admission:	Free
Hours:	Sunrise to sunset
Water:	None for horse or rider
Rest room:	Portable toilet
Trail length:	Approximately 4 miles
Trailer parking:	Off Holland Road and Route 35
Terrain:	Fairly level; dirt

Location: From the Garden State Parkway, take exit 114 and turn east onto Red Hill Road. Go 1 mile to the Red Hill Activity Center entrance. Or turn left from Red Hill Road onto Van Schoick Road; go to Holland Road and turn right to the Holland Activity Center entrance on the right.

Several nice, short trails have been set aside for use by hikers, bikers, and equestrians on this 368-acre property amid rolling hills, open fields, and groves of red and chestnut oaks and tulip trees. Maps are available at the trailheads at the Red Hill Road and Holland Road parking lots. Indian Springs Trail (0.9 mile) follows an old farm road up to Red Hill Road; Tatum Ramble Trail (2.3 miles) explores fields and forests; and Meadow Run Trail (1.0 mile) rambles through interesting fields that sport a new look with each season.

The park is named for Charles Tatum, a businessman who purchased this property in 1905 as a summer home for his family. His Keyport and Millville factories manufactured laboratory glassware, bottles, decanters, paperweights, and glass insulators—many of which can be seen at the park's Holland Activity Center. His widow donated seventy-three acres of the property to the county in 1973; the remainder was purchased with federal Land and Water Conservation funds. Additional acres have been acquired through federal funding, via donations, and with the help of the New Jersey Conservation Foundation.

Contact: Tatum Park, Red Hill Road, Middletown 07748, 732-671-1987; Monmouth County Park System, 805 Newman Springs Road, Lincroft 07738, 732-842-4000, www.monmouthcountyparks. com.

59. THOMPSON PARK

County:	Monmouth
Admission:	Free
Hours:	8 a.m. to one-half hour before dusk
Water:	Horse, none; rider, at Craft Center
Rest room:	At Craft Center
Trail length:	At least 5 miles
Trailer parking:	At Craft Center. Enter the park on Route 520 at the sign marked "Maintenance"; go to the end of the road, turn right, and head to the Craft Center parking area.
Terrain:	Mostly flat; dirt trails

Location: From the Garden State Parkway, take exit 109 for Route 520 (Newman Springs Road) west. Continue 2.2 miles to the park entrance in Lincroft.

Thanks to Geraldine Thompson, who bequeathed Brookdale Farm to the citizens of Monmouth County in 1967, equestrians throughout the state can enjoy the tranquility offered along old farm roads, a former horse exercise track, and hiking trails (where allowed). Although most of the trails in this 665-acre park are maintained simply by hikers walking them, you'll find the trip worthwhile—particularly the area around the lake and the exercise track. Before leaving, you might want to visit the Craft Center and sign up for a pottery or ceramics class.

If you're here during May through October, don't miss the opportunity to visit the Lambertus C. Bobbink Memorial Rose Garden. Named in memory of the dean of commercial rosarians, this official All-America Rose Selections Display Garden has a variety of prize-winners that will captivate you with their beauty and aroma.

Contact: Monmouth County Park System, 805 Newman Springs Road, Lincroft 07738; 732-842-4000; www.monmouthcountyparks. com.

60. TOURNE COUNTY PARK

County: Morris
Admission: Free
Hours: Sunrise to sunset
Water: None for horse or rider
Rest room: Yes
Trail length: 3 miles
Trailer parking: At the McCaffrey Lane entrance on the Mountain Lakes side
Terrain: Hilly and rocky, with flat areas

Location: At 40 McCaffrey Lane, Powerville Road, and Old Denville Road in the Townships of Boonton and Denville. From northbound I-287, take exit 43 for Intervale Road (Mountain Lakes). Turn left at the end of the ramp, cross over I-287 to the traffic light, and turn right onto Fanny Road. Continue to the second stop sign and turn right onto West Main Street. Bear left at the Y onto Powerville Road. At the first road on the left, McCaffrey Lane turn left and look for the sign for the park.

This well-kept park derives its name from the Dutch word meaning "lookout" or "mountain." It is the only remaining undeveloped fragment of the Great Boonton Tract. David Ogden, attorney-general of New Jersey in 1759, originally purchased the land. According to park literature, "Clarence Addington DeCamp (1859–1948) inherited and acquired during his lifetime much of the land now preserved as Tourne County Park. Using hand tools and levers, he built two roads to the top of the Tourne and encouraged the citizenry to enjoy the forests and fields with him, thereby becoming one of the first conservationists in Morris County."

The park is especially attractive during spring, when wildflowers dot the forest floor with vibrant colors.

Contact: Morris County Park Commission, 53 East Hanover Avenue, Morristown 07960; 973-326-7600; www.morrisparks.net.

61. TURKEY SWAMP PARK

County: Monmouth
Admission: Free
Hours: Sunrise to sunset
Water: Horse, none; rider, yes
Rest room: Yes
Trail length: Approximately 4 miles around the perimeter of the park
Trailer parking: Any parking lot
Terrain: Level; gravel roads

Location: From the intersection of Routes 9 and 524 in Freehold, take 524 west; turn left onto Georgia Road to the park entrance.

Don't be disappointed if you fail to encounter wild turkeys as you ride around the perimeter of this park. In fact, the park was named for the town of Turkey, now known as Adelphia! However, this short trail has lots to offer, for you'll be passing through lovely grassy fields and wooded areas. You'll even have partial views of the lake.

If you want to explore the interior of the park after your ride, start at the office next to the parking area and follow the blazed hiking trails. During the summer you can rent a paddle boat and relax on the lake.

Contact: Park Ranger, Turkey Swamp Park, Nomoco Road, RD 4, Freehold 07728, 732-462-7286; Monmouth County Park System, 805 Newman Springs Road, Lincroft 07738, 732-842-4000, www.monmouthcountyparks.com.

62. WATCHUNG RESERVATION

County:	Union
Admission:	Free
Hours:	Sunrise to sunset
Water:	Horse, in barn; rider, fountains in barn building
Rest room:	Yes
Trail length:	Approximately 20 miles
Trailer parking:	Take the first right along the driveway
Terrain:	Hilly; crushed gravel or rocky in places

Location: From I-95, take I-78 west to exit 43 (New Brunswick/ Berkely Hts.). At light, turn right onto McMane Avenue. Turn left onto Glenside Avenue and continue for 1.2 miles. Turn right into the Watchung Reservation (Route 645).

The Lenape Indians traveled widely through this area, which they referred to as the "Wach Unks," meaning "high hills"—or, as we know them today, the beautiful Watchung Mountains. Relax and enjoy the ride. You'll see birds, deer, a babbling brook, and much more. Spring is a great time to be here, for that's when the wildflowers form a colorful carpet beneath the trees. The dense woods offer relief on hot, sunny days in summer, while in autumn they glow with vibrant reds, yellows, and oranges.

The Watchung Stable offers special activities and lessons, boards and rents horses, and holds annual events, including the Watchung Troop Horse Show each May and October. After your ride, you may wish to visit the Trailside Nature and Science Center to learn more about the flora and fauna of the area.

Contact: Watchung Stables, 1160 Summit Lane, Mountainside 07092; 908-789-3665 or 908-273-5547.

63. WELLS MILLS COUNTY PARK

County:	Ocean
Admission:	Free
Hours:	8 a.m. to sunset
Water:	Horse, streams; rider, in the nature center
Rest room:	In the nature center (open daily 10 a.m.–4 p.m.)
Trail length:	From 1 to 8 miles
Trailer parking:	At the main parking lot near the nature center or at the boat launch area adjacent to Wells Mills Lake
Terrain:	Hilly; sandy

Location: Waretown. From the Garden State Parkway northbound, take exit 69 for Route 532 west; proceed 2.5 miles to the park entrance on the left. From the Parkway southbound, take exit 67 (Barnegat, Chatsworth) and turn right on Route 554 (West Bay Avenue); continue about 5 miles to Route 72; travel west on Route 72 for a short distance to Route 532 east; turn right and proceed 3.8 miles to the park entrance on the right.

Equestrians are welcome to ride on numerous trails within this beautiful 900-plus-acre park. Trails go through fantastic scenery, including pine and oak forests, Atlantic white cedar swamps, freshwater bogs, and maple gum swamps. Watch for rare curly grass fern, pitcher plants, sundews, cranberries, sphagnum moss, and turkey beard spread out beneath the trees.

Leave time to explore the Wells Mills Nature Center, where, from the observation deck atop the building's third story, there's a great view of the surrounding Pine Barrens and Wells Mills Lake. Inside, numerous displays describe the history of the area. The park is named for James Wells, who dammed Oyster Creek and built the first sawmill here in the late 1700s. The large stands of Atlantic white cedar surrounding the property were used for building ships and constructing homes and fences. Two more sawmills were built here in the late 1800s, and it was around this time that the Estlow family turned clay mining into a successful venture. After the land was sold in 1936, the property was used as a recreational retreat until it was acquired by the New Jersey Conservation Foundation in the late 1970s. Today it is owned by the Ocean County Department of Parks and Recreation.

Contact: Wells Mills County Park, 905 Wells Mills Road, Waretown 08758; 609-971-3085; www.co.ocean.nj.us/parks/wellsmills. html.

Wildlife Management Areas

In addition to enjoying the trails described above, equestrians may ride on the multiuse public lands known as wildlife management areas (WMAs). In New Jersey, these lands are administered by the Division of Fish and Wildlife and managed by the division's Bureau of Land Management for fish and wildlife habitat. The trails open to equestrians range from rugged terrain to level woods roads, as well as sandy tracks through the Pinelands and coastal marshes.

Listed below are fourteen WMAs where horseback riding is allowed to individuals who purchase an annual permit. Currently the fee is $25 per person, plus a $2 application fee. The permit holder is responsible and liable for any damage and must abide by WMA regulations. Furthermore, horses may not be ridden over any wildlife food area, dam, fireline, or cultivated field. Carriages are restricted to main and secondary roads and cannot drive off-road or on any established horseback riding trail. At the Assunpink WMA, recreational riders are not allowed to use the jumps, which belong to the Monmouth County Hunt Club.

Permits may be obtained by contacting the Division of Fish and Wildlife, Central Region Office, One Eldridge Road, Robbinsville 08691; 609-259-2132. When applying by mail, include your phone and license plate numbers.

Because each WMA can be reached via several approaches, it's best to purchase a copy of the Bureau of Land Management's map of *New Jersey's Wild Places and Open Spaces.* Call 609-984-0547; e-mail wmamaps@dep.state.nj.us; or inquire when applying for your permit.

64. ASSUNPINK WILDLIFE MANAGEMENT AREA

Location: Monmouth County. Access from Routes 524, 571, and 539, and from exit 11 off I-195.

This tract encompasses more than 5,600 acres of fields, hedgerows, and woods.

65. BEVANS (EDWARD G.) WILDLIFE MANAGEMENT AREA

Location: Cumberland County. South of Millville and bisected by Route 555.

This WMA is among the largest owned and managed by the Division of Fish and Wildlife. Acquisition began in 1932. Today, this WMA boasts 12,000 acres of woodlands and fields.

66. BLACK RIVER WILDLIFE MANAGEMENT AREA

Location: Morris County. Headquarters on Route 513 (North Road), 2 miles northeast of Chester.

This tract of 3,057 acres is managed primarily for upland game species through the planting of annual food patches and hedgerows.

67. COLLIERS MILLS WILDLIFE MANAGEMENT AREA

Location: Ocean County. Southeast of the intersection of Routes 539 and 529.

The majority of the upland portion of this WMA of 12,250 acres consists of stands of pitch pine and scrub oak. A white cedar swamp covers the lowland area.

68. FLATBROOK WILDLIFE MANAGEMENT AREA

Location: Sussex County. Approximately 6 miles west of Branchville at the town of Bevans.

Fields and upland areas make up this 2,334-acre tract.

69. GLASSBORO WILDLIFE MANAGEMENT AREA

Location: Gloucester County. South of the city of Glassboro on Route 47.

The state has been acquiring land here since 1935. Today, the WMA encompasses 2,337 acres of woodlands and fields.

70. GREENWOOD WILDLIFE MANAGEMENT AREA

Location: Ocean County. North of the intersection of Routes 539 and 72.

The major portion of this 27,298-acre tract consists of stands of upland pitch pine and scrub oak. A white cedar swamp covers the lowland area.

71. HIGBEE BEACH WILDLIFE MANAGEMENT AREA

Location: Cape May County. On Delaware Bay, south of the Cape May Canal, approximately 4.5 miles from the southern end of the Garden State Parkway.

The 634 acres of this WMA include beachfront, dunes, marsh, woodlands, fields, and ponds.

72. MACNAMARA (LESTER G.) WILDLIFE MANAGEMENT AREA

Location: Cape May County. East of Tuckahoe on Route 50.

This tract of 13,337 acres includes six lakes created by impoundment, in addition to areas managed for many game species.

73. MEDFORD WILDLIFE MANAGEMENT AREA

Location: Burlington County. Between Mt. Laurel and Vincentown in Medford Township.

Purchased by the Division of Fish and Wildlife in 1936, this tract covers 214 acres, is fairly flat, and has hedgerows, cover crops, and other plantings for wildlife.

74. PEASLEE WILDLIFE MANAGEMENT AREA

Location: Cumberland County. Between Routes 522 and 49, about 7 miles east of Millville.

This tract consists of 17,988 acres of pine-oak woodlands and lowlands.

75. UNION LAKE WILDLIFE MANAGEMENT AREA

Location: Cumberland County. Between Vineland and Millville.

An 898-acre lake is part of this tract, along with an additional 4,677 acres of woodland.

76. WHITTINGHAM WILDLIFE MANAGEMENT AREA

Location: Sussex County. South of Newton and west of Route 206 in Fredon and Green Townships.

This tract, with both upland and lowland habitat areas, consists of 1,514 acres.

77. WINSLOW WILDLIFE MANAGEMENT AREA

Location: Camden County. South of County Route 720 and north of Winslow-Williamstown Road.

The 6,566 acres of this tract are almost entirely covered with woods. Two ponds and four small fields of crops provide food for small game species.

CREATING NEW TRAILS

Each year, the state of New Jersey sets aside funds for clubs and associations that want to build, renovate, and preserve the state's trail system. For details, contact the New Jersey Horse Council/New Jersey Trails Coordinator, 25 Beth Drive, Moorestown 08057; 856-231-0771; njhorse@aol.com.

As an individual or as a member of a club, you can take positive steps to enhance trail riding for all New Jersey equestrians:

- Join trail advocacy organizations, such as Rails-to-Trails, and lobby within the group to have more trails opened to horseback riding. Remember, there is power in numbers!

- Contact your local park superintendent or ranger and express the willingness of you or your club to sponsor a trail maintenance program in return for use of local trials.

- Be proactive. Know which laws and regulations are up for a vote and be involved no matter what your equine activity may be— whether it's land use, animal rights, trailering, grants, and so on. Attend hearings to offer input or volunteer to serve on a board or commission. Invite a politician to go trail riding with you or your group!

- Ask a private property owner for permission to clear a new trail.

- Write to anyone who can help grant permission for equestrians to use a particular trail.

The Equestrian Land Conservation Resource (ELCR) is a national, proactive organization that can help you learn how to be successful in gaining access to public lands. It offers valuable information on how to organize locally to preserve land for equestrian use and how to practice good stewardship for trail riding and protecting land. Contact ELCR at Box 335, Galena, Ill. 61036; 815-776-0150; www.elcr. org.

6

A man may well bring a horse to the water,
But he cannot make him drink without he will.

John Heywood

Therapeutic Riding

Horseback riding was used in England after World War II as a therapy for treating war injuries. However, its effectiveness was not generally recognized until Denmark's Liz Hartel, who had been paralyzed from polio, won a silver medal in dressage at the 1952 Helsinki Olympic Games. Since then, horseback riding has become the most popular form of animal-assisted therapy, and it is recognized by both the American Physical Therapy Association and the American Occupational Therapy Association as a treatment that can help people recover from certain injuries. Individuals of all ages, with a wide range of physical, cognitive, and/or emotional disabilities, as well as those who cannot walk unassisted, can learn to maneuver independently on a horse and thus enjoy the same freedom and exhilaration as able-bodied riders. They can benefit as well from other horse-related activities. In addition to gaining confidence and self-esteem, individuals can form lasting friendships with peers, trainers, and volunteers, and learn patience and empathy in the special bond that usually develops with the therapy horses.

THE THEORY BEHIND THE THERAPY

The first centers for therapeutic riding in the United States were started by individuals in Michigan and Massachusetts. In 1969 they established the North American Riding for the Handicapped Association (NARHA), which disseminates information and conducts accreditation programs. Today, NARHA has more than 700 member centers nationwide—including many in New Jersey—with more than 35,000 riders receiving help from 2,000 instructors, 30,000 volunteers, 600 licensed therapists, and 5,500 therapy horses.

According to Michael Kaufmann, NARHA's educational director, "The Equine Facilitated Mental Health programs bring together mental health professionals, instructors, and individuals who have hidden disabilities such as eating disorders, anxiety, substance abuse, Alzheimer's, depression, and many psychological disabilities. While some mental health programs offer traditional riding lessons (known as therapeutic riding) to children with physical disabilities, others concentrate on a variety of activities, including ground work and barn work where riding is not involved. Another beneficial activity for individuals with disabilities is driving, especially for those who have trouble maintaining balance. Each activity is aimed toward different goals, with different credentialed professionals administrating them." Simply being around horses often proves therapeutic.

When a trained therapist uses the movement of a horse as a treatment tool, the practice is known as *hippotherapy*. By carefully monitoring a patient's reactions on a horse that has a calm temperament and good, athletic walk, the therapist can modify the horse's movement to help improve the patient's neuromuscular functioning and sensory processing. The American Hippotherapy Association, a section of NARHA made up of licensed professionals, believes that the lessons learned during these riding sessions can be combined with other treatment strategies and applied to everyday activities. The association notes that "patients respond enthusiastically to this enjoyable experience in a natural setting."

According to Octavia J. Brown, professor of equine studies at Centenary College, "The key to understanding why the horse's movement is so useful lies in understanding the three-dimensional movement of its back. When you sit on a walking horse, your pelvis moves forward and back, side to side, and in rotation—all depending on which leg the horse happens to be moving forward. This same movement in the pelvis happens when the non-handicapped person walks. The therapist can see clearly where the client's movements are influenced by his or her disability and work to help the client react to the horse's input in a more normal way. Theoretically, the brain will integrate the new movement reaction patterns into a more fluid way of moving when off the horse." This type of therapy often helps to stretch and strengthen the rider's spine and leg muscles gently while improving balance and coordination.

In 1972 Brown established New Jersey's first riding facility for the disabled, the Somerset Hills Handicapped Riding Center in Oldwick. Eight years later, with sponsorship from the New Jersey Department of

Megan Goss, who rides with the Handicapped High Riders Club at Riding High Farm to help her cerebral palsy, is proud of the blue ribbon she won for best lead at the horseback riding for the handicapped competitions.

Agriculture, Jersey Fresh, and the New Jersey Equine Advisory Board, Brown and Barbara Isaac cofounded Horseback Riding for the Handicapped of New Jersey (HRH). The mission of this state organization is to educate the public about horse programs for individuals with disabilities; support the establishment of new programs in accordance with NARHA standards and policies; sponsor training programs for instructors, therapists, and interested individuals; provide opportunities for competition; and collect data for research on the benefits of therapeutic horse programs.

Isaac, now executive director of Handicapped High Riders Club, Inc., an umbrella facility under HRH, notes that the success of therapeutic riding is measured in different ways. "For some, it's a success just getting on the horse. When someone is lifted out of a wheelchair and put on a horse, suddenly they're looking down at everyone else. They get a sense of independence and freedom and can move equally with another person. Riding can be used in many ways, such as competition, Special Olympics, trail riding, and sharing with families while on vacation because it's lots of fun."

Therapeutic riding is indeed lots of fun in New Jersey. Besides providing opportunities for competition at all levels for riders with disabilities, many of the state's therapeutic riding centers feature in-house shows where any rider can compete, some using a leader and two sidewalkers, and some independently. The Horse Park of New Jersey puts on an exciting regional show each October (see chapter 8).

THERAPEUTIC RIDING PROGRAMS IN NEW JERSEY

Regardless of age or disability, almost any person with a disability can benefit by participation in the numerous therapeutic riding programs throughout the state. A physician's written authorization and an individual evaluation are required. Programs vary; some operate part-time, others do not employ certified therapists or use hippotherapy. It is best to check with NARHA or HRH for the latest information, hours, and fees, if any:

North American Riding for the Handicapped Association, P.O. Box 33150, Denver, Colo. 80233; 800-369-7433; www.narha.org.

Horseback Riding for the Handicapped of New Jersey, 145 Route 526, Allentown; 609-259-3884.

NARHA Premier Accredited Centers

To be accepted as an NARHA Premier Accredited Center, a facility must comply with a rigorous set of guidelines. These include: employing NARHA-certified therapeutic riding instructors to work with horses and students; meeting required safety standards; qualifying for insurance; and submitting to on-site inspections by NARHA professionals. The facilities listed here are approved by NARHA and are members as well of HRH.

Some facilities may choose not to be accredited by NARHA because they are too small to meet all requirements. To be a member of NAHRA, however, they must still comply with NARHA minimum standards. They have three years to apply for accreditation.

Atlantic Riding Center for the Handicapped (ARCH), 214 Asbury Road, Egg Harbor Township 08234; 609-926-2233.

Handicapped High Riders Club, Inc. (HHR), Riding High Farm, 145 Route 526, Allentown 08501; 609-259-3884.

Special People United to Ride, Inc. (SPUR), Monmouth County Park System, 805 Newman Springs Road, Lincroft 07738; 732-460-1167.

Special Therapeutic Education through Equestrian Development (STEED), Box 84, Allendale 07401; 201-327-2284 or 201-447-4692.

Unicorn Handicapped Riding Association, 40 Cooper-Tomlinson Road, Medford 08055; 609-953-0255.

Additional Members of NARHA

Challenged Horsemen and Special Equestrians Riding, Box 102, Franklinville 08322; 856-728-4134.

ECS Therapeutic Riding Program (Hunterdon County Educational Services Commission Riding Program), Sandhill Center, 215 Route 31, Flemington 08822; 908-735-5912.

Mercer County Equestrian Center, 431B Federal City Road, Pennington 08534; 609-730-9059.

Pony Power of New Jersey, Inc., Three Sisters Farm, 1170 Ramapo Valley Road, Mahwah 07430; 201-934-1001; www.ponypowernj.com.

Special Strides Therapeutic Riding Center, 118 Federal Road, Monroe Township 08831; 732-446-0945.

Therapeutic Riding at Centenary (TRAC), Centenary College, 220 Middle Valley Road, Long Valley 07853; 908-852-1400 ext. 2174 or 908-979-4271.

Additional Members of HRH

Chariot Riders Inc., 3179 Chariot Court, Lakehurst 08733; 732-657-2710.

Helping Horseshoe Therapeutic Riding Club, 12 Dahn Drive, Sparta 07871; 973-209-4331.

Somerset Hills Handicapped Riding Center, Box 455, Bedminster 07921; 908-234-2024.

Water Wheels Handicapped Olympian Athletes (W.H.O.A. Riders), 40 Lincoln Laurel Road, Blairstown 07875; 908-362-1194.

Other Therapeutic Riding Centers

Bancroft Algonkin Stables, Route 581, Box 367, Mullica Hill 08062; 856-769-5229.

Garret Mountain Equestrian Center Therapeutic Riding Program, 311 Pennsylvania Avenue, Paterson 07503; 973-279-2974.

7

> *But he, mighty man, lay mightily in the whirl of dust, forgetful of his horsemanship.*
>
> Homer

Owning a Horse in the Garden State

Owning a horse requires owning up to the responsibility of caring for it. If you have any doubts about your ability to fit a horse into your life, but want to try, you might consider half-boarding or leasing a horse. Some stables where lessons are given will offer these options to students who wish to gain more experience and/or compete in horse shows. Your instructor can give you advice and may know owners who are willing to make such arrangements.

Before purchasing a horse, it is wise to select a board-certified veterinarian who specializes only in equine health. He/she should be available to examine your prospective horse and to answer any questions you may have. To help you choose a veterinarian, ask your horse-owning friends for recommendations or contact the American Veterinary Medical Association (800-248-2862; www.avma.org).

Should you have a question concerning proper horse care and management, a multitude of additional resources are available to help. For example, reference books can be found on almost any equine topic (check appendix C for suggested reading). You can also seek the most up-to-date information from the New Jersey Equine Advisory Board; the Rutgers Equine Science faculty; the New Jersey Horse Council; your breed group; your county agricultural extension office; and your riding club.

CHOOSING A STABLE: YOUR OWN OR AWAY

Perhaps you've never thought about living arrangements for the more than 49,000 privately owned horses in New Jersey. In the nation's most densely populated state, however, it is essential that horse owners maintain certain standards of care to ensure the health of their animals, to live peacefully with their neighbors, and to conform to the law.

Most owners, of course, board their horses at stables owned and operated by others. The cost varies with the facilities offered. Do you want an indoor riding barn, lighted outdoor rings, a cross-country course, instruction for you, training for your horse? In choosing a stable, you are placing your horse's daily care in the hands of others. Take time to talk to the stable owner, other boarders, and your veterinarian. Don't hesitate to ask questions about on-site supervision and emergency plans. Your horse's health and safety depend upon your choice.

If you decide to keep your horse on your own property, you must abide by local and state laws (see below). The New Jersey Horse Council and the New Jersey Agricultural Experiment Station have also established guidelines for private, noncommercial owners. These maintenance procedures apply not only to horses and ponies but also to donkeys and mules.

A shelter must be built to protect the horse from rain, wind, and hot sun, with barn or stable floors made of skid-proof material (clay, asphalt, or rough gravel). For boarding a single horse, the box stall should be at least 10 x 10 feet square; a tie stall should be at least 5 x 8 feet. Straw or shavings should be used in the stall as bedding material. A free or run-in shed should be large enough to cover completely all the animals that will use it. No matter which shelter you use, it is important to keep it free of protruding nails, sharp edges, broken glass, low clearings, or other potential hazards.

NEW JERSEY REGULATIONS
FOR STABLE OWNERS

According to state regulations, a structure housing horses should be no closer than forty feet to adjacent property lines and one hundred feet from a neighboring residence. The stall, barn, or pen should be located and managed where it will not become muddy due to weather conditions, surface drainage, or activity of confined horses. Drainage should be such that standing water does not accumulate. An outside lot, when used to provide exercise or grazing, should be fenced in a manner that is safe to both animals and humans, and located so that horses will not cause damage to a neighbor's property. Fences at the exterior property line should be constructed of wooden materials, woven wire, or pipe or PVC materials, be forty-eight inches high, and be supported by posts not more than ten feet apart. The pen or corral may have appropriate footing other than grass.

The amount of land set aside to maintain a horse is not as significant as the care of the animal and its use. The criteria should be cleanliness in disposing of manure and sufficient exercise space for the welfare of the animal. Adequate space is contingent to a great extent on the intended use of the animal; for example, show horses are confined to stalls and exercised in a ring, whereas brood mares roam open paddocks. Horses smaller than 48 inches can be housed more densely. Municipalities may determine that in areas where there are ample trails and/or many neighbors who also keep horses, less land is required to maintain each horse.

New Jersey's fire and building codes are applicable to outside buildings and structures. In addition, the New Jersey Board of Health is empowered by statute to:

Regulate, control, or prohibit the keeping of animals or the accumulation of manure. Did you know that a 1,000-pound horse will defecate from four to thirteen times each day? According to Michael Westendorf, an animal scientist at the Rutgers University Extension, a horse "produces thirty-five to fifty pounds of manure (feces and urine) daily, or approximately nine tons per year." He reminds horse owners that "horse manure may contain internal parasites." For this reason, it is important "not to spread horse manure on pastures where horses could become re-exposed to parasites. When spreading, manure should be harrowed or otherwise incorporated into the soil. Composting of horse manure will result in the destruction of internal parasites; the composted product could then be spread on pastures." Westendorf recommends that manure storage piles should be "kept in a dry area not affected by runoff, and not stored on a stream bank or near a wetland, but on level ground, if possible."

According to code, a manure disposal lot must be located in a low-profile area, cause no nuisance, and be at least fifty feet from a property line and no closer than one hundred feet from any permanent residential structure, attached garage, swimming pool, tennis court, or patio on adjoining premises.

Manure should be removed daily from all interior housing and/or exterior lots. Once the manure is removed, it should be handled in one of the following manners:

- Used immediately by incorporation daily into the soil of a garden or by spreading on neighboring fields. If manure is to be spread on neighboring fields, application is not to exceed 10 tons per acre (or the latest recommendations from the state's land grant college).

- Incorporated into a bona fide composting procedure so that odors and flies do not become a problem. A manure pile does not qualify as a composting procedure.

- Stored in an undercover (rain-free), well-drained, screened, and fly-free storage area located 50 feet or more from the property line, until the manure can be handled according to one of the above alternatives.

- Placed daily in empty feed bags, shavings bags, or other biodegradable bags, tightly closed, for periodic removal from the premises with normal garbage collection or stored for later incorporation into the soil. Stored manure should not accumulate for more than three weeks.

As of this writing, the New Jersey Horse Council is researching new uses for manure. One possibility, the council notes, is that manure may be processed for fuel cell generators that can be "used on farms as a way to generate electricity." Straw bedding, Westendorf believes, may be useful to mushroom farmers, "compost or stack manure to landscapers, home gardeners, or farmers."

Prevent any accumulation of animal or vegetable matter in which fly larvae exist or any accumulation of filth or source of foulness hazardous to health or comfort of people. Stagnant pools and puddles, as well as high weeds and grass, provide breeding grounds for flies, mosquitoes, and rodents. Therefore, it is important to keep pastures and other areas well clipped and drained to minimize odor, fly, and rodent problems. Elimination of flies requires a constant, aggressive program every spring: each fly killed will mean hundreds fewer in the weeks to come. Repellents are of limited value; one of the most effective tools is a flytrap—simply a jar with bait. Fly strips that are periodically replaced can also reduce the frequency of fogging with chemicals.

Rodents, often found nesting in stables, can be discouraged by the use of covered containers for feed.

Prohibit any nuisance, offensive matter, foul or noxious odors. To live harmoniously with your neighbors and local officials, heed the regulations about manure disposal and follow the advice of the New Jersey Horse Council:

- Be considerate of your neighbor.
- Do not litter your property or the property of others.
- Fence your horse in strong, attractive fencing to prevent it from escaping onto the property of others and to exclude children or pets from your corral.
- Do not ride on the property of others without permission, and be considerate of the landowner when riding with permission.

KEEPING YOUR HORSE HEALTHY

Whether you've just acquired a horse or are a seasoned owner, familiarize yourself with the characteristics of a healthy horse. It should relish small amounts of food throughout the day; be alert, with pricked ears and bright eyes when observing activity around it; move freely and easily, placing each foot firmly and squarely on the ground; mingle with other horses if in a herd; have pink and moist mucous; excrete firm and moist feces and clear urine; and exhibit normal rectal temperature and respiratory rate.

Feeding, Grooming, and Dental Care

With proper care, your horse can live a healthy life for several decades. Nutrition plays an important role. Consult your veterinarian for advice on the best combination of food and supplements for your horse. What goes into its mouth will depend on the horse's age, type of use, reproductive status, and even how it's boarded. The New Jersey Equine Advisory Board cautions that "not all green plants are good for horses. Some can make a horse extremely ill or even kill it. Plants that are toxic to horses include wild and black cherry, red maple, oak, Jimson weed, nightshade, and bracken fern." For detailed information, check with your county agricultural agent.

Remember that a horse's stomach is very small. It's best to offer small quantities of food at frequent intervals each day. Know the difference between the two kinds of hay, legume and grass. Legume hays, including alfalfa and clover, are higher in protein and calcium than grass hays (timothy, orchard grass, broom grass, and Kentucky bluegrass). A mix of high-quality timothy and clover is a good bet for most horses. Buy from a reputable dealer or farmer. Is the hay clean, green, fresh-smelling, and free from mold, weeds, and stems?

The average horse drinks up to ten to twelve gallons of water daily. Fresh water should always be available, but do not allow a horse that is hot to drink too much at one time. Access to a trace-mineralized salt block is also necessary.

Daily grooming creates a special bond between you and your horse, while allowing you to examine its body closely for any signs of injury or disease, stimulate its circulation, and make its coat shine. New Jersey veterinarian Dan Keenan recommends using "a good stiff curry worked well into the coat, followed by brushing the loose dander away with a stiff brush, ending with a soft brush."

Taking care of your horse's hooves is essential. Picking should be done on a daily basis to avoid hoof diseases and to dislodge any foreign objects, such as stones or nails. If your horse wears shoes, check to be sure they are firmly attached. Although the schedule for trimming hooves and shoeing varies for each horse, it should be done at least every six weeks.

Just as people need well-maintained teeth to chew and digest food properly, so do horses. A horse's jaw is wider on the top than on the bottom; if the teeth do not line up properly, serious problems can occur. For example, a horse must grind food between its molars with a side-to-side motion in the lower jaw. When its teeth don't mesh, food may fall out or be swallowed mostly whole. Also, a horse's teeth continue to erupt and grow throughout its life; if the upper incisors do not

Deb Parks of Desperado Acres checks her horse's teeth
to ensure it can chew properly.

hit the lower teeth properly, they will not wear down and will further hamper chewing. Without regular dental care, the upper teeth will form hooks that can dig into the cheeks, forming abrasions in the lining of the mouth that can allow bacteria and toxins to enter the horse's bloodstream, thereby putting stress on the heart, liver, and immune system.

Most horses, according to veterinarian Thomas Allen, "will not show symptoms of dental problems, although all will develop sharp, pain-inflicting points on their teeth." To help horses live longer and perform better, Dr. Allen urges frequent dental checkups, with an oral exam every six months. During a thorough equine dental visit, notes Dr. Allen, any long, sharp teeth that may cut the tongue, cheeks, or lips will be "shortened and rounded by means of filing, a procedure known as *floating*. Points will be removed, along with any *waves* (humps in the lower line of cheek teeth), *ramps* (ski-jump-like structures on the lower cheek tooth right behind where the bit sits), and *hooks* (spikelike long sharp daggers common on the fronts and back ends of the rows of cheek teeth)."

By age three and one-half, a horse has acquired all of its permanent teeth. Surprisingly, a horse's teeth are a fairly accurate indicator of age until about the eighth year; after that time, the shape, degree of wear, and angle of the front teeth give a rough estimate of age. Marks are another aid in determining age. *Dental cups*, the dark marks on the tooth surfaces, tend to disappear as the horse ages. The *Galvayne's groove*, a mark on the upper incisors, appears after a horse reaches ten years of age and then heads further down on the tooth until, at around age twenty, it can be seen at the end of the tooth.

Preventive Medicine: Vaccinations a Must

Many of the diseases that horses contract are similar to those that infect humans. Fortunately, just as for humans, vaccines are available to enable your horse's immune system to produce antibodies against some of the most deadly diseases. Be sure to maintain a health record for each horse, with the date and type of vaccines administered, and the dates when further preventive vaccinations and/or medications are due.

According to Dr. Dan Keenan, "Although some vaccines are a mandatory part of all routine horse health programs, others are dependent upon the type of horse(s) you have, their use, and your geographic location. For this reason, it is necessary to consult with your veterinarian, who can formulate a specific program." The following vaccination schedule is recommended by Dr. Keenan for all horses in New Jersey.

Botulism

Of the three forms of botulism, two are found in New Jersey. The toxin that causes this disease—a soil-borne bacteria called *Clostridium botulinum*—is transmitted in feed and may occur frequently in certain areas. Fortunately, the vaccine for the two types is very effective, reports Dr. Keenan. Your horse will need an initial three-shot series, followed by a yearly booster.

Coggins Test (Equine Infectious Anemia)

Although there is no vaccine against equine infectious anemia, the blood test for it, known as the Coggins test, should be a part of your horse's regular preventive medicine program. The state of New Jersey requires that any horse on other than the owner's private property must have had a negative Coggins test within the last twenty-four months. Furthermore, any horse changing ownership within the state must have had a negative Coggins test within the previous ninety days. Horses changing residence should have a negative test from the previous twelve months. Managers of horse shows, sales, or barns may require more frequent testing than mandated by the state.

Equine infectious anemia is caused by a virus similar to the AIDS virus in humans. Because there is no cure for it, the state of New Jersey requires that a horse diagnosed with the disease be completely isolated from other horses or destroyed. Signs of the disease can include weight loss, anemia, fever, weakness, and edema.

Equine and Western Encephalomyelitis (Sleeping Sickness)

Horses need an initial series of two shots for this disease, which is caused by a virus transmitted by mosquitoes. The initial vaccination is effective for only six months, but encephalitis is a problem in New Jersey only from August through October. Dr. Keenan recommends "once yearly vaccination in May or early June, and, if your horse did not receive the initial two-shot series or you are not sure of his vaccination history, it's best to start again with the initial series."

There is no known treatment for viral encephalomyelitis, so it's important to watch for clinical signs of the disease. At first, symptoms may be very mild, including transient fever and depression for about five days. Further signs involve the central nervous system, ranging from depression and sleepiness to aggression and agitation. Later, affected horses may exhibit blindness, circling, head tilt, quivering face and leg muscles, and paralysis of the throat and tongue. Terminal horses will usually be down for several days before dying, and death occurs in 75–80 percent of horses that develop neuralgic signs. Survivors show gradual improvement over weeks to months, but complete recovery is rare. Horses that recover often continue to show depression, abnormal behavior, and difficulty in walking.

According to the Bayer Corporation's Agriculture Division of Animal Health, "humans are also susceptible to this illness if bitten by mosquitoes carrying the disease in their salivary glands." However, although both people and horses can contract this disease, "it cannot be spread from horse to horse or from horse to people."

Influenza and Rhinopneumonitis

Both of these diseases are caused by viruses and are transmitted directly from an infected animal. Vaccinations administered at an early age, with adequate booster shots and frequent revaccination, offer some protection against infection and can reduce the severity should the disease occur. Vaccines should be administered to all horses age two and under, to all horses traveling to shows, sales, racing events, and so on, and to all horses kept in stables where horses are always coming and going. Dr. Keenan notes that the vaccines "are not 100 percent effective, and last only ten to twelve weeks, so revaccination at frequent intervals is necessary." Because the virus causes abortion, the rhinopneumonitis vaccine should be given to all pregnant mares.

Early recognition of the horse's ill health and immediate isolation can reduce the chance of other horses catching the virus, and new horses brought into a stable or farm should be quarantined for up to six weeks to avoid the introduction of equine influenza. Bayer Corporation points out, however, that "the illness may not be apparent for several days, even though a horse is infected and contagious." The first symptom is a sudden high fever, followed by a dry, harsh cough that may last for weeks. At the onset, the nasal discharge is watery, but soon after usually becomes yellow and heavy owing to a secondary bacterial infection. "The horse may also have watery eyes, enlarged lymph nodes between the mandibles, edema and stiffness in the legs, plus breathing difficulty. It can suffer from depression, weakness, and loss of appetite."

Your veterinarian may recommend laboratory tests to identify the disease positively. The good news is that horses with a mild case usually recover in about a week. However, severely ill horses may require weeks to months to recover fully. A horse not allowed to rest, or one under stress, may develop secondary pneumonia, a chronic cough, or inflammation of the heart muscle, possibly resulting in death.

Rabies

The rabies virus is transmitted to horses through contact with the saliva of infected animals. Moreover, rabies can be transmitted from horses to humans! The New Jersey Association of Equine Practitioners (NJAEP) recommends that horses receive the rabies vaccine—which is very effective—at three months of age; thereafter, an annual booster is required to maintain immunity.

Signs of rabies in the horse include weakness, fever, lack of appetite, lameness, colic, facial nerve paralysis, restlessness, depression, excessive salivation, aggressive behavior, and progressive lack of co-ordination, vocalization, drooling, and paralysis. A horse exhibiting any of these symptoms should be examined by a veterinarian immediately. If the neurologic signs are consistent with rabies, the case will be reported to the local health department, which will then assist the veterinarian and horse owner with the protocol for collecting a specimen and transporting it to the New Jersey Department of Health and Senior Services Public Health Laboratory in Trenton for absolute diagnosis. There is no treatment to stop the progress of rabies. Once a positive diagnosis is made, the horse must be euthanized immediately.

During the period from first symptoms to final diagnosis by the state laboratory, take care not to handle the horse unless necessary, wear gloves, immunize yourself against the disease, and notify anyone who has been in recent contact with the horse. The local health department will investigate and consult with individuals who may have been exposed to the rabid animal and determine if treatment is necessary for them.

Tetanus (Lockjaw)

Tetanus is described by Dr. Keenan as "a bacterial toxin that is secreted only under specific conditions, such as deep puncture wounds, and is transmitted through contamination of wounds with *Clostridium tetani*—commonly found in horse manure and in the intestinal tracts of people and animals." Following an initial two-shot series, the tetanus vaccine should be given once yearly.

Bayer Corporation's Agriculture Division of Animal Health points out that in a horse with an infected wound, "it may take several days to several weeks for the clinical signs of tetanus to appear, depending on how close the contaminated wound is to the central nervous system." Among signs to look for are: saliva dripping from the horse's mouth; food or water regurgitated from the nostrils when the horse tries to eat or drink; paralysis or rigidity in the face, neck, trunk, and legs; violent reaction to external stimuli, such as loud noises or sudden light; and profuse sweating, colic, and difficulty in walking and breathing. Bayer notes that "pneumonia may develop as a secondary complication."

The good news is that treatment is available. Besides the tetanus antitoxin and tetanus toxoid (a vaccination given as soon as tetanus is suspected, to induce antibody production), antibiotics may also be administered to kill the bacteria. Bayer advises that "cleansing of all wounds should be tended to immediately, and necrotic tissue or any foreign bodies should be surgically removed promptly."

West Nile Virus

Before 1999, West Nile Virus (WNV) was known to occur only in Africa, the Middle East, the Mediterranean region of Europe, and western Asia. Unfortunately, this virus, which is transmitted by mosquitoes, has since appeared in the Western Hemisphere. During 2000, WNV claimed its first equine casualty, a thoroughbred in Cape May, New Jersey. Consult your veterinarian about a vaccine that has recently been approved and is 95 percent effective against the virus in horses.

The mosquitoes that carry this virus have infected humans, horses, and birds. A horse bitten by an infected mosquito may not get sick, but the odds are not good. In Europe and North America, notes the Monmouth County Mosquito Extermination Commission, horses infected with encephalitis have "a moderate to high fatality rate." Clinical signs may include malaise, anorexia, lethargy, or other indications that the nervous system has been affected, such as stumbling, lack of coordination, weakness of limbs, convulsions, circling, hyperexcitability, partial paralysis, paralysis, or coma. If you suspect that your horse is unwell, notify your veterinarian immediately, because supportive care given early enough may be beneficial.

By taking a few preventive measures, you can protect your horses and other animals from exposure to this virus. Most important: eliminate areas of standing water, such as old tires, buckets, tin cans, and other water-catching items; change the water in birdbaths and wading pools frequently; clean gutters; cover containers holding water; install screens; and use horse sheets and fly masks. Insect repellent applied to horses, horse sheets, stalls, and handlers can help to decrease exposure, but be certain to follow the directions on all labels. Horses should be kept indoors from dusk to dawn, during the mosquitoes' most active feeding period. Mowing pastures and fields regularly can also help.

Although no cases of transmission of WNV from horse to human have been confirmed, the Monmouth County Mosquito Extermination Commission suggests taking the following personal precautions:

- Avoid shaded areas where mosquitoes may be resting.
- Limit evening outdoor activity when mosquitoes are most active.
- Wear protective clothing, such as long-sleeved shirts and pants.
- Keep trash cans and stored boats covered.
- Fill or drain depressions.
- Stock ponds with fish.

For more information on West Nile Virus, contact your personal physician, veterinarian, or local health department.

The following vaccinations are indicated in certain situations and are recommended by Dr. Keenan. Consult your veterinarian for further information:

Equine Protozoal Myeloencephalitis

This disease, a very common one in New Jersey, is caused by *Sarcosystis neurona* and spread through opossum droppings. An initial two-shot series, followed by yearly vaccination, is recommended.

Potomac Horse Fever

The parasite *Ehrlichia risticii*, which causes this disease, can be transmitted to a horse when it ingests small land snails in the pasture. The disease occurs most commonly in wet areas and is not contagious. The vaccine is given only to horses living or going to areas with known problems. An initial series of two shots is followed by one every three months during the summer in problem areas or annually in nonproblem areas.

Strangles (Distemper, Barn Fever)

This highly contagious disease of the upper respiratory tract is caused by the *Streptococcus equi* bacteria and is spread directly from horse to horse or by contamination. Vaccination begins with two-shot series, followed by an annual intranasal dose.

Signs of the disease—named because the lymph nodes can swell to a point where they actually restrict breathing—include depression, loss of appetite, high fever, cough, thick yellow nasal discharge, and swelling of the head and neck lymph nodes. To diagnose the disease, bacteria cultured from the abscess material is examined. Serious illness due to strangles is rare and occurs most often when the bacteria spreads beyond the upper respiratory tract and invades lymph nodes throughout the body. This form is known as "bastard strangles." *Purpura hemorrhagica*, a rarer and more serious complication of the disease, is an immune reaction that can damage the horse's blood vessels and prove fatal.

When a case of strangles is confirmed, contaminated boots, tack, hay, stall, and soil should be cleaned and disinfected or discarded because the discharge from the abscesses is infectious. The Bayer Corporation warns that "clinically recovered horses may shed the bacteria in nasal secretions up to several months after illness. Recovered horses should not be considered free of infection until bacterial cultures are negative. If an outbreak occurs, all exposed or contact animals should be monitored for temperature rises or other signs of illness."

Other Conditions and Diseases

It is recommended that *pregnant mares* be vaccinated against rhinopneumonitis, a viral, highly infectious disease, at three, five, seven, and nine months from the last breeding date. Pre-foaling vaccinations should be administered at nine and one-half to ten months from the last breed date (six to four weeks before the foaling date). However, at farms that have had a problem with Rotavirus (an extremely dangerous and contagious virus that is shed in the feces), Dr. Keenan recommends that pregnant mares be vaccinated with the Rotavirus vaccine at eight, nine, and ten months from the last breeding date.

Foal vaccinations should begin at twelve weeks of age and and continue on a schedule set up by your veterinarian.

Other diseases and illnesses to watch for include *Equine Gastric Ulcer Syndrome*, where high levels of acid can cause damage to the stomach lining. The symptoms—colic, poor appetite, decreased performance, poor body condition, and tooth grinding—may be alleviated with appropriate management and medication.

An episode of *colic*, a painful upset of the horse's intestinal system, is signaled by lack of appetite, kicking and/or looking at the belly and flank, frequent lying down and getting up, rolling, thrashing, or violent behavior. Call your veterinarian immediately.

Do not hesitate to seek advice from your veterinarian whenever your horse has an oral or nasal discharge, severe diarrhea, or a condition that seems unusual.

Emergency Healthcare Measures

In case of emergency, stay calm and do not administer any medication without consulting your veterinarian. The American Association of Equine Practitioners recommends that horse owners take the following measures to be prepared at all times in case of emergency:

- Keep your veterinarian's telephone number by each phone, along with after hours contact information.

- Consult with your veterinarian regarding a back-up or referring veterinarian's number, just in case.

- Know in advance the most direct route to an equine surgery center.

- Post the names and phone numbers of neighbors and nearby friends who can assist you in an emergency.

Dr. Keenan advises all horse owners to know "how to take temperature, heart, and respiration rates; what to look for when checking mucous membrane for color and capillary refill time; and what the normal ranges are for these parameters." Know in advance what is average for your horse by taking these measurements "at different times of day and in different weather." As Dr. Keenan explains:

"The *temperature* range for an adult horse is from 99 to 100° F and up to 102° F in foals. Generally, a horse's temperature is lower in the morning and higher in the evening. To take a horse's temperature with a mercury thermometer: shake it down; apply K-Y Jelly, Vaseline, or saliva to the end; gently insert it into the rectum; and wait up to three minutes to read. Digital rectal thermometers will beep when ready."

Heart rates in adult horses range from thirty to forty beats per minute. To take your horse's pulse, Dr. Keenan suggests that you "locate the facial artery just under the mandible, place two fingers on it, count the number of times you feel the pulse within a fifteen-second period, and multiply the number by four to get the beats per minute."

Respiration rates in adult horses range from fourteen to twenty breaths per minute. Take this rate only when the horse is calm. Observing the abdomen or the nostrils, count the breaths for fifteen seconds and multiply by four to get the breaths per minute. (If you place your hand near the nostrils to feel the breaths, your horse may ruin the count by sniffing your hand.)

Capillary refill time (CRT) is the time it takes for the blood to fill back into the capillaries after some pressure has been applied. To take the CRT, lift your horse's lip and note the color of its gums. They should be pink. Press your finger on the gums for a few seconds, release, then count the seconds until the pink color returns.

In case of an emergency, assess the nature of the problem and, if possible, check the horse's temperature, heart rate, breathing rate, and CRT. If the horse is violent, ensure your own safety. Then call your veterinarian. Until you can speak directly to your veterinarian, you can follow these procedures:

For bleeding wounds: Apply direct pressure to the area and, if you can, apply a pressure bandage. If you cannot contact your veterinarian, gently clean in and around the wound with iodine surgical scrub and wet cotton. Dr. Keenan adds: "Rinse it well, smear K-Y Jelly around and in the wound, and clip away the hair. If severe bleeding isn't a problem, use a garden hose and gently hose the wound out with lots of water. This is the best way for getting bacteria out of a wound. Pack the wound with water-soluble antibiotic salve and apply a pressure bandage, if possible. If you cannot bandage the wound and your veterinarian will be coming out to suture it, keep it moist until he/she arrives."

For high fever: If necessary, hose down the horse with cold water (during warm weather) or stand it in cold water. If it's shivering, put on a blanket. Let the horse rest in a stall, and do not force it to walk.

For choke: Signs of choking are profuse nasal and oral discharge. Remove all feed, hay, and water from the horse immediately and try to keep the horse quiet. If you can see the obstruction, gently massage the underside of the lower portion of the neck, but do not try to force the obstruction (lump) in any direction.

Lacerated or infected eye: Place the horse in a dark stall. If untended, some types of infections and lacerations may cause the horse to lose the eye within twenty-four hours.

Severe lameness: Place the horse in a stall. Apply cold water to the affected area and wrap it if swollen. Do not give any pain killers until you've spoken to your veterinarian.

For more equine health information, contact the New Jersey Division of Animal Health (609-292-3965; http://www.state.nj.us/agriculture/animal.htm).

DISASTER PLANNING: BEFORE AND AFTER

Natural disasters can occur at any time and any place. Hurricane Floyd reminded us that New Jersey is not immune to lethal calamities. During Floyd's rampage, numerous horses drowned in a boarding stable, power was lost at the Horse Park of New Jersey, laboratory animals died when their water supply became contaminated, and many pets were lost because their owners were at work and could not return home in time to save them.

Planning Ahead

Advance preparation is a must if lives, both human and animal, are to be protected in the event of a flash flood, hurricane, fire, gas explosion, or other disaster. Thankfully, veterinarians, concerned citizens, and the New Jersey Animal Emergency Preparedness and Response Committee (AEPARC) are working hand-in-hand with the personnel of each county office of emergency management to coordinate animal issues during a disaster. Created in 1996, AEPARC has developed guidelines to help horse owners formulate a disaster plan. Its recommendations include an *emergency disaster kit* that should be kept on hand at all times and contain the following items:

- Plastic trash barrel with lid
- Water bucket
- Leg wraps
- Fire-resistant non-nylon leads and halters
- Sharp knife
- Portable radio and batteries
- Flashlight
- Wire cutters
- Tarpaulins
- Lime and bleach
- First aid items (rectal thermometer; Phenylbutazone [bute] paste, powder, or tablets—to be used *after* conferring with your veterinarian; hair clippers; four rolls of 6-inch gauze; two 1-pound rolls of 10- or 12-inch roll cotton; water-soluble antibiotic salve; four rolls of 4-inch Vetrap®; iodine surgical scrub; tube of K-Y Jelly; twitch; blunt tipped scissors)

The kit should be stored in a clean, dry, readily accessible place, and everyone in your household should know where it is. Also keep a first aid kit in your horse trailer or towing vehicle (see chapter 4).

Study your property to determine what you would do with your animals in the event of a disaster. In a flood situation, for example, is there high ground where they would be safe? Automatic watering systems and pumps will fail during a power outage; check for alternate water sources and have enough fresh water and hay on hand for forty-eight to seventy-two hours.

Additional preparations should include:

- Making advance arrangements for evacuation. Know all evacuation routes and host sites before needed, and map out alternate routes.
- Permanently identifying each animal by tattoo, microchip, brand, photograph, and/or drawing. Take photographs from all sides.
- Placing a permanent tag on each halter, with your name, phone number, and animal's name.
- Ensuring that all vaccinations and medical records are in writing and up to date. At a minimum, each horse should have current Coggins documentation.
- Keeping trailers and vans well maintained, full of fuel, and ready to move at all times.

Practice your disaster plan by acclimating your horses to trailers and vans and to unusual clothing you might wear during a disaster. Take your animals to the predetermined location to familiarize yourself with the route. Develop a priority list of which animals to save if not all can be rescued. Keep your disaster insurance coverage current on both your property and your animals.

When Disaster Strikes

It is of utmost importance to keep calm and follow the disaster plan you've practiced. On your portable radio, listen to an Emergency Broadcast System station for information on how to locate a lost horse and for livestock care providers offering services during the disaster. If you have an emergency on your property, call your local office of emergency management and tell the operator to dispatch the call to an individual handling animal emergencies. Be persistent, because the operator may be unaware of the county veterinary coordinator. For livestock and equine-related emergencies, you should also call the New Jersey Department of Agriculture.

If you leave home, take your animals' health records with you. If you must evacuate with your animals, take all records, your emergency kit, and sufficient hay and water for a minimum of forty-eight hours.

Call ahead to make certain your emergency destination is still available. If you must leave your animals at home, put them in the safest place available, with enough water for the length of time you expect to be gone.

When the Emergency Is Over

Your animals may behave unexpectedly after the emergency is over because the odors they're familiar with and the landmarks they've grown accustomed to may have changed. In this situation, the New Jersey Department of Agriculture, in cooperation with the Department of Law and Public Safety, Division of State Police, Office of Emergency Management, and the New Jersey Veterinary Medical Association make the following recommendations:

- Observe your animals until they are relaxed.

- Carefully check your property for anything that may have been deposited on it during a windstorm, tornado, or other calamity, particularly downed power lines or wild animals that may have entered your property.

- If fences are down or damaged, keep your horses in a safe area.

- Should any animal have strayed, contact your veterinarian, humane society, local stable, equestrian center, farm neighbors, and other facilities as soon as possible.

- Check with your veterinarian about the possibility of a disease breaking out.

- If you find a frightened animal, use caution in approaching or handling it.

For further information on caring for your horse and on disaster preparedness, subscribe to *New Jersey Horse Health News,* a newsletter published by the New Jersey Department of Agriculture and the New Jersey Association of Equine Practitioners (Department of Agriculture, Division of Animal Health, Box 330, Trenton 08625; 609-984-2251). You can also contact the Humane Society of the United States (2100 L Street, Washington, D.C. 20037; 202-452-1100).

LEGAL MATTERS FOR HORSE OWNERS

Disputes in the horse industry can occur over a variety of matters, including, but not limited to: the purchase and sale of equipment and tack; equine safety; health matters; property damage; personal injury; partnership and syndication agreements; and lease and purchase agreements. Even your own equipment may be cause for a lawsuit. For example, if you offer a friend a ride on your horse and he/she falls, that person can file a lawsuit against you, claiming that part of the bridle broke or the saddle was too loose. In *Equine Law and Horse Sense*, attorney/author Julie Fershtman notes that unsafe equipment is an almost certain basis for a lawsuit, and she offers many practical suggestions for avoiding liability, such as inspecting equipment on a regular basis, whether or not you lend your horse to friends or are engaged in a horse-related business activity.

Sadly, there are risks whether you are a rider, a riding instructor, a stable operator, a carriage driver, or just an individual trying to do a friend a favor by lending your mount or equipment. Thankfully, forty-three states, including New Jersey, have passed equine activity liability laws, thereby reducing individuals' risk in some cases and under certain conditions. For example, litigation is disallowed if you can prove that you had no knowledge of equipment defects or had a valid, legally enforceable written release or waiver of liability signed by the complainant. However, these defenses depend on the facts and applicable law, so you should check with your attorney and the New Jersey Horse Council for the latest interpretation.

Since Governor Christie Whitman signed the Equine Activity Liability Law in 1998, frivolous lawsuits against equestrians have been reduced. This law acknowledges that equine activities can be dangerous and defines the responsibilities of stables and other equestrian businesses. However, it is still prudent to check what conditions your insurance company covers. Remember that you may be liable for an "attractive nuisance"—defined as a potentially harmful object or condition that can attract children. At the sight of a horse, young children—and sometimes their parents—may be oblivious to your warning signs. Therefore, know what your town requires with regard to fencing and gates, and, if you allow visitors to be near your animals, have them sign a legal release form. Remember, too, that you should prominently display this message in large print: WARNING: UNDER NEW JERSEY LAW AN EQUESTRIAN AREA OPERATOR IS NOT LIABLE FOR AN INJURY TO OR THE DEATH OF A PARTICIPANT IN EQUINE ANIMAL ACTIVITIES RESULTING FROM THE INHERENT RISKS OF EQUINE ANIMAL ACTIVITIES PURSUANT TO P.L. 1997, c. 287 (C.5:15-1 et seq.)

For recommendations on attorneys who have expertise in handling equine disputes, contact the New Jersey State Bar Association.

All in green went my love riding
on a great horse of gold
into the silver dawn.

E. E. Cummings

Equine Entertainment for All Ages

As far back as anyone can remember, the Garden State has offered a multitude of equestrian entertainment and events. One truly unique event, billed in 1905 as the High Diving Horse Show at Atlantic City's Steel Pier, drew hundreds of spectators. Each evening they impatiently waited for Lorena Carver and her horse to plunge from a sixty-foot tower into a pool. Her father, a Wild West showman, thought that featuring a beautiful young woman atop a handsome horse would attract attention—and it did. Lorena took the plunge several times a day and suffered at least one broken bone a year. After retiring in 1930, she trained new jumpers, telling them not to worry because the horses knew what to do. She wasn't kidding—the horses were so well trained that even a blind jumper was employed! The only problem was trying to hold the horses back for a few minutes to build audience suspense. Frequently, when the horses got to the platform, they'd just jump.

Although high-diving horses are no longer featured in Atlantic City—the show ended in the 1950s—horse-related events throughout the state are bound to keep all ages entertained year-round.

LIVING HISTORY FARMS

Fosterfields Living Historical Farm

A visit to Fosterfields is not only a trip back in time but also an opportunity to learn about farming methods at the turn of the twentieth century. Charles Foster, a successful New York City commodities

At Fosterfields Living Historical Farm, visitors can learn
about farming as it was done a century ago and watch
the carriage competitions that are held there annually.

merchant, purchased this farm in 1881 and introduced many agricultural innovations. His daughter Caroline later managed the farm and
lived on it for 98 of her 102 years, until her death in 1979. An avid outdoors woman who loved horses, she is once supposed to have said,
"Good manure smell—you can't beat it!" Caroline treasured the 200-
acre farm so much that she bequeathed it to the Morris County Park
Commission to be preserved as a "living historical farm."

In the early 1900s, local transportation was by foot or horse-drawn
carriage. The Fosters hired Andrew Gibbons, a coachman, to care for
their horses and carriages, drive the family to appointments, and go on
errands. Almost every morning, Gibbons would hitch the horses to one
of the family's carriages and drive Charles Foster 2.4 miles to the Morristown train station. At the end of the day, he would return to fetch
Foster home again. Gibbons's chores included feeding and grooming
the horses, and cleaning the stalls, blankets, and tack. He was on call
twenty-four hours a day, seven days a week.

A visit to the Carriage House is a must. Here you'll find Foster's
regal Rockaway, a popular middle-class vehicle of the era, identified by
its characteristic roof projecting over the driver's seat. A speaking tube
was used for communicating between the driver and passenger. The

family's Side-Bar Runabout was used as basic transportation. It's a fine example of the carriage maker's economy of parts and was known for its symmetry, balance, and proportion, combined with serviceability and durability. Caroline's sporty High Tandem Cart was used with two horses "in line," or head to tail, which required the carriage to be quite high so that the driver could see and direct the lead horse. The Albany Sleigh, with a curved dash that practically enfolds the occupants, was used when the roads were covered with snow.

Through regularly scheduled events and demonstrations at Fosterfields, you'll find out how farming, butter churning, sheep shearing, and cooking were done yesteryear. Without doubt, one of the most popular events is the annual carriage driving competition. When I visited the farm in September 2000, the Hunterdon County Horse and Pony Association had organized this educational and exciting event. While member Tricia Haertlein delivered knowledgeable commentary, drivers expertly demonstrated the types of skills needed around 1910. In negotiating the obstacle course, the driver must carefully pass through tightly spaced, paired markers and halt the carriage with the rear axle on the start/finish line, all while trying to make the fastest time. There are also grooming and harnessing demonstrations, as well as a skills test, in which each driver must execute four basic driving skills, including a tight circle, the drop-off, driving a "chute" for accuracy, and a backing turn.

For details of upcoming events, contact Fosterfields Living Historical Farm, Box 1295, Morristown 07962; 201-326-7645; www.parks.morris.nj.us/parks/ffmain.htm.

Historic Longstreet Farm

This nine-acre working farm is a great place to spend a morning or afternoon watching farmhands tend to chores as they did in the 1890s, observe horses and mules plowing the fields using old-fashioned tools, or take a hayride through the property.

For details and events, contact the Monmouth County Parks System; 732-842-4000; www.monmouthcountyparks.com/parks/longstreet.html.

Howell Living History Farm

At this living history farm, a restoration in progress, you'll be transported back to the year 1900, a time when horses and buggies traveled local lanes and when farms were bordered by snake fences and Osage orange trees. The farming methods handed down by previous generations are nurtured here today, along with animals that are modern-day descendants of breeds raised in the area a century ago. Visitors of all ages are encouraged to watch the farmers drive teams of horses and oxen. Best of all, you can join in helping with some of the chores.

Here, too, you'll learn how farmers in 1900 depended on physical labor and real horsepower. In the main barn, dating to the beginning of the nineteenth century, you'll get a close-up look at a huge purebred Belgian draft horse, the same breed used in the Middle Ages as war horses because they were strong enough to carry their own heavy armor plus that of a knight. Bill and Buster and the rest of the farm's working horses provide the power for the various plowing, fertilizing, planting, mowing, reaping, and carrying jobs. On certain days, carriage rides through the historic Pleasant Valley area are offered, and on Valentine's Day rides in the farm's circa 1900 sleigh or carriage are available for married or courtin' folk only, on a first-come, first-served basis. On the Saturday before Labor Day, families can enjoy the old-time plowing match and driving competition featuring highly trained teams of Belgians, Clydesdales, and Percherons.

For details, contact Howell Living History Farm, 101 Hunter Road, Titusville 08560; 609-737-3299; www.howellfarm.com.

HORSE-DRAWN CARRIAGES AND RIDES

Driving is one of the fastest-growing equine sports (see chapter 9). That's easy to understand, because commanding a single horse or team pulling a carriage (a four-wheeled vehicle) or a cart (a two-wheeled vehicle) is lots of fun. Of course, horse-drawn vehicles aren't new on the scene. The ancient Assyrians fought wars from chariots; the kings and queens of Europe traveled in style in lavishly furnished carriages; pioneers made their way across the United States in covered wagons; and passengers and mail were brought from one town to the next via stagecoaches. Until motorized vehicles became affordable, horses pulled streetcars, funeral hearses, delivery wagons, and fire engines in cities throughout our country.

Carriages are still used today in parades, entertainments, and special events, for who can resist admiring an elegant carriage pulled by one or more stately horses? Interest in reviving the art and pleasure of carriage driving has skyrocketed in recent years. When the American Driving Society was established nearly three decades ago, only 100 individuals signed up. Today, the society has more than 3,000 members, with more joining each year!

Museums

To travel back to yesteryear, when horses were an important means of transportation, visit the museums in New Jersey that feature historical collections of carriages and related items.

Frelinghuysen Arboretum

In addition to enjoying the arboretum's beautiful trees, flowers, and garden nooks, you can view a collection of Brewster vehicles in the coach house, as well as harnesses in the attached harness room.

53 East Hanover Avenue, Morristown 07962; 973-326-7600; www.parks.morris.nj.us/parks/frelarbmain.htm.

Museum of Early Trades and Crafts

Here you'll find harnesses, carriage wheels, horseshoes, and tools for harness makers, wheelwrights, and farriers.

Main Street and Green Village Road, Madison 07940; 973-377-2982; www.rosenet.org.

Ranch Hope Carriage Museum

Built in 1981 by Alvin Lippincott in memory of his wife, Grace, this museum features carriages, wagons, sleighs, and various other horse-related items.

Telegraph Road, Alloway 08001; 856-935-1555; www.ranchhope.org.

Waterloo Village

Besides hosting exciting events all year, this fascinating 200-year-old village maintains a collection of carriages.

Allamuchy Mountain State Park, Stanhope 07874; 201-347-0900; www.waterloovillage.org.

Holiday Traditions

Around the Christmas and Hanukah season, check your local newspaper for information about towns that offer carriage rides as part of their seasonal celebrations. Not only are these towns perfect places to spend the day browsing for gifts and admiring holiday displays, but they invite families to climb aboard an old-fashioned carriage for a horse-drawn ride through the decorated streets. *Historic Manahawkin Village, Summit, New Brunswick, Chester*, and *Cape May* are just a few of the towns where you can hop aboard (for free or for a nominal charge) and have a delightful return to days long gone.

What started out as fun for Beverly Carr is now a tradition in Cape May. In 1992 she invited a few of her friends to parade through the streets with their horse-drawn carriages as a way to celebrate the holiday season. Today this annual free event—celebrated the Sunday before Thanksgiving—is witnessed by hundreds of people from miles around. Huge, ribbon-adorned Clydesdales and miniatures alike pull with pride. If you long to experience what it feels like to be a privileged guest in one of these fine carriages, Carr can accommodate you. As owner and operator of the Cape May Carriage Company (609-884-4466), she runs frequent tours through the historic district.

Climb Aboard

If you've been hankering for an old-fashioned ride in the country or through a lovely town, check out rides offered in your neighborhood. In addition to carriage rides, many hayrides take place around Halloween; and when there's snow on the ground, sleigh rides are plentiful. All are advertised in local newspapers. Also, consult the historic farms listed above for their schedules of carriage and wagon rides. One historic house/museum that offers carriage rides in season is Emlen Physick Estate (1048 Washington Street, Cape May; 609-884-5404).

To ensure memories that will last a lifetime, and to lend stateliness to any special occasion, consider hiring a horse-drawn carriage. For example, Don Gargiulo at *Brook Valley Farm* (908-479-6456) will deliver a bride and groom in style on their big day. He'll send a luxury nine-passenger coach, complete with elegantly dressed coachmen, and an impressive team of huge, handsome Belgian draft horses. He'll also provide fantastic rides for passengers through business or shopping districts.

Other horse-drawn carriage rentals include *New Horses Around* (732-938-4480), which offers hayrides, dinner rides, and moonlight and sunset rides; the *Cape May Carriage Company* (609-884-4466; see above, "Holiday Traditions"); *Greyhorse Carriage Co., Inc.* (609-259-2791); and *Highlawn Pavilion Carriage Rides* (973-325-3023), which offers 30- and 60-minute horse-drawn carriage rides through scenic Eagle Rock Reservation in West Orange.

Vacation Getaways Featuring Carriage Rides

Many of the delightful accommodations in New Jersey's most historic and scenic areas can arrange a memorable carriage ride for you. The partial list below will give you ideas for great getaways.

CAPE MAY AREA

Abbey Bed & Breakfast, 34 Gurney Street, Cape May 08204; 609-884-4506.

Abigail Adams' Bed & Breakfast by the Sea, 12 Jackson Street, Cape May 08204; 609-884-1371.

Alexander's Bed & Breakfast Inn, 653 Washington Street, Cape May 08204; 609-884-2555; www.alexandersinn.com.

Angel of the Sea Bed & Breakfast Inn, 5–7 Trenton Avenue, Cape May 08204; 800-848-3369.

Bedford Inn, 805 Stockton Avenue, Cape May 08204; 609-884-4158.

Cameo Rose Bed and Breakfast, 109 East 24th Avenue, North Wildwood 08260; 609-523-8464.

Candlelight Inn, 2310 Central Avenue, North Wildwood 08260; 609-522-6200.

Carroll Villa Hotel, 19 Jackson Street, Cape May 08204; 609-884-9619.

Gingerbread House, 28 Gurney Street, Cape May 08204; 609-884-0211.

The Inn on Ocean, 25 Ocean Street, Cape May, 08204; 800-304-4477.

John F. Craig House, 609 Columbia Avenue, Cape May 08204; 609-884-0100.

Linda Lee Bed & Breakfast, 725 Columbia Avenue, Cape May 08204; 609-884-1240.

The Mission Inn Bed & Breakfast, 1117 New Jersey Avenue, Cape May 08204; 800-800-8380.

The Mooring, 801 Stockton Avenue, Cape May 08204; 609-884-5425.

Queen Victoria Inn, 102 Ocean Street, Cape May 08204; 609-884-8702.

Saltwood House, 28 Jackson Street, Cape May 08204; 609-884-6754.

Sealark Bed & Breakfast, 3018 First Avenue, Avalon 08202; 609-967-5647.

Southern Mansion, 720 Washington Street, Cape May 08204; 800-381-3888.

Trellis Inn, 822 Washington Street Cape May 08204; 609-884-3361.

Victorian Lace Inn, 901 Stockton Avenue, Cape May 08204; 609-884-1772.

RIVER TOWNS

Lambertville House, 32 Bridge Street, Lambertville 08530; 609-397-0200.

REENACTMENTS

Black River & Western Railroad
(Flemington and Ringoes)

The annual Great Train Robbery is a must for train buffs and horse fans. Don Western gear, bring cap guns, and help the sheriff protect the train you're riding through the Hunterdon County countryside. The fearsome Covered Bridge Gang will ride their mounts at unbelievable speed and try to board the train and rob the passengers. It's a thrill a minute as costumed members of the Somerset County Horse and Pony Association succeed in getting your adrenaline flowing. You may gasp when one of the gang is "shot" off his horse, but he'll quickly remount and continue galloping beside the train.

The fun began in the late 1950s, when William Whitehead and his sons decided to do something with their steam engine and collection of rolling stock. They incorporated in 1961 and named the line for the Black River in Chester, where they originally intended to operate excursions. Today, the Black River & Western is the only regularly scheduled steam-powered passenger railroad in the state.

The Great Train Robbery is staged twice on a weekend in May; for dates and directions, contact: Black River & Western Railroad, Box 200, Ringoes 08551; 908-782-6622; www.brwrr.com.

Medieval Times Dinner and Tournament
(Lyndhurst)

From the moment you pull up to this European-style castle, where colorful banners fly from soaring turrets, you'll feel as though you've stepped back in time. And as you watch the unbelievable performance within the 80,000-square-foot re-created castle, you'll gain a feeling for what it was like when medieval kings ruled the land and chivalrous knights traveled from near and far to defend the honor of the kingdom and win the favor of fair maidens.

The evening's festivities—full of sorcery, pageantry, and food—culminate as each of the brave knights competes in an authentic jousting tournament that requires incredible skill and riding competence. Mounted on magnificent horses, the knights charge each other at full gallop while the crowd cheers them on. The weapons used during the tournament are handcrafted replicas of the ones used during the Middle Ages, including: the bola, a spiked ball attached to a wooden handle by a short chain and used from atop a horse or on foot to deliver a powerful blow to an opponent; a short sword used one-handed on horseback or, on foot, in combination with a shield or another weapon; the mandoble, a two-handed sword, five to seven feet long, that's longer and heavier than the three- to five-foot Spanish espada sword and used by knights on foot; the lance, used to knock an enemy from his horse; and the alabarda, a cross between a battleaxe and a spear, used by foot soldiers to keep enemies at a distance (a point added to the back of the weapon ensured that if the enemy was missed on the forward stroke, he could be stabbed with a backward thrust!).

If you're wondering about the beautiful Andalusian horses, they're kept in temperature-controlled stables and cared for by trained employees. All of show's stallions were bred on a ranch in Texas and trained in the movements of the Spanish Riding School, so they can perform "airs above the ground" and carry their riders in grand style.

For directions, ticket information, and show times, contact: Medieval Times, The Castle, Box 327, 149 Polito Avenue, Lyndhurst 07071; 800-828-2945 or 201-933-2220.

Wild West City (Netcong)

Why travel out West to watch cowboys perform when you can sample "the best of the West in the Heart of the East" at Wild West City? Sure,

The old-fashioned stage coach at Wild West City
is a must for all ages.

The sheriff of Wild West City opens the show
along the main street of the re-created town.

the continuous live-action shows that have been running for more than
four decades at this Western heritage theme park are mostly kid stuff.
But if you're young at heart, you'll have a great time in a setting
inspired by Dodge City of the 1880s. Celebrate the legend and lore of
the American frontier by watching cowboys perform twenty different

shows that dramatize Western adventure, re-create historic and legendary events, and demonstrate traditional cowboy skills. Take a ride on the horse-drawn stagecoach, put your child on a pony, or sit back and relax while cowboys hold up the stagecoach, demonstrate a deft touch with the bullwhip, and change Pony Express mounts faster than you can blink!

The opening ceremony is dramatic. Watch the "dancing horse," and raise a glass of root beer at the Golden Nugget Saloon. One thing is for sure: you'll have lots of fun walking the broad, dusty, main street lined with hitching rails, old wooden sidewalks, and a series of nineteenth-century-style buildings containing a variety of exhibits. The Stabile family of Sussex County conceived everything in the 1950s. Wear comfortable shoes and don your cowboy hat (or buy one at the shop) to explore the re-created Old West town and much more.

For hours and information, contact: Wild West City, Box 37, Netcong 07857; 973-347-8900; www.wildwestcity.com.

DANCING HORSES

If you haven't experienced the magic of watching a horse dancing with a human partner, consult the newspaper for the next time *Dancing with Horses* comes to New Jersey. This large-scale event for dancers, horses, and their riders was created by Manhattan-based choreographer JoAnna Mendl Shaw. A dancer from childhood, Shaw previously worked with ice dancers, gymnasts, and in-line skaters. She spent countless hours watching riders school their horses before creating this unique production. The physicality of the work and the deep connection between rider and horse inspired her to imagine the possibilities for fusing equestrian work and dance choreography. As Shaw began her work with a horse, she realized that, indeed, it was taking cues from her. Her equestrian collaborators agreed that the horse was forming a bond as if the dancer were the alpha member of the herd. It was an engagement based on mutual play.

Trained in Laban Movement Analysis, a technique used by psychologists, dancers, social workers, and psychotherapists to read body language, Shaw first observed the physical language of the horse, then began matching trained dancers with equine partners. For the dancers, the experience has been a source of great pleasure. One dancer in particular, whose family was caught in Turkey's earthquakes, found dancing with horses to be a valuable therapy for healing. Shaw herself believes that many riders realize that riding is about healing. "You ride the perfect horse, one to help you work out things you don't understand in your life. The psychological implications of this work are very interesting to me."

The end result is nothing short of fantastic. Sometimes the horse follows the dancer; at other times, the dancer follows the horse! As Shaw notes, "Nothing is static; nothing is guaranteed. There is an energy flow between the dancer and horse leading to fluid movements."

For more information, contact Shaw at jmsnyc@aol.com or visit www.dancingwithhorses.org/performance/future_projects.html.

THE RODEO, STATE AND LOCAL FAIRS, AND MORE

Cowtown Rodeo (Pilesgrove)

Reputed to be the longest-running Saturday night rodeo in the United States, and the oldest one on the East Coast, the Cowtown Rodeo attracts up to 3,000 visitors each year from May through September. Cowboys and cowgirls display expertise in bull riding, calf roping, steer wrestling, saddle bronc riding, barrel racing—and much more. I was glued to my seat watching some of the best riding I've ever seen.

Few people realize that the owners, Grant and Betsy Harris, raise their own horses and that much of their bucking stock—rated with the best in the country—has gone on to the National Finale Rodeo for many years. Raising livestock is a tradition that has been passed from one generation of Grant's family to the next since colonial times. Needing more income, the family began the Saturday night rodeo in 1926, which has been a success from the start and is one of the best entertainment buys in New Jersey. And it continues to be a family affair. Courtney and Katie, the Harris's daughters, are excellent riders and participate in the rodeo. Even Grant's dog Buddy, an Australian Blue Heeler, takes part. In fact, he's one of the stars! Everyone cheers when this small dog rounds up the bulls and broncos and herds them to the exit gate.

Put on your jeans, grab your cowboy hat, and plan on arriving early so you'll have time to visit the Cowtown flea market (open Saturday only, from 8 a.m. to 4 p.m.) before purchasing tickets to the rodeo. Once inside the arena (gates open at 7 p.m.; show starts at 7:30), head for the high rows, where you'll have the best view. Take a picnic basket, purchase food from the stands in the food court, or wait for the vendors to come around with the delicious hot peanuts that have become a tradition here. If you stay until the very end, you'll see the performing horses, Brahma bulls, and calves being guided through a tunnel beneath the street to the quiet fields on the other side.

For directions, showtimes, and tickets, contact: Cowtown Rodeo, 780 Route 40 Cowtown, Pilesgrove 08098; 856-769-3200; www. njsouth.com/index-cowtown.htm.

Horse Park of New Jersey at Stone Tavern, Inc.

The Horse Park of New Jersey—the state's first major facility devoted to equine activities—is located in Monmouth County. That's understandable, because this beautiful county is home to more horses than any other of New Jersey's twenty-one counties.

Nestled on 147 acres and bordered by the 5,000-acre Assunpink Wildlife Management Area, this unique operation opened in 1988 thanks to a partnership that brought together the New Jersey Department of Environmental Protection, the New Jersey Department of Agriculture, and private not-for-profit groups. The land was purchased by the Department of Environmental Protection with Green Acres funds, while the park is operated under contract with the Department of Agriculture by the Horse Park of New Jersey at Stone Tavern, Inc., a not-for-profit educational organization. Forty acres have been developed with state-of-the art facilities for horses in all disciplines, riders (including disabled riders), judges, show managers, and spectators. One hundred acres are kept as open fields and wooded areas for the cross-country and driving courses.

The Horse Park's brochure boasts, "The Horse Park Has Something for Everyone"—and that's the truth. As part of its mission to assist the state of New Jersey in the development and operation of a world-class facility for the benefit of all citizens, the Horse Park offers a wide range of educational, competitive, and recreational equine activities from March through November, including clinics, trail rides, horse shows, exhibitions, and other events. Most shows are free and afford all ages the opportunity to watch riders conditioning their horses and demonstrating their skills. One of the most popular events is the Festival of Horses, a showcase for more than three hundred New Jersey Standardbreds and Thoroughbreds, which compete in mare, foal, and yearling classes. In addition, festival visitors will find demonstrations and contests, free pony rides, horse and pony information, a 4-H petting zoo, and much, much more. In September, the National

Standardbred Pleasure Horse Show features retired Standardbred race horses in various classes, including driving, jumping, and barrel racing.

Future plans for the park may include shows for other animals, such as cattle, sheep, and goats. The managers also hope to purchase a trailer that can be used as a traveling classroom for year-round lectures and seminars. One of the ongoing projects, run by volunteer and park trustee Alle Lamphier, is the Memorial Tree Program. For a donation to the park, a commemorative granite plaque can be placed in front of a beautiful shade tree or flowering Bradford pear tree to remember or honor a loved one. The program has planted more than 200 trees so far, adding to the beauty of this precious open space.

For a show schedule, contact: Horse Park of New Jersey, Box 548, Allentown, 08501; 609-259-0170; www.horseparkofnewjersey.com. It is a wheelchair accessible facility.

Sussex County Farm and Horse Show/ New Jersey State Fair

Every August for more than six decades the Sussex County Farm and Horse Show has presented entertainment for all ages. Over several days you can enjoy a garden tractor and farm tractor pull, top singers and bands, a demolition derby, agricultural events featuring sheep, poultry, swine, potbellied pigs, dairy goats, and beef and dairy cattle, and a thrilling late evening fireworks display. There are also livestock shows, interactive farm activities for children, landscape gardening competitions, a milking parlor, and a baby animal nursery.

The fair offers something for everyone—clown acts, butter sculpture, racing pigs, crafts, petting zoo, pony rides, and almost any kind of food you can imagine—but the majority of those who return year after year come to see the horse show. It's jam-packed with hunters, miniature horses, team pulling, family and costume classes, Friesians, draft horses, Tennessee Walking horses, plus an exciting grand prix jumping event.

According to author Alex Everitt in *Living on the Farm*, the fair originated in 1919, and the horse show officially became part of it in 1936. The fair assumed its present name in 1940, when a nonprofit organization was incorporated to operate the show, to promote agriculture, and "to encourage the leadership, sportsmanship, and development of the youth of our country." The fair had to be postponed during the war years from 1942 to 1945, but in 1946 a huge show held over several days made up for lost time. In 1986 the Sussex County

Farm and Horse Show/New Jersey State Fair celebrated its fiftieth anniversary.

For dates, times, admission fee, directions, and other information, contact: Sussex County Farm and Horse Show, Box 2456, Branchville 07826; 973-948-5500; www.sussex-county-fair.org.

Watchung Troop Horse Show

Each May and October, no fewer than four hundred young members of the Watchung Mounted Troop put on one of the largest junior horse shows in the state. The action takes place at the Watchung Stable, and tests riders' ability to negotiate obstacle courses and ride bareback on horses selected by lottery. Each day brings new thrills and challenges, from riding in teams of threes and pairs to competing individually in horsemanship classes.

For more information, contact: Watchung Stable, 1160 Summit Lane, Mountainside 07092; 908-789-3685; http://students.dqinc. com/webdev13/watchung.

Farms

Former Governor Christie Whitman declared June as the "Month of the Horse" in New Jersey, and many farms invite the public to attend special events, with lots of horses on hand to admire. Consult your local newspaper for a listing of dates and times, or call these participating farms for information:

Baymar Farm, Harbor Road, Holmdel; 732-591-4600

Briarwood Farm, 161 Pleasant Run Road, Flemington; 908-806-8044

Campbell Farm, Pilesgrove; 856-769-8925

Dorsett Farms, 169 Russell Mill Road, Gloucester; 856-467-0870

Garoppo Farm, 1259 Tuckahoe Road, Tuckahoe; 856-697-4444

Liberty Bell Farm, Elmer; 856-358-2892

Riding High Farm, Allentown; 609-259-3884

Snowbird Acres Farm, Long Valley; 908-876-4200

Johnson Park (Piscataway)

If you love to watch trotters, head over to the track in Johnson Park. On almost any weekend, you can observe drivers exercising their horses. The entertainment is free, and the owners and trainers are usually willing to answer any questions. As a bonus, you can stroll alongside the Raritan River, only steps away from the paddock and ring.

For details, contact Johnson Park, River Road, Highland Park/ Piscataway; 732-745-3926; www.co.middlesex.nj.us/parksrecreation/ johnson.asp.

HORSE TROOPS

With a name reminiscent of the famed troop that guarded General George Washington during the American Revolution, the Jersey Light Horse Brigade, Inc., is dedicated to improving public awareness of the versatility of the horse. The accomplished equestrian members of this nonprofit organization can provide: a parade unit, color guard, musical precision drill team, security patrol, search and rescue team, and a riderless horse and solemn guard for burial/funeral services. Members are also available to entertain and instruct during charity benefits, social club activities, and at sports half-times. They have worked in school systems to supplement health, science, and/or vocational courses, and they are equipped to travel with or without their mounts. Needless to say, their horses are "streetwise."

The group has its own liability insurance and provides all necessary equipment and teaching aids. New members are welcome so long as they possess adequate riding skills and a devotion to the ideals of the club. Nonriding members can help out with a variety of chores.

For details, visit the link to "Mounted Training" at www.gleason-mountedsupply.com.

CAROUSEL RIDES

Young or old, it's hard to resist a ride on a carousel. I still remember the "good old days" when, as a child, I would delight in mounting a horse on the giant carousel at Coney Island's Steeplechase Park. If I was lucky enough to catch a brass ring, it made my day, even though I had to return it once the horses stopped going round and round. Happily, my reward for catching and returning the ring was another ride— for free.

The origin of the carousel goes back to sixteenth-century France, when knights needed a way to practice their wartime skills. From decorated wooden horses suspended from a mechanism turned by hand or horsepower, they could spear gold rings and imagine themselves expertly stabbing enemies. In the late 1700s, similar devices, created by European wood-carvers, were used for amusement and profit.

It was only a matter of time before these rotating wooden horses caught the fancy of the general population. A huge carousel at New York's Coney Island drew tourists from miles around in the late 1800s. Between 1867 and 1928, thousands of wooden carousels were crafted by hand, and the horses people loved were joined by an assortment of other animals, including giraffes, lions, and tigers. Production ceased in the Great Depression and never revived after World War II.

Because so few of the original wooden horses are left, a single one from an old-time carousel can fetch tens of thousands of dollars. Fortunately, in New Jersey you can still mount a carousel horse, either a rare wooden masterpiece or one of the new plastic models, and go round and round to melodious tunes. Thanks to carousel buff Dr. Floyd Moreland, a handsome example from 1910 still delights all ages at the *Casino Pier* in Seaside Heights. It sports fifty-eight hand-carved wooden animals, including fifty-three horses, and a few of these animals date to the 1890s. According to Moreland, this is one of only two American-made wooden carousels left in New Jersey, and one of approximately 130 nationwide. Another carousel featuring wooden horses operates on the boardwalk at *Ocean City*.

One of the most beautiful modern carousels I've seen is inside *Van Saun County Park* in Paramus. Built in Kansas in 2000, it includes thirty-two horses among its sixty animals. Each animal is constructed of fiberglass and was painted by hand. One of the largest carousels in the state, it offers disabled patrons a ramp leading to a chariot. Co-owner Jim Arfakelian, who grew up in Bergen County, feels "great joy in watching children on the carousel with big smiles on their faces."

Smaller carousels can be found in some of New Jersey's shopping malls, including *Woodbridge Mall* and *Freehold Raceway Mall*.

FIRE MUSEUMS

In colonial times, fire equipment consisted of buckets, ladders, and small hand pumps. As the equipment grew in size and complexity over time, the weight became too much for a team of men to pull quickly and safely. For that reason, according to Don Mulligan, vice chairman of the Volunteer Committee for the State Fire Museum, horses became vital to the state's fire departments. Two or three horses could pull a larger load of hoses and ladders and move it faster than a team of men. The horse became absolutely essential when the steam boiler, used to operate a piston pump to draw and shoot water, came on the scene.

For about fifty years, horsepower dominated in all New Jersey municipal fire departments. Between 1905 and 1915, however, the horse was slowly replaced by motorized vehicles, and by the early 1920s, horses were gone from the fire departments.

A visit to the *Newark Fire Department Historical Association Museum* (49 Washington Street, Newark; 201-596-6550) and the *New Jersey Firemen's Home Museum* (565 Lathrop Avenue, Boonton; 201-334-0024) will take you back in time. A firemen might recount how retired fire horses pulling delivery wagons would take off wildly racing after a motorized fire truck when they heard the clanging bell.

At the time of this writing, plans were in the works to construct the *New Jersey State Fire Engine Museum and Fire Science Center* opposite Allaire State Park. Once completed, it will house firefighting apparatus used in days long gone and display many fire department photos taken around the turn of the century: teams of three horses pulling steamers and ladder wagons; two horses pulling hose and chemical wagons; and single horses pulling the chief's buggy. You can also find photographs of these loyal animals adorning the walls of other fire museums around the state, including the ones listed here:

Chief John T. Brennen Fire Museum, 10 West 47th Street, Bayonne; 201-858-6199.

Cape May Fire Department Museum, 643 Washington Street, Cape May; 609-884-9512.

Dover Fire Museum, 209 North Sussex Street, Dover; 201-366-0301.

Engine Company No. 5 Museum, 415 North Essex Avenue, Margate.

Eureka Fire Museum, 39 Washington Avenue, Milltown; 908-828-0221.

Fire District No. 3, 39 Throckmortan Lane, Old Bridge.

Firefighters Museum of South New Jersey, 8 East Ryon Avenue, Pleasantville; 609-641-9300.

Friendship Fire Company Museum, 29 Delaware Street, Woodbury; 609-845-0066.

Haddon Fire Company Museum, 15 North Haddon Avenue, Haddonfield; 609-429-4308.

Hoboken Exempt Firemen's Association Museum, 213 Bloomfield Street, Hoboken; 201-420-2397.

Meredith Havens Fire Museum, 244 Perry Street, Trenton; 609-883-1569.

North Plainfield Exempt Firemen's Association Museum, 300 Somerset Street, North Plainfield; 908-769-2932.

Newton Fire Museum, 150 Spring Street, Newton; 201-383-0396.

Schierle's Fire Museum, 825 Grant Avenue, Westfield; 201-233-3838.

Somerville Exempt Firemen's Museum, North Doughty Avenue, Somerville.

Union Fire Company #1 Belmar Fire Department, Ninth Avenue and E Street, Belmar; 732-280-2085.

For more information, visit www.firemuseumnetwork.org/directory/nj.html.

9

*To turn and wind a fiery Pegasus
And witch the world with noble
horsemanship.*

Shakespeare, *Henry IV, Part I*

Equine Games and Sports
for Participants and Fans

For an experienced rider, nothing is more challenging than playing games or competing in sports while riding high in the saddle on a favorite mount. Interestingly, many of the equine sports and competitions enjoyed today were handed down from yesteryear's needs. For example, fox hunting was a means for farmers to track down marauders that could attack their domestic animals; tent-pegging, a popular contest in the 1800s, tested a soldier's ability to spear a tent peg from the ground while riding at a full gallop; and roping cattle from a horse was an everyday part of the cowboy's job.

In competitions where performance determines the winner, scoring depends on the judges' evaluation of how closely a horse and/or rider comes to reaching an ideal. In sports like polo, horse racing, and show jumping, winning is a matter of strength and stamina. Before engaging in any equine sport or competition, it's wise to contact the sponsoring organization and familiarize yourself with the rules, health requirements for you and your horse, and the necessary equipment. Of course, if you wish only to be an observer, the rules are simple—dress comfortably and enjoy!

Below are a few sports and games popular in New Jersey for equestrians and observers.

BAYER/UNITED STATES EQUESTRIAN TEAM
FESTIVAL OF CHAMPIONS

Since 1952, the United States Equestrian Team (USET) has represented the United States in the Pan American and Olympic Games,

154

*Ribbons displayed in front of a stall at the annual
Bayer/USET Festival of Champions.*

World Championships, and other international competitions. This
nonprofit organization is financed solely by contributions from individuals, organizations, and corporate sponsors. Donated monies are
used to select, train, and equip equestrian teams representing our
country in the disciplines of dressage, driving, endurance, eventing,
reining, show jumping, and vaulting.

USET horses and riders have achieved great success through the
decades, winning more than thirty Olympic medals, sixty-two Pan-
American Games medals, and numerous World Championships. In
1980 the USET entered its first World Driving Championship. Since
then, one of its teams has participated in this event each year, and in
1991 the USET driving team won the Pairs World Championship in
Austria.

Hamilton Farm in Gladstone is the USET's headquarters and principal training center. The public is welcome to enjoy free guided tours
Monday through Friday. Exploring the property is an unforgettable
experience: not only are the grounds magnificent, but the ornate
stable, built by New York financier James Cox Brady, is probably the
only one of its kind in the nation.

Brady first purchased 180 acres here in 1911 to build a lodge for
his family's summer hunts. He soon added a two-and-one-half story,

sixty-five-room house, an athletic building with a fifty-foot-long tiled pool and squash and tennis courts, a bull barn, a horse barn, and a blacksmith shop. After purchasing an additional 5,000 acres, he kept a crew of one hundred men busy planting a variety of crops, harvesting hay, and raising sheep, pigs, ducks, geese, chickens, and cattle. Already a breeder of Thoroughbred racehorses on a farm in Kentucky, Brady decided to build a stable here. When it was completed in 1916 at a cost of $250,000, the result was nothing short of astonishing. Today, it still takes in sunlight from fifty dormer windows, and the large clock continues to keep time over the entrance where Brady's Shetlands, Clydesdales, and Percherons once passed. Visitors will be amazed by the magnificent terrazzo floors, vaulted ceilings, glazed tile walls, and fifty-four stalls, each twelve feet square, with high metal railings and posts topped by ten-inch brass orbs. Among the forty rooms for humans are eight bathrooms, recreation rooms, and a kitchen once used to prepare special food for the horses. And it's all fireproof, thanks to the brick, concrete, and reinforced steel construction.

The USET offices are located in the building's right wing. On the second floor, ten small rooms where Brady's farmhands once slept are reserved for equestrians entered in the international contests held on the grounds. In the trophy room, you can examine the hundreds of trophies and photographs related to the USET's history and victories. On one side of the room, a balcony overlooks the dressage arena. At the center of the room, you can look up at an impressive glass floor overhead. This is where those invited to Brady's home would dance. Just above the glass floor is a skylight made of Tiffany glass.

Hamilton Farm was an extremely successful enterprise for local merchants and workers as well as for Brady. It all came to an end in 1927, however, when Brady died of pneumonia at the age of forty-eight and his heirs shut down the entire operation. Thanks to Brady's widow, Elizabeth Jane Hamilton Brady, the stable was put to good use again from 1941 to 1947 as a hospital for wounded Merchant Marines. She fondly named it Hamilton Farm Base Hospital No. 1. She also donated the family's silver trophies to the war effort.

In the 1970s Hamilton Farm was sold to the Beneficial Corporation, and sold again to Daylar Properties in 1998. That Connecticut-based firm has since developed a golf club on the site. The good news is that the USET headquarters and Olympic training center, including competition arenas and equestrian courses in Bedminster and an adjoining parcel in Gladstone, will remain forever dedicated to equestrian activities, thanks to easements in favor of the USET and the Nature Conservancy.

Each June, hundreds of equestrians from around the world compete in the Bayer/USET Festival of Champions. For a small admission fee, spectators can watch riders and horses of international caliber perform in a variety of disciplines. In between the competitive events, children are free to attend the Country Fair and Children's Corral presented by the New Jersey Department of Agriculture, while parents can inspect and purchase the items offered by dozens of vendors. The disciplines featured in the 2003 festival were:

Dressage. Spectacular to watch, high-level dressage requires years of training for both horse and rider. Judges evaluate the horse for controlled paces, flexibility, and obedience. The advanced movements, which can look like ballet, include: the *piaffe*, an elevated trot in place; the *passage*, a suspended trot in slow motion moving forward; the *pirouette*, a rhythmic circle in place at the walk or canter; the *half pass*, a forward and sideways movement at the trot or canter; and the *flying change*, a skipping movement at the canter, where the horse changes its leading front and back leg every fourth, third, second, and, finally, single stride.

Dressage, with the exacting movements we know today, attracted attention during the nineteenth century as a way for European cavalry units to test their skills. Its place in horsemanship has an even longer history. Between 430 and 355 B.C.E., the Greek general Xenophon devised a series of dressage-type movements for use in wartime.

Endurance or Long Distance Riding. As in competitive trail riding events, which cover from twenty-five to one hundred miles, the endurance horse and rider are expected to complete the journey without encountering a problem. Endurance riding, however, is extremely demanding and competitive. The horse and rider must complete a predetermined number of miles each day over a several-day period through a variety of terrain on marked trails. The first to arrive at the finish line is the winner—except that a rider who overextends and comes in too early will be penalized. Any breed or type of horse or mule is eligible, but it must be at least five years of age and in top shape.

This exciting sport, a challenge to both rider and horse, began in the cavalry. Soldiers had to practice and "endure" riding over long distances, just as the Pony Express rider had to endure all kinds of hardships, including inclement weather, as he rode countless miles to deliver the mail.

Reining. This event tests the athletic ability of a ranch-type horse, of any breed, within the confines of a show arena. Contestants are required to perform approved patterns at controlled speed, and they are judged on smoothness, finesse, attitude, quickness, and authority.

Movements include small slow circles, large fast circles, flying lead changes, roll backs over the hocks, 360-degree spins in place, and the sliding stops that are the hallmark of the reining horse. In freestyle reining, the maneuvers are set to music and choreographed by each competitor.

Top reining horses are often descended from specific bloodlines bred for generations for performance, and they are chosen as well for their calm disposition and intelligence.

Show Jumping. In a designated order and within a maximum time, riders and their mounts must clear numerous obstacles ranging in height from approximately 4'3" to 5'6". Faults are counted for any portion of an obstacle dislodged by the horse's front or back feet. Jumps include: the *vertical*, a rail fence with no extra width; the *wall*, composed of individual blocks; the *oxer*, two elements paired to create a spread; the *triple bar*, a spread with three elements of graduating height; the *combination*, a series of fences one or two strides apart; the

*A knight in shining armor parades before the audience
at the Bayer/USET Festival of Champions Invitational
Freestyle Reining Competition.*

Show jumping is one of the competition disciplines at the Bayer/USET Festival of Champions, held annually at the U.S. Equestrian Team headquarters in Gladstone.

water jump, with a low hedge usually marking the leading edge; and the *gate*, a vertical made to appear solid by using planks, brush, or balustrades.

Show jumping riders balance themselves in a forward position that distributes their weight optimally for the horse's takeoff and landing. This "natural" technique originated with the training devised for the Italian cavalry by Federico Caprilli in the 1890s.

The Bayer/USET Festival of Horses takes place at the USET Headquarters and Olympic Training Center in Gladstone. For details, contact the festival hotline (908-234-0555) or visit www.uset.org.

Note: In the future, the festival may take place at other locations; confirmation was not available at the time of this writing.

RACING

Thoroughbred and Harness Racing

The two most popular types of horse racing are Thoroughbred racing, where a jockey on the galloping horse guides it around an oval track, and harness racing, where a driver sits behind the trotting or pacing horse in a light two-wheeled cart known as a sulky. Another difference between the two types of racing is the starting gate. In harness racing, the horses and sulkies hit the starting line already trotting behind the "mobile starting gate," a contraption with winglike appendages, mounted on a truck. At the moment the gate reaches the line, the starter folds the wings and the truck speeds off the track. Thoroughbreds, on the other hand, start from narrow, individual compartments in a "standing gate." Once the starter springs the doors, the horses must leap straight forward into a gallop.

While watching a race, you may wonder how the horses are ordered across the starting line. In fact, a horse's "post position" is determined by a random drawing overseen by a racing judge. The name of each horse entered in a race is put on a slip of paper, and then one name at a time is blindly selected and assigned to a position, usually from outside to inside (next to the inside rail). A position close to the rail is considered beneficial. Particularly on shorter harness tracks, where more turns are required for a mile race, a horse and driver on the outside will have to travel farther to maneuver to the front.

The length of a race is measured by fractions of a mile or by the number of one-eighth-mile furlongs (originally a "furrow long," the length of a plowed field). Each furlong is marked by a green and white pole along the track's inside rail. A red and white pole notes each quarter-mile point. The "quarter pole" is the red and white pole located on the last turn, a quarter mile from the finish line.

Often referred to as the "sport of kings," Thoroughbred racing has been enjoyed for centuries. The sport really took off in the eighteenth century, when the breed was improved in England and earned a reputation for speed. In America, horse racing has been popular since colonial times, but it was not until 1873 that the American Jockey Club was organized to register Thoroughbreds and certify their eligibility for approved races. Since then, the Kentucky Derby, patterned after the original Derby at England's Epsom Downs, has become the most famous Thoroughbred race in the world.

For American Standardbreds, the most famous harness race is the Hambletonian, which is run every August at New Jersey's Meadowlands Racetrack. Why the name Hambletonian? As the story goes, a farmhand became so attached to a particular colt that the owner sold him both the mare and the foal. Convinced that the colt was special, the young man named the colt Hambletonian after a village in Yorkshire, England, where race meets were held, and started racing him in 1851 at the age of two. Before the horse died in 1876, he had sired more than 1,300 foals, the best of whom formed the basis of the American Standardbred registry. In the 1920s, when promoter Harry Reno thought of holding a race for three-year-old trotters, he named it for this great father of the Standardbred. The Hambletonian was first run in 1926 in Syracuse, New York. It later moved to Goshen, New York, and then, in 1957, to Illinois, where it remained until Governor Brendan Byrne brought the race to the Meadowlands in 1981.

If you're planning to place a bet at one of New Jersey's racetracks, you won't be betting against the track. Instead, in what's known as pari-mutuel wagering, you bet against everyone else who makes the same kind of wager you do in a particular race. The racetrack holds all the money in a pool; after the race, it deducts a small fixed percentage, known as the takeout, before returning the balance of the pool to winning bettors. This system originated in France around 1865, when a lottery operator and perfumist collected wagers in a common pool and determined the odds on individual horses by the amount of money bet on them. The perfumist took a small percentage from the total pool as his fee for overseeing the event and called his system "pairier mutuel," or "betting amongst ourselves." This idea was later adopted in England, where it was known as Paris Mutuels. In New Jersey, the takeout is used to fund state equine programs, track expenses, and purses for the races.

To place a bet on a race is a fairly simple matter, especially if you understand the following terms: *win*, you pick the horse that finishes first; *place*, the horse that finishes first or second; *show*, the horse that finishes first, second, or third; *exacta*, you pick the exact order of the first two finishers; *trifecta*, the exact order of the first three finishers; *superfecta*, the exact order of the first four finishers; *daily double*, you picking the winners in two designated, consecutive races; *pick 3*, the winners in three designated, consecutive races.

Horse racing is especially alive and well in New Jersey, where racetracks are more than just places to watch exciting action and bet on your favorite horse. In fact, they play a significant role in supporting the state's economy and maintaining open space for everyone to enjoy. The breeding farms and training facilities that send horses to the tracks keep large areas of land free of asphalt and chemicals, and at the same time they and the tracks employ a variety of workers and patronize local businesses and professionals.

For a great day (or night) at the races, visit one of New Jersey's beautiful racetracks:

Freehold Raceway

The nation's oldest and fastest daytime half-mile harness racetrack, established in 1853, Freehold features live Standardbred races for trotters and pacers from August through May. The facility also stays open year-round, seven days and nights a week for Thoroughbred and harness racing simulcasts from tracks throughout North America. Admission is free every afternoon, with free parking every evening and all day Sunday, Monday, and Tuesday for simulcasts.

For details and directions, contact: Freehold Raceway, 130 Park Avenue, Freehold 07728; 732-462-3800; www.freeholdraceway.com.

Meadowlands Racetrack

The New Jersey Sports and Exposition Authority operates two racetracks at the Meadowlands: the original one-mile main course for harness and Thoroughbred racing, and a newer seven-furlong turf course for Thoroughbreds only. The main course has seen many record-setting races and is home to the million-dollar Hambletonian championship for three-year-old trotters (see above). Originally built as a summer-only track, the Meadowlands is now a state-of-the-art, climate-controlled facility and features television monitors, food concessions, stands for 40,000 guests, a clubhouse with 1,800 seats, teletheaters, a nonsmoking level, and 400 wagering locations. During warm weather months, many events—including Family Days on Sundays—take place in Paddock Park, which occupies seven acres outdoors. For a $1 admission fee, children are treated to pony rides, clown acts, and more. Among the many family activities offered during the annual open house, held in conjunction with the Hambletonian, are free tours of the backstretch.

Traditionally, harness racing is a nighttime sport, and most of the races here are held during evening hours. It's a perfect time to experience the races while enjoying the offerings at one of the dining rooms overlooking the track.

For information, contact: Meadowlands Sports Complex, 50 State Highway 120, East Rutherford 07073; 201-843-2446; www.thebigm.com.

Monmouth Park Racetrack

More than 700,000 visitors come here each year to enjoy world-class Thoroughbred racing and to relax on beautifully landscaped grounds. Over the years, there have been three Monmouth Park racetracks. The first, opened in 1870 in an effort to lure visitors to Long Branch, was

Horses charging from the starting gate at one of the Thoroughbred races at Monmouth Park Racetrack, which draws more than 700,000 visitors annually.

forced to close three years later. When the completely refurbished park opened in 1882, it was the largest facility of its kind in the nation. Almost immediately, it became a favorite summer vacation spot, attracting such notable visitors as President Ulysses S. Grant and the British actress Lilly Langtry (who owned racehorses herself). In 1893, however, antigambling legislation forced the park to close and nearly killed the sport. The efforts of Amory Haskell and others eventually persuaded the New Jersey Legislature to legalize wagering for Thoroughbred and Standardbred horse racing in 1941. Five years later, a new Monmouth Park Racetrack opened under Haskell's leadership. Shortly after the park's revival, horse-breeding farms began springing up throughout the state.

From Memorial Day through Labor Day every Sunday is Family Day at Monmouth Park, when free pony rides, face painting, clowns, a petting zoo, and more activities are offered to visitors at no charge. Another free event, the Dawn Patrol held on Wednesdays and Fridays during summer months, offers visitors an opportunity to witness a "day in the life of a racehorse." The visitors' day begins at 7 a.m. with morning training and includes a tour of the stable area and starting gate, a peek at the jockeys' quarters, and complimentary coffee, juice, and donuts. (Reservations required; call 732-571-5542.) At other times, visitors are encouraged to admire the horses and jockeys close up as they are paraded along the tree-shaded English Walking Ring on their way to their races.

Each August, Monmouth Park is home to the million-dollar Haskell Invitational Handicap, a one-and-one-eighth-mile race for the nation's top three-year-olds, named in memory of Amory Haskell. Racing fans can sit in grandstand or clubhouse seats or rent luxury boxes that accommodate eight to ten people. Nonsmoking areas, video games, a pinball arcade, playground, picnic area along most of the homestretch, more than a hundred umbrella tables, and a teletheater are just some of the many features of this park.

For information, contact: Monmouth Park Racetrack, 175 Ocean-port Avenue, Oceanport 07757; 732-222-5100; www.monmouth-park.com.

Far Hills Race Meeting

Each October, for the past eight decades, this festive steeplechase meeting has drawn thousands of visitors to Somerset County and ben-efited various charities, including the Somerset Medical Center. Among the races held on this one day each year is the Breeder's Cup Steeple-chase, which attracts world-class horses and riders.

Originally a small neighborhood picnic sponsored by equestrians as a thank-you to farmers for access to their land, the occasion nowa-days is an extravaganza complete with tents, tailgate parties, people dressed in their finest, ice sculptures, and an assortment of tabletop decorations. It's a time to outdo one another with the fanciest foods and wine while enjoying the races and, most important, raising funds for charities. During the 2001 race, eagles, American flags, and red, white, and blue decor were everywhere, even on the fifty-foot tower where officials sit, as a tribute to those who lost their lives in the Sep-tember 11, 2001, tragedy.

The annual race takes place at Moorland Farms in Far Hills. For information, call 908-685-2929 or visit www.farhillsrace.org.

COMPETITIVE MOUNTED ORIENTEERING

Competitive Mounted Orienteering (CMO) was introduced to New Jersey in 1995 by Janice Elsishans, who officially represents the state on the board of the National Association of Competitive Mounted Orienteering (NACMO). This part scavenger hunt/part road rally on horse-back originated in Minnesota in 1981 and is also known as the "Thinking Horse Sport." Although "competitive" is part of its name, this innovative sport is ultimately about equestrians and their horses enjoying themselves. It's great exercise for body and mind, an excellent opportunity to meet other riders, and a terrific way to get rid of everyday stresses while playing amateur detective and learning compass and map-reading skills.

To participate, all you need is a compass and a horse, pony, or mule of any breed and at least three years of age—plus a passion for riding the trails. Before a CMO event begins, a free clinic is offered on compass and map reading. Then each competitor is given a map with the approximate locations of five to ten "objective stations" laid out in a six- to eight-square-mile area. An objective station is basically a nine-inch paper plate with two letters and a station number written on it. On the back of the rider's map, after each objective station number, at least three compass bearings are given to or from a described identifiable landmark. The object of the ride is to plunge into the woods, find as many of the objective stations as possible, and return to the starting point in the least amount of time, usually under four hours for five sites. Teams are sent out in intervals. No one is alone, and so far, no one has been lost! Competitors can find their way from one objective station to the next in any order they please. When one is found, the rider records the station's letters to prove he or she was there.

Horses must stay on the trail; be willing to go through woods and brush; cross bridges, creeks, streams, rivers, and wet, spongy ground; step over logs; and be conditioned for speed and distance. Riders must also be in good condition. Frequent dismounting may be necessary to read the compass or abide by local park rules and/or environmental conditions. CMO events are planned with consideration to the speed appropriate not only for the terrain but also for the riders' safety. Also, organizers endorse the "Leave No Trace" ethic (see chapter 4).

In addition to the rewards of being outdoors and enjoying beautiful surroundings on a horse, NACMO members receive points according to the number of stations they find during a sanctioned event. Points continue to accrue year after year, leading to different levels of awards for horse and rider. Ribbons, wall plaques, patches, and horse blankets are some of the forms of recognition.

For information, contact Janice Elsishans (973-948-3814; gldg@nji.com) or the National Association of Competitive Mounted Orienteering (www.nacmo.com).

COMPETITIVE TRAIL RIDING

Competitive trail riding and driving isn't about speed. Rather, riders must complete a marked course within a given period of time. Horses are judged on condition, soundness, and trail ability, while riders are judged on presentation (not showmanship), trail equitation (without prettiness), trail safety, courtesy, and stabling, among other details. According to the North American Trail Ride Conference (NATRC), the pace, length, and duration of the ride vary, depending on the division. In the Open Division, a one-day ride of twenty-five to thirty-five miles will be paced at about 4–6 mph, whereas a one-day ride for the Novice and Competitive Pleasure divisions will be approximately twenty to twenty-five miles, paced at 3.5–5 mph. Rides in the Open Division can be as long as eighty to ninety miles over three days.

The NATRC's philosophy is to stimulate greater interest in the breeding and use of horses possessing the stamina and hardiness needed for trail use; to demonstrate the value of type and soundness in the selection of horses for competitive riding; to teach proper methods of training and conditioning horses for competitive trail riding; to encourage good horsemanship; and to demonstrate the best methods of caring for horses during and after long rides without the aid of artificial methods or stimulants. For more information, visit www.natrc.org.

In New Jersey, the most exciting competitive trail riding and driving event has to be the *New Jersey 100*. This competition, sponsored by the New Jersey Trail Ride Association, takes place in the Pine Barrens over the Memorial Day weekend. Forty miles must be covered in 6 1/4 hours to 6 3/4 hours on days 1 and 2, with the final twenty miles covered in 2 3/4 hours to 3 hours on the final day. A time penalty of one point is assessed for every three minutes of a finishing time that is earlier or later than the day's given time window. Furthermore, a competitor will be disqualified for finishing more than thirty minutes early or late on any day. Competitors are judged 100 percent on the condition of their horses.

Spectators are warmly welcomed and may observe the horses at various points along the course. For information, contact Nancy Milne Haff (609-726-9050; NAMilne@aol.com).

DRIVING

We have already seen in chapter 8 that horses pulling wagons were a necessity for everyday life for centuries in the United States. Today, pleasure driving is a leisurely activity, with driver and passengers enjoying the scenery, fresh air, and wistful stares of onlookers while exercising a single horse or team. This type of driving can also be enjoyed by the physically challenged and the elderly. On the other hand, competitive driving is a demanding sport for the hearty soul. The trails may be rough, far, and dusty and the obstacles tricky or frightening. In either case, driving requires skill, a well-groomed horse and driver, and a fancy, well-kept carriage. With seats placed back-to-back, the carriage is called a *trap*; with seats facing each other, it is a *wagonette*. The number of horses varies. Two horses abreast are a pair; in single file they are a multiple. A team of four is known as a four-in-hand. A unicorn is one horse followed by two. Proper attire, required for competitive driving, includes brown gloves, a hat, and lap apron.

Like combined training (sometimes called three-day eventing), combined driving is a multiday challenge that tests driver and horse on all-around horsemanship and athletic skill in three different driving phases.

The first phase, *dressage*, is the most formal part of the competition and demonstrates the horse's strength, flexibility, and obedience as it is guided through a mandatory series of movements. In addition, the drivers are judged on the presentation of their turnout (horse, harness, carriage, and driver).

The *marathon*, the second phase, challenges the horse's stamina, endurance, and agility, as well as the driver's ability to pace the horse over more than twenty kilometers (about twelve miles) of cross-country driving so that the team's finishing time is neither too fast nor too slow. Obstacles along the last section of track test the courage and quick thinking of horse and driver.

The last phase, *obstacles* or *cones*, again requires stamina and obedience from the horse and judgment and horsemanship from the driver. Drivers are allowed to examine the course in advance, but the horse sees the hazards for the first time during the competition. Paired cones are set only about eight inches wider than the carriage wheels, making this a test of skill and nerves.

The *Gladstone Driving Event*, held each September at the United States Equestrian Team's headquarters at Hamilton Farm in Gladstone, is the nation's premier driving competition. The host for the event is the Gladstone Equestrian Association (GEA), which was formed in 1985 and sponsors clinics on driving, course design, equine health, and endurance training to educate the public on the diversity of horse sports. The driving event is accompanied by the annual *Youth Day and Equine Expo*, hosted by the New Jersey Department of Agriculture, the

New Jersey Equine Advisory Board, and the GEA. Youngsters can learn about grooming and tack, breeds, horse history, and horse health care.

Another exciting opportunity to witness expert driving and highly disciplined horses is the *Garden State Horse and Carriage Society's Combined Driving Event*, held each October at the Horse Park of New Jersey at Stone Tavern. For information, contact the Horse Park (609-259-0170; www.horseparkofnewjersey.com).

GYMKHANA

The word *gymkhana* (pronounced *jim-ka-na*) comes from India and means "games on horseback." Once you've seen these games, you'll want to return again and again. They're fast, exciting, and lots of fun to watch! Gymkhana events include:

Barrel Racing. During this event, one of the most popular in Western games, the horse and rider gallop in a cloverleaf pattern around three barrels set up in a large triangular formation. In one pattern, barrels 1 and 2 are placed 60 feet apart, with the third barrel 120 feet away. The tight turns at high speed require good timing, balance, and agility.

Flag Race. Here the rider's hand-eye coordination, balance, and reining skills come into play. Although the patterns vary, the horse and rider must carve a figure-eight pattern while galloping between markers and around barrels, plus pick up a flag in one part of the pattern and spear it into a bucket before crossing the finish line.

Keyhole. Horse and rider must gallop into the narrow neck of a keyhole pattern marked with chalk, turn quickly within the 20-foot-diameter top circle, and gallop out.

Pole Bending. Negotiating six poles placed 21 feet apart in a straight line requires twelve turns. Expert timing of aids (cues to the horse) plus skilled reining are needed as horse and rider run the poles four times, weaving through the line twice in each direction.

Stake Race. Here a team has to run a figure-eight pattern with two tight turns around stakes placed 80 feet apart. Speed, balance, and proper aids count greatly.

HUNTING

Fox hunting is one of the oldest known horse sports. Although I have never had an opportunity to try this exciting sport myself, I have had the pleasure of watching the enthusiastic members of the Amwell Valley Hounds in Hopewell prepare for one of their hunts. Here, the strict

*Members of the Amwell Valley Hounds
waiting for the fox hunt to begin.*

rules of the Master of the Foxhounds Association were carefully observed. When the master gave the signal for the dozens of hounds to be released from their cages, the excited but obedient hounds sat at the horses' feet until the master made certain that everyone was dressed in proper attire: hunt jacket, breeches, high boots, and hunt cap. Once everyone was assembled, the master sounded his hunting horn—and the mounted followers took off so quickly after the hounds, they seemed to be gone in the blink of an eye!

Hunts can last for as little as a half hour to more than several hours. Both rider and mount must be physically fit to cover long distances and jump over obstacles. It's rare for the hounds to catch the fox, but that doesn't matter. The sport is all about catching the scent and enjoying the thrill of the ride.

Check your local newspaper or horsemen's association to find out about hunts in your area.

POLO

I witnessed my first polo match in the fall of 2001. While watching the Colts Neck Polo Club team, I was captivated by the excitement of this thrilling and very dangerous sport. I was also impressed by the friendliness of the spectators, who immediately offered me a chair and snacks.

Members of the Colts Neck Polo Team
engage in this exciting and dangerous game.

After I admitted to knowing nothing about the game, announcer Carol Stahl took me under her wing and, during each intermission, described what was taking place. For openers, I learned that the nonprofit Colts Neck Polo Club was organized by community residents in 1994 not only to have fun but also to raise funds for the town's first aid squad and fire department. Today, the team is a charter member of the United States Polo Association. Its home field is Bucks Mill Park, and the team's objective is to "foster community unity and benefit local volunteer groups through playing polo."

Horse and player work as one in this fast-paced game. Frequently, as the horses galloped at speeds of up to thirty-five miles an hour, I prayed they wouldn't come crashing into the spectators! Take an animal that weighs at least a thousand pounds, ride it at top speed with your reins in one hand and your mallet in the other, risk getting hit with the ball or mallet—and it's clear why polo is highly dangerous!

Polo may be the world's oldest game on horseback. It supposedly originated in Pakistan more than 2,500 years ago for training warriors' agility, quick thinking, and combative skills on horseback. By 600 C.E., the game had spread to Persia, Constantinople, and even into China, but it died out around 1500. Thanks to India's princess of Bengal, it was revived in the 1850s, and officers of the British cavalry codified the rules. After noted American publisher and adventurer James Gordon Bennett witnessed the game in 1876, he quickly introduced it to New York. Polo clubs soon started springing up all over the United States, and in the 1930s, polo became an Olympic sport. Today, more than 3,000 players are affiliated with 225 clubs belonging to the United States Polo Association, and there are numerous international polo clubs as well.

Lasting less than two hours, a polo match is divided into six seven-minute periods known as chukkers. The game is played on a field 300 yards long and 160 yards wide, the equivalent of almost eight football fields. The rules are simple—even a first-timer can understand what's going on. The four players on each team take either offensive or defensive positions. Positions are changed frequently, depending on where the ball lands, with right-of-way determined by the route the ball travels. Players are allowed to push each other off the line, bump into an opposing player's horse, steal the ball, or hook an opponent's mallet. The game is supervised by two mounted umpires on the field and a referee in the stands. When a rule is broken, the penalty is a free hit; depending on which rule was broken, the referee places the ball closer or further from the untended goal.

Polo is among the most expensive of equine sports. Because the horses cover two to three miles per chukker at high speed, they need time to rest, and so players must bring a minimum of three horses to each game.

It's best to dress comfortably for a polo match, bring a blanket or chair to sit on, and pack a picnic lunch, snacks, and lots of water. The atmosphere is friendly, exciting, and informal, and during breaks the players are very willing to answer questions. When I watched the Colts Neck team, I spoke to its captain, Christopher Gerberding. Like other team members, Gerberding doesn't get paid to play; rather, he "does it for the satisfaction and fun." Gerberding takes six horses to each game, which makes it possible for him ride a different horse for each chukker. On this outing, he allowed his ten-year-old son to play a round with the team for the first time. I wondered how a parent could watch such a small child participate in such a dangerous game. Gerberding explained that he himself learned to ride in Germany at the age of six and that his son has been riding since age four. "With an early start, my son has the opportunity to become a very good player," Gerberding commented. "The game takes concentration, an awareness of what's going on all around you, and you must keep moving." Both father and son proved they can do it all—and very well.

For information about the Colts Neck Polo Club call 732-946-4243 or visit http://members.aol.com/cnpolo/life1/index.html.

The *Cowtown Polo Club* in Elmer (732-946-4243 or 609-358-7200; e-mail frankenpolo@cowtownpolo.com) is reputed to be the oldest active polo club in the state. It invites beginners to learn the basics, from preparing the horse for the game by wrapping its legs and tail, to securing yourself in the saddle during the game. Demonstrations show the various strokes, and there is a discussion about the game afterward.

Each year, the *Far Hills Polo Club* in Lebanon (908-647-0800 or 908-439-2761) hosts the Bonnie Brae Polo Classic. This event raises funds for the Bonnie Brae nonprofit residential treatment and special education center, which serves emotionally disturbed adolescent males from throughout the state.

Other *active polo clubs in New Jersey* include: Amwell Valley Polo Club, Princeton (908-369-3322); Brookview Polo Club, Holmdel (732-275-0808); Shannon Hill Polo Club, Liberty Corner (908-604-4817); Tanglewood Polo Club, Vineland (609-696-8251); Tinicum Park Polo Club, Somerville (908-996-6449); Valley Polo Club, Princeton (609-921-7655; this club holds benefit games for various charities).

SIDESADDLE RIDING

No one knows for certain when or where sideways riding originated. It is thought that during the Middle Ages, the attire of noblewomen was so cumbersome that they rode sideways with their feet supported by a tiny platform atop a saddle pad. In 1382, Anne of Bohemia, wife of King Richard II, introduced this style of riding to England. By the fifteenth century, a central horn was added to the padded seat, but the original foot rest was left intact. Paintings from the Middle Ages show ladies of royal blood riding sidesaddle. Although they were in full control while riding, a servant usually led them along the road or trail. By the eighteenth century, riding sidesaddle—with a rail attached at the side and sometimes a velvet-covered slipper stirrup—became commonplace for upper-class women. Various safety stirrups were introduced to replace the slipper stirrup. The flat seat invented for sidesaddle riding in the early 1900s incorporated two horns in order to make it easier for the rider to sit straight to the front of the horse.

Today, riding sidesaddle is once again enjoyed by female equestrians, who love to display their expertise and finery at parades and horse shows, but who no longer need anyone to lead them! The customary nineteenth-century riding habit—wool coat, canary yellow vest, white shirt and tie, black pants and boots, and an apron to cover the legs like a huge skirt—is always worn. Authentic used sidesaddles are not only difficult to find but also costly.

New Jersey sidesaddle rider Susan Samtak won the International Side Saddle Organization's (ISSO) Paso Fino division in 2000 and 2001 and the trail ride division in 2002. For more information, contact the ISSO (90 Cumberland Avenue, Estell Park, N.J. 08319; 609-476-2976; www.sidesaddle.com).

VAULTING

In 2001 the United States Equestrian Team added vaulting, the sport of gymnastics on a moving horse, to its core disciplines. A training technique for soldiers and hunters in ancient times, vaulting became a youth sport in Europe in the years after World War II. Since the 1970s, the United States has been the major non-European country that competes in international vaulting events. The American Vaulting Association is the national governing organization that maintains the rules for

A member of the American Vaulting Team,
one of the competitive disciplines supported by
the U.S. Equestrian Team, shows how it's done.

competition and sponsors clinics and demonstrations to promote the sport. Today, vaulting is included among the activities of many Pony Club, 4-H, and therapeutic riding programs because it assists riders in developing balance, confidence, and poise.

It's mind-boggling to watch individuals, pairs, and teams perform the compulsory moves and freestyle routines (*Kürs*) to music. The routines are practiced on a stationary barrel, then on a horse at a walk and trot. Eventually, the athlete performs on a horse that canters in a circle on a longe line held by the longeur. For information about the vaulting clubs in New Jersey, visit www.americanvaulting.org.

WESTERN RIDING COMPETITIONS

Western riding originated in America and was developed by the pioneers who depended on horses for hunting, transportation, and, later, herding cattle. Their horses had to be strong, fast, calm, and responsive, and have comfortable gaits.

Many of the events at Western-riding competitions are based on the jobs that cowboys of the Old West had to excel in, such as cutting out and controlling cattle, 360-degree turns, reining, roping, and tests of the horse's ability to manage numerous hazards and tasks, such as opening and closing gates, jumping over logs, and dragging objects. Popular horses used in these competitions include the American Quarter horse, Appaloosa, paint, and pinto.

According to rules established by the National Reining Horse Association (www.nrha.com), riders must wear long-sleeved shirts and Western hats or safety helmets while performing. Ties or scarves are optional; chaps are traditional, as are Western boots.

HORSESHOES

Almost everyone has pitched horseshoes, either on a regulation court in a local park or on a backyard lawn. Fun, relaxing, and great exercise, this activity for all ages is believed to have derived from a game Roman soldiers played to improve their aim. Now gaining in popularity, horseshoes can be played by one person or in doubles, either competitively or simply for pleasure.

When played for recreation, a horseshoe court requires a level area with two stakes located thirty to forty feet apart. A game sanctioned by the National Horseshoe Pitchers Association of America (NHPA) must be played on courts that meet certain specifications. Other official requirements are: horseshoes weighing not less than 2 lbs. and not more than 2 lbs. 3 oz.; stakes eight inches high; and a pitcher's box six feet square. The game consists of twenty-five innings, and each player must pitch two horseshoes each inning. A "ringer" is a thrown shoe that rests encircling the stake; it receives the highest point award, whereas a shoe that comes to rest within the court and within six inches of any part of the stake earns a point. The player scoring the most points wins the game.

For more information visit the NHPA website: www.horse-shoepitching.com.

A horse! A horse! My kingdom for a horse!

Shakespeare, *Richard III*

Learning More

JOIN A NEW JERSEY EQUESTRIAN ORGANIZATION

The Garden State offers a myriad of clubs and associations dedicated to equestrian-related activities for both novices and experts, and for individuals who just enjoy being around horses. Below are several organizations guaranteed to spur you to join, including some in neighboring states. These breed- and activity-related groups may also conduct trail rides, offer regularly scheduled performances, or sponsor guest speakers and contests. Please note that contact information is subject to frequent change.

Breed Associations

Appaloosa

Formed in 1991 by the merger of earlier organizations, the *Garden State Appaloosa Association* promotes the Appaloosa breed in New Jersey through horse shows, trail rides, and various activities. Three annual shows draw competitors from Maine to Florida. As well, the association holds an awards banquet, beach ride, and poker run. For details, visit www.gardenstateapps.com.

National associations are the *Appaloosa Horse Club*, Box 8403, Moscow, Idaho 83843, 208-882-5578, www.appaloosa.com; and the *International Colored Appaloosa Association*, Box 99, Shipshewana, Ind. 46565, 219-825-3331, www.icaainc.com.

Arabian

Individuals who simply admire the Arabian horse, as well as those who own Arabians, are invited to join the *Arabian Horse Association of New Jersey*. The association sponsors an annual show in June at the Horse

A leopard Appaloosa.

Park of New Jersey, as well as clinics, seminars, and trail rides. For more information, contact 116 Wingate Drive, Hackettstown 07840; 908-684-0514.

In addition to holding an annual show in May at the Horse Park of New Jersey and presenting a bimonthly meeting schedule, the *New Jersey Half Arabian Horse Association* sponsors trail rides, selects a queen or king for state title in January, and publishes a newsletter. For details, contact the association at 210 Brindletown Road, New Egypt 08533; 609-758-7032.

More information about Arabian horse associations in New Jersey and the Middle Atlantic states can be found through the national *Arabian Horse Association*, 10805 East Bethany Drive, Aurora, Colo. 80014; 303-696-4500; www.arabianhorses.org.

Draft Horses and Mules

The *New Jersey Draft Horse and Mule Association* promotes and supports ownership of draft horses and mules within New Jersey. Members participate in equine activities around the state and in Pennsylvania, Ohio, and New York. For more information, contact the association at 82 Sanford Road, Rosemont 08556; 908-996-4836.

The *American Donkey and Mule Society* can be reached at Box 1210, Lewisville, Texas 75067; www.lovelongears.com.

Miniature Horses

Since 1994, the *Keystone Miniature Horse Club* has been dedicated to promoting miniature horse ownership and activities in Pennsylvania and surrounding states. Membership is open to anyone who owns miniature horses and who is interested in the organization's activities, which include parades, nursing home visits, driving, 4-H participation, fun shows, club picnics, demonstrations, and tours of members' farms. For more information, contact the group at 520 Coal Street, Lehighton, Pa. 18235; 610-377-8160.

The *American Miniature Horse Association* can be reached at 5601 South I-35 West, Alvarado, Tex. 76009; 817-783-5600; www.amha.com.

Morgan

Formed to stimulate interest in the breeding, showing, and pleasure use of this versatile horse, the *Morgan Horse Association of New Jersey* supports the mission of the national organization by providing a united voice on behalf of this breed, promoting good fellowship among owners and friends of the breed, and sponsoring activities for youths. In addition, it publishes a bimonthly newsletter and presents a show, two annual membership meetings, and an awards program. For details, visit www.geocities.com/newjerseymorgan.

The *American Morgan Horse Association* can be reached at Box 960, Shelburne, Vt. 05482; 802-985-4944; www.morganhorse.com.

New Jersey Bred Hunter

If you're searching for hand and performance classes, the *New Jersey Bred Hunter Association* can help. To be eligible, a horse must be a Thoroughbred, one-half Thoroughbred, or a sport horse of the Hanoverian, Holsteiner, Trakehner, Oldenberg, Swedish Warmblood, Danish, Dutch, or Selle Francais breeds, and must be foaled in New Jersey or sired by a stallion standing the full breeding season in New Jersey. For details, visit www.njbha.homestead.com.

Paint

Paint and pinto horses may bear similar coat patterns. But to be registered with the American Paint Horse Association, a horse must prove parentage from one of three registries: American Quarter horse, Thoroughbred, or American Paint. The horse must also meet a minimum color requirement. The tobiano pattern (dark patches on a white base) features: a dark head, either solid or with a blaze, star, strip, or snip; all four legs white below the knees and hocks; regular oval or round spots that extend down the chest; and a tail of two colors. By contrast, the markings of the overo pattern (white patches on a dark base) are generally scattered and irregular; one or all of the legs will be dark; and the tail is generally dark.

The *Garden State Paint Horse Club* was established in 1967 to promote and recognize this popular breed. Today, the club sponsors

A friendly painted pony greets a passerby.

fourteen horse shows, an annual banquet, and meetings on the first Monday of the month from September through April. For details, visit www.gsphc.com.

The *American Paint Horse Association*, formed in 1962 and based in Fort Worth, Texas, can be reached at 817-834-2742 or www.apha. com.

Palomino

The *New Jersey Palomino Exhibitors Association* (NJPEA) is a state affiliate of the *Palomino Horse Breeders of America* (PHBA). A nonprofit organization formed in the late 1960s, the NJPEA promotes the breeding and showing of palomino horses throughout the state. All horses registered with PHBA are eligible to participate at any of the shows held annually by NJPEA. For details, visit www.njpalomino.com.

The national organization is based in Tulsa, Okla.; visit www. palominohba.com.

Paso Fino

New Jersey owners of Paso Fino horses can join the regional *Mason Dixon Paso Fino Association*. The association sponsors a trail log program that recognizes members for achievements in trail riding. For more information, contact the association c/o B. J. Schuler, 750 Cowpath Road, Telford, Pa. 18969; 215-723-5621.

The national *Paso Fino Horse Association* can be reached at 101 North Collins Street, Plant City, Fla. 33566; 813-719-7777; www. pfha.org.

Pinto

Pintos belong to a color registry and may be of any breed. Among the many activities of the *New Jersey Pinto Horse Association*, established in 1956, is its breeder awards program. Its shows feature a wide variety of disciplines, including driving, hunter, saddle horse, games, cutting, dressage, and more. For details, visit www.newjerseypintohorse.com.

The *Pinto Horse Horse Association of America* in Fort Worth, Texas, maintains a registry for horses, ponies, and miniatures throughout the United States, Canada, Europe, and Asia. Visit www.pinto.org.

Pony

Established in 1957, *New Jersey Pony Breeders and Owners, Inc.*, accepts members who have ponies of all breeds, registered in New Jersey or out of state, and bred in New Jersey or elsewhere. Ponies must stand no higher than 14.2 hands. Member owners of New Jersey–bred ponies are eligible to compete for year-end awards and prize money through the New Jersey Department of Agriculture's Non-Racing Breeder Awards Program. Club activities include an annual clinics and youth programs.

For more information, contact Sharon Stewart (973-579-5141) or Donna Raquet (973-383-0456).

Quarter Horse

The *New Jersey Quarter Horse Association* (NJQHA) was founded in 1961 in Sussex County "to educate [and] promote in all ways the interest of the New Jersey Quarter Horseowners, to increase the number of New Jersey breeders and owners of Quarter Horses registered by the American Quarter Horse Association and to advance New Jersey to a position of a leading Quarter Horse state." NJQHA has grown tremendously over the past few years and currently sponsors a wide variety of English and Western show events for youths and adults. The association also distributes information about the breed and holds an annual awards banquet to recognize members for their achievements. For details, visit www.njqha.com.

The *American Quarter Horse Association* (AQHA), the largest breed association in the country, requires horses to meet both bloodline and performance standards. Visit www.aqha.com.

Saddlebred

Formed in 1968, the *American Saddlebred Horse Association of New Jersey* devotes its activities to promoting interest in the breeding and showing of registered American Saddlebreds in the state. This group also sponsors a youth club and holds the Jersey Classic Horse Show on the second weekend in June at the Horse Park of New Jersey. Although new members are always welcome, membership is not required to attend the association's monthly meetings. For more information, contact Mike Ryan, 11 Forest Hill Drive, Titusville 08560; 609-737-0927.

The *American Saddlebred Horse Association* may be reached at 4093 Iron Works Parkway, Lexington, Ky. 40511; 859-259-2742; www.asha.net.

Standardbred

"They're not just for racing anymore," says the *New Jersey Standardbred Pleasure Horse Organization*. That's because these fine animals participate in many other events, including pleasure driving, pleasure riding, jumping, dressage, saddle seat equitation, drill teams, 4-H clubs, endurance, barrel racing, competitive trail riding, and mounted police work. In addition to an awards program for members who compete in a variety of disciplines, this Standardbred organization offers a certificate program for members engaged in noncompetitive activities and holds retraining clinics for horses retired from racing. Its monthly newsletter also features training articles. For more information, contact Box 38, Howell 07731; 732-901-8001.

The *Standardbred Breeders and Owners Association of New Jersey* (SBOA) is the backbone of the harness racing and breeding industry in New Jersey. Established in 1961, it oversees legislation and policy, stallion and foal registration, promotion of the industry, and benefits for individuals involved in harness racing. Its programs also include an annual show for yearlings and mares with foals; equine training and horse farm management courses; forums and symposiums; and major stakes races for New Jersey–sired horses at the state's tracks, notably the $500,000 SBOA/NJ Pacing Classic at the Meadowlands. For details, contact Box 839, Freehold 07728; 732-462-2357; e-mail SBOANJ@monmouth.com.

The *United States Trotting Association* promotes the Standardbred industry in the United States and Canada. A horse must be registered with the association before it is permitted to race or be bred, and the registration must be completed before the animal's second birthday on January 1. For more information, contact the association at 750 Michigan Avenue, Columbus, Ohio 43215; 614-224-2291; www.ustrotting. com.

Tennessee Walking Horse

As part of its mission to promote the enjoyment of the naturally trained Tennessee Walking Horse on the trail, in the field, and in the show ring, the *Tennessee Walking Horse Association of New Jersey* (TWHANJ) also supports the humane treatment of horses, good sportsmanship, and camaraderie among enthusiasts of this breed. TWHANJ sponsors numerous clinics, shows, and trail rides, and publishes a newsletter. For more information, visit www.geocities.com/twhanj.

The *Tennessee Walking Horse Breeders and Exhibitors Association* may be reached at Box 286, Lewisburg, Tenn. 37091; 931-359-1574 or 1-800-359-1574; www.twhbea.com.

Thoroughbred

The *Thoroughbred Breeders' Association of New Jersey* promotes the breeding and ownership of Thoroughbred horses in the state. The association's incentive program provides bonuses to breeders, stallion owners, and owners of registered New Jersey–bred horses that finish first to third in open or restricted races. For more information, contact the association at Ursula Plaza, 444 North Ocean Boulevard, Long Branch 07740; www.njbreds.com.

The *Jockey Club* maintains the American Stud Book, which is the registry of all Thoroughbreds foaled in the United States, Canada, and Puerto Rico, and of all Thoroughbreds imported into those countries from nations around the world that maintain registries recognized by the Jockey Club and the International Stud Book Committee. For more information, contact 821 Corporate Drive, Lexington, Ky. 40503; 800-444-8521; www.jockeyclub.com.

Carriage Driving

Garden State Horse and Carriage Society

The mission of the Garden State Horse and Carriage Society, founded in 1990, is to promote the sport of carriage driving both competitively and for pleasure; to educate and inform its members and the public about proper driving methods, safety, and events; to organize driving events; and to engage in social, intellectual, and recreational events to strengthen sociability and good fellowship among members. The club is affiliated with the American Driving Society, the New Jersey Horse Council, and the New Jersey Equine Advisory Board. Membership is open to anyone interested in equine activities, and meetings are held on the first Tuesday of the month.

The society sponsors two main events each spring and fall. (See chapter 9 for the society's Combined Driving Event.) Other activities include pleasure drives in New Jersey and surrounding states, plus driving clinics. For more information, contact 177 Pointers-Auburd Road, Salem 08079; 856-935-1616; www.americandrivingsociety. org.

The *Carriage Association of America* claims to be "the oldest and largest organization dedicated to the preservation, restoration, and use of horse-drawn carriages and sleighs." The association introduces individuals to the pleasures of collecting these vehicles and learning to drive them. For more information, visit www.caaonline.com.

The *American Driving Society* promotes the sport of driving, whether for competition or for pleasure. The society can be reached at Box 160, Metamora, Mich. 48455; 810-664-8666; www.american-drivingsociety.org.

Hunterdon County Horse and Pony Association
Organized to promote interest in equine activities among residents of Hunterdon and adjoining areas, the Hunterdon County Horse and Pony Association offers programs in carriage driving, particularly combined driving. For more information, see below under "Competitive and Fun Riding Organizations" or contact the association c/o Haertlein, 3 Lynwood Drive, Lebanon 08833; 908-236-6843.

Community Service

The horse lovers who belong to the *Friends of Morristown National Historical Park* are dedicated to preserving this important Revolutionary War site, where General George Washington and his troops withstood the freezing winter of 1779–1780. In addition to raising funds to support various projects throughout the park, the organization is working to bring horses to the park as part of a program to help grieving families in New Jersey. Members hope that, through caring for and riding horses that would be housed at the park, bereaved children and adults will have an easier time dealing with the grief process. For details on joining this fine group, visit www.nps.gov/morr, or contact Glenn Kendall (973-540-0345; restorepeace@optionline.net).

For information about the *Equestrian AIDS Foundation*, a national organization based in New Jersey, see "National Equine Associations" below.

Competitive and Fun Riding Organizations

Central Jersey Horseman's Association
The goal of the nonprofit Central Jersey Horseman's Association (CJHA) is to teach interested people the basics of competitive horseback riding and to foster the skills to excel. Six shows are sponsored annually, with each designed to attract all skill levels and disciplines. Competitions cover driving as well as English and Western riding. Riders are judged on horsemanship, control, and poise and appearance. An unofficial competition division, known as "leadline," is open to children under seven years of age. Here, adults lead the horses by a rope so that children will become comfortable and gain confidence while on a horse. Exhibitors at the shows receive award points for their performances.

The CJHA also sponsors monthly meetings with guest speakers, fashion shows, tack swaps, and more. The year is topped off with a banquet featuring awards for high-point champions and others. For more information, contact Martha Rahming at 732-928-5087.

Delaware Valley Horseman's Association

Established in 1947, the Delaware Valley Horseman's Association (DVHA) is dedicated to "fostering horsemanship by furthering the art of riding and promoting the welfare of horses and ponies; generating and enhancing general public interest and participation in equestrian activities in the State of New Jersey; and providing an incentive for competition through participation in the DVHA Annual High Score Awards." All members of the family are eligible to join, and all are invited to the DVHA's monthly meetings. At its show grounds, located between Ringoes and Sergeantsville, the DVHA sponsors English/Western shows almost every week on Sundays from April through October. Seven disciplines are judged at the shows—hunter, jumper, dressage, Western, youth, driving, and draft—and each discipline is featured at six or seven shows each season. There are no admission or parking fees for spectators. For membership details and show times, contact Box 69, Ringoes 08551; Wanda Howell, 609-397-1626; 609-397-8080 (show days only); www.dvha.org.

Game Horse Association of New Jersey

Having fun is the main goal of the family-oriented Game Horse Association of New Jersey. Its members, ranging in age from six to sixty, compete in several gymkhanas from April through October, and new members are always welcome. The shows at Piney Hollow, near Vineland, are free to spectators, who may also enjoy breakfast, lunch, and dinner at the onsite concession stand. For more information, visit www.gymkhanarider.com/clubhouse/ghanj.html.

Hunterdon County Horse and Pony Association

Since 1969, the Hunterdon County Horse and Pony Association (HCH&PA) has welcomed members who share an interest in riding and driving horses. Its many activities include an early spring Headstart Driving Seminar, a fall ride/drive day, exhibitions, a winter brunch, a monthly newsletter, and trips to horse-related museums and equine clinics and demonstrations. The club's monthly meetings cover a broad range of topics, from health issues and stable management tips, to barn tours and specific training techniques.

For more information, contact the association at Box 84, Pluckemin 07978; 908-725-9649.

Intercollegiate Horse Show Association

The Intercollegiate Horse Show Association (IHSA) was founded in 1967 at Fairleigh Dickinson University and originally involved students from the New York metropolitan region. Today, teams from the College of St. Elizabeth, Centenary College, Drew University, Princeton University, Rider University, and Rutgers University compete against other college teams in zone 2, region 1, and zone 3, regions 1 and 2.

The purpose of IHSA is to promote competition for riders of all skill levels, regardless of financial status. Individual colleges host each event, pay entry fees, and provide the horses; the student riders are responsible only for their own clothing. Competition is both individual and team oriented. Classes are geared to specific experience levels— from beginner walk-trot to open—in four disciplines: hunter equitation, equitation over fences, Western horsemanship, and reining. Riders draw lots for mounts, must use the tack on the horses, and go into the ring without schooling time. Points are awarded to individual riders and accumulated by both individuals and teams. The national championships, held each May, test the individual riders who have won in their zones and the college teams that have accumulated the most points in their regions.

For more information on how to join a team or start one, contact the IHSA National Zone Director, 2019 Stillwell-Beckett Road, Hamilton, Ohio 45013; 513-529-2352; www.ihsainc.com.

New Jersey Horse Shows Association

One of the main missions of the New Jersey Horse Shows Association (NJHSA) is to "represent the exhibitor-members in those matters of concern where a forum is needed." Open meetings are held on the second Monday of each month at 7:30 p.m. at the Lamplighter's Inn, Route 24, Chester. The NJSHA sponsors an annual horse show in September and a high-score awards dinner and dance in January. For more information, visit www.njhsa.org.

Tewksbury Equestrian Committee

Among the newest associations to foster horse-related activities is the Equestrian Committee in the town of Tewksbury. Formed in 2002, the group hopes to provide leadership in coordinating community-based equestrian activities in this rural area, where horseback riding is especially popular among residents. For more information, contact the Tewksbury Trail Association, Box 173, Oldwick 08858; 908-439-9142.

Equine Information Organizations

New Jersey Equine Advisory Board

Created in 1961 as a unit of the New Jersey Department of Agriculture, the Equine Advisory Board represents various breed groups and other agricultural organizations. The board's primary function is to recommend horse-breeding and development programs to the state Board of Agriculture. The advisory board also addresses issues concerning youth, research, promotion, and trails, and it contributes to the operation of the Horse Park of New Jersey. For more information, contact Lynn Mathews, New Jersey Department of Agriculture, Box 330, Trenton 08625; 609-984-4389; www.state.nj.us/agriculture.

New Jersey Horse Council

Established in 1970, the New Jersey Horse Council is an independent, nonprofit corporation composed of horse associations and individuals dedicated to serving the interests of the horse industry within the Garden State. It acts independently of state government, and, through lobbying and other activities, it works to influence government for the benefit of the horse industry.

Thanks to this group, the economic and social importance of the horse in New Jersey is better understood by local and state governments. Among the council's legislative successes is the Equine Activity Liability Law, which recognizes the inherent risks in such activity and limits horse owners' liability (see chapter 7). The council was also responsible for legislation that defines the responsibilities of car and truck drivers when approaching equestrians or horse-drawn carriages in the roadway (see chapter 5). And, thanks to the council, the horse was named the state animal in 1977.

In addition to its bimonthly meetings, the council holds annual seminars at Rutgers University that bring eminent speakers to address current issues facing the horse industry. As a virtual clearinghouse for information on horses and horse activities, the council keeps the public informed about horse farms; facilitates the education of horse owners; monitors zoning codes to permit and encourage the keeping of horses; preserves and expands public trails; works with horse owners and animal welfare agencies to assure humane treat of animals; and offers free literature on a variety of topics, ranging from horse care and farm keeping to trail riding and more. The council supports the American Youth Horse Council, as well as research on horse health and proper nutrition. Members have access to all information published by the American Horse Council and the American Youth Horse Council, and they receive updated information on current horse legislation, taxes, zoning, trail preservation issues, and farmland assessment and preservation. Most important, horse owners have a strong, unified voice in Trenton for the development of laws and regulations.

To join, contact the New Jersey Horse Council, 25 Beth Drive, Moorestown 08057; www.njhorsecouncil.com.

Rutgers University Cooperative Extension

The Rutgers University Cooperative Extension (RCE) is a major force in New Jersey's horse industry. Its outreach programs include: 4-H programs throughout the state, which introduce youths to horses and afford them an in-depth opportunity to learn how to care for and appreciate them; farm visits for adults; analysis and advice on management problems. At the Equine Science Center, RCE conducts research on horse-related topics ranging from stress management to nutrition, and it offers classes in equine science at Cook College and education programming for youths, horse owners, and industry professionals.

For more information, contact RCE at Martin Hall, 84 Lipman Drive, New Brunswick 08901; 732-932-9306; www.rce.rutgers.edu.

Trail Clubs

Allaire Trail Users Group

Trail maintenance in Allaire State Park is the heart and soul of the Allaire Trail Users Group (ATUG). Members spend time each month mapping all the trails within the park, building new access trails, and closing worn-out trails and planting pine trees on them. Members also work closely with the mountain bikers who use this park. For more information, contact the ATUG hotline (732-918-1970) or follow the link at www.bicyclehub.com.

Central Jersey Trail Riders

Organized to provide fellowship and promote general interest in horses and horse-related activities, the Central Jersey Trail Riders Association (CJTRA) holds meetings each month at the Jobstown Fire Station. Club activities include Sunday trail rides, weekend camping trips, competitions, and social gatherings. For more information, contact Kathleen McKernan (609-294-3439) or visit http://members.tripod.com/cjtra.

Colts Neck Trail Riders Club

In addition to enjoying trail rides throughout the state and beyond, members of the informal Colts Neck Trail Riders Club (CNTRC) engage in barrel racing, driving, showing, and more. You're welcome to join even if you don't own a horse! Annual events, held mainly at Bucks Mill Park in Colts Neck and at Hope Brook Farm in Holmdel, include hunter paces, poker rides, fun days, and trail and beach rides. Besides promoting the preservation and safe use of horse trails in the Monmouth County area, CNTRC raises money for SPUR (Special People United to Ride; see chapter 6) and for the state farmland preservation program. For more information, contact CNTRC via e-mail (cntrc@yahoo.com) or visit www.cntrc.org.

Hudson Riding Club

Formed in 1901, the Hudson Riding Club begins its weekly rides from various stables in the northern part of the state. The club's riding season runs from October through June. For more information, contact B. Reinhart (201-915-0107) or visit www.hudsonridingclub.com.

New Jersey Trail Ride Association, Inc.

Each year, the New Jersey Trail Ride Association (NJTRA) holds exciting endurance events sanctioned by the Eastern Competitive Trail Ride Association. For more information, see chapter 9 (under "Competitive Trail Riding") or visit www.members.tripod.com/njrta2/.

Readington Trail Association

Members of the Readington Trail Association (RTA) are dedicated to maintaining the trails they have created within Deer Path Park and alongside the South Branch of the Raritan River (see chapter 5, trail 33). This nonprofit organization holds monthly meetings to determine what work needs to be done and where; takes group rides for maintenance work and for fun; educates car drivers about safe speeds and courtesy when passing horses on the roadways; creates and maintains trails on private lands; and insures private property owners who allow equestrian crossings. Currently, members are working to connect trails leading from Deer Path Park and the river to Stanton Station; from there, it's approximately three-quarters of a mile to the extensive Pittstown trails (see chapter 5, trail 22). One of the RTA's top goals is to have a trail leading from Deer Path Park to Round Valley Recreation Area.

Membership in the RTA is restricted to Readington Township residents. For more information, contact Janet Agresti (908-788-3075).

Skylands Trails Association

This newly formed nonprofit organization serves northern Warren and southern Sussex Counties. Its mission is to identify and maintain trails now in use while working with state and local governments to create new trails that will link as many parks, forests, and open spaces as possible. Members are needed to help mark and maintain existing trails so they can be used and enjoyed by everyone. For more information, contact the association at 14 Turpin Road, Blairstown 07825; 908-459-4177; www.skylandstrails.netfirms.com.

Somerset County Horse and Pony Association

The Somerset County Horse and Pony Association (SCHPA) places great emphasis on horse access to public trails and participation in trail maintenance. Member activities include trail rides, patrols on horseback, and adopt-a-trail programs. The SCHPA also participates in nationally sanctioned mounted orienteering events in New Jersey and surrounding states. Other member interests include team penning, parades, and the Great Train Robbery (see chapter 8).The association publishes a monthly newsletter. For more information about this enthusiastic group, contact Box 84, Pluckemin 07978; 908-725-9649.

Tewksbury Trail Association

With a membership of more than 250 riders and nonriders, the Tewksbury Trail Association (TTA) is dedicated to keeping the town of Tewksbury picturesque and horse friendly. Through local events and patronage, members support the town's equine hospitals, horse boarding businesses, and feed and hay farmers. Among the chief aims of the TTA are to preserve open space, renovate historic farms and barns, and gain trail easements. Tewksbury's privately owned trails are restricted to TTA members and those who board their horses here, but the public trails may be used by nonresidents. The association is open to nonresidents who board their horses in Tewksbury and to supporting members who do not live in Tewksbury. For more information, contact Box 173, Oldwick 08858; 908-236-9339.

NEW JERSEY EQUINE EDUCATIONAL PROGRAMS
For Youths

4-H

Mention 4-H, and immediately the familiar green four-leaf clover, with the letter H in white or gold printed on each leaf, comes to mind. This symbol, registered with the U.S. Patent Office in 1924, signifies the organization's primary purpose: to attain positive youth development through teaching youngsters to use the *Head*, representing knowledge; the *Heart*, for community service and leadership; the *Hands*, to become expert at tasks; and *Health*, for better living.

In New Jersey, the 4-H Youth Development Program is overseen by the Rutgers Cooperative Extension of Cook College. Clubs are organized in each county through the local Rutgers extension office. According to Margie Margentino, equine program associate for Rutgers and the Cooperative Extension Service of New Jersey, "4-H offers informal, educational programs to youths from kindergarten through the first year out of high school at limited or no cost." Many of the 4-H clubs in New Jersey are devoted to woodworking, cooking, livestock and small animal husbandry, gardening, and a variety of other projects; but there are also 4-H clubs devoted solely to equine programs. As of 2003, 1,500 youths throughout New Jersey belonged to ninety 4-H equine clubs supported by more than 300 volunteer adult leaders who are knowledgeable about horses. According to Margentino, "4-H programs incorporate a fun, learn-by-doing approach, thus enabling youths to develop the knowledge, attitudes, and skills they need to become competent, caring, and contributing members of the equine industry and general society."

Membership in the 4-H Equine Program is open to all youths who meet the age requirements, regardless of sex, race, national origin, or disability. Best of all, owning a horse isn't necessary! When Margentino took over the New Jersey 4-H program in 1988, she expanded the equine component to include activities for individuals who love horses but don't own one. Today, one-third of those enrolled in the equine program do not own horses.

Although riding and horse shows are part of the 4-H curriculum, the major focus is on the educational programs held throughout the year. Events that do not require the use of live horses, but showcase participants' equine knowledge, include the *Horse Bowl*, a project that enhances study skills and encourages teamwork. In preparation for a contest similar to a college quiz bowl, participants use reference materials to learn about such equine topics as anatomy, conformation, nutrition, evolution, breed characteristics, reproduction, management, tack and equipment, styles of riding, and exhibition. The skills and knowledge gained in this project can be carried forward to other 4-H projects and, possibly, into a career field.

Another project that does not require live horses is the *4-H Horse Judging Contest*, which provides youths with an opportunity to develop and/or improve their ability to envision the ideal horse. Contestants must use deductive reasoning and decision making to evaluate the conformation and performance of a group of horses in a typical show setting. Giving oral reasons for their choice of winners helps the participants to improve memory skills, thought organization, and public speaking.

Hippology, introduced by Margentino in 1994, combines the skills and knowledge acquired in the Horse Bowl and the Horse Judging Contest and tests competency in practical horse management. Participants must demonstrate their equine learning through written quizzes, oral presentations, team problems, and hands-on stations.

All 4-H members are also welcome to participate in the annual New Jersey State 4-H Model Horse and Equine Arts Projects. In the *Model Horse Project*, members are judged on the model horses and tack they've purchased, made, or customized, and the realism of their photographed scenery. Leading up to this event, participants gain knowledge of breeds, tack, horse show requirements, anatomy of the horse, colors, markings, and other horse behaviors and attitudes. They also learn new math skills by measuring fabric and patterns or calculating distance and light settings on a camera.

The *Equine Arts Project*, held each year as part of the 4-H Championship Horse Show, encompasses all aspects of the art world. Members may enter any type of art, from graphics, sculpture, and photography, to woodworking and clothing. It's a time for members to display their artistic talent and imagination.

Choosing the New Jersey State *4-H Equestrian of the Year* is an opportunity to showcase the top equestrians from each county and encourages candidates to express themselves and demonstrate their abilities before a public audience. This event takes place at the Horse Park of New Jersey in Stone Tavern in conjunction with the New Jersey State 4-H Championship Horse Show. The winner then serves as an "ambassador" for the state's 4-H horse program and represents the 4-H at the New Jersey Department of Agriculture's "Equestrian of the Year" competition. The individual may also represent New Jersey in the public speaking contest held at the Eastern or Western National 4-H Horse Round-Up—a national competition to which each state sends its top 4-H members to compete in a variety of events.

The New Jersey State *4-H Competitive Trail Ride* serves to stimulate greater interest in trail riding. The project teaches appropriate selection of horses, methods of training and conditioning for trail riding, and proper care for horses during and after each trail ride. Throughout the program, good sportsmanship, horsemanship, and safety on trail rides is encouraged.

Volunteers can serve 4-H in a number of ways and are essential to the program. After receiving training, at no cost, volunteers may participate as club leaders, teachers, project judges, community resource persons, camp counselors, mentors, and in many other capacities.

For information on how to become a club member or volunteer leader, contact Margie Margentino, New Jersey 4-H Horse Program, 4-H Dept., Home Ec. House, 71 Lipman Drive, Rutgers University, New Brunswick 08901; 732-932-9794; www.rce.rutgers.edu. For the National 4-H Council, contact 7100 Connecticut Avenue, Chevy Chase, Md. 20815; 301-961-2945; www.fourhcouncil.edu.

Pony Club

Say "pony club," and most people think of youngsters on ponies. Not so. The Pony Club is open to children and young adults up to age twenty-one who ride both ponies and horses. Created by the British Horse Society in 1929, the program is intended to help boys and girls, through fun instruction, learn to ride, be responsible, and develop a good sense of horse management, leadership, and team participation. Today, there are more than 100,000 Pony Club members worldwide.

The United States Pony Clubs, Inc., program—which the United States adopted in 1953—emphasizes horsemanship, sportsmanship, and safety. Safe tack, safe horses, safe riding, and safe barn rules are the constant focus points.

New Jersey is home to several nonprofit Pony Clubs; together they make up the New Jersey Region Pony Clubs, which are affiliated with the United States Pony Clubs. Programs are offered in dressage, eventing, show jumping, cross country, road safety, tetrathlon, polocrosse, hunter trials, and a host of mounted games known as gymkhana. (See chapter 9 for horse sports and games.) Several of the Pony Clubs also teach driving, vaulting, and fox hunting. All competitions are team riding events, but the Pony Clubs also have an unmounted competition known as *Quiz* (formerly Knowdown), which involves identifications and demonstrations of horse management.

Pony Clubs give members the opportunity to practice important skills and gain confidence in their performance. The rating system provides for testing at increasing levels of proficiency, and it rewards progress. Beginners start at level D1: walking and trotting in an enclosed area without being led; and the ability to answer simple questions about horses and safety rules when working with horses. Individuals advance through D2 and D3, before reaching the C level. Progress from level C1 through C3 requires higher degrees of knowledge and riding ability, until the member is considered safe and competent to ride a trained horse and care for it without hurting the horse or undoing its training. D1 through C2 ratings are conducted by the club, whereas the C3 rating is evaluated by the regional office. The three highest ratings are awarded by the national office and are major tests of skill and horsemanship. Those who gain the B and HA rating are certified instructors; those who achieve the A rating are also certified horse trainers.

In New Jersey, the Amwell Valley Hounds Pony Club (AVHPC), founded by Joan Toigo in Hunterdon County in 1964, is the tenth oldest club in America and one of the largest. Its more than four dozen male and female members, ranging in age from six to nineteen, usually come from New Jersey's Hunterdon and Mercer Counties, and from Bucks County in Pennsylvania. Although the AVHPC's original affiliation with the Amwell Valley Hounds fox hunting group has since dissolved, Pony Club members are still invited to join the Hounds each fall for the Junior Hunt.

Two outstanding Pony Club members, Kate and Gus Huebner, joined the AVHPC at seven and nine years of age, respectively. Their natural urge to ride was no doubt inherited from their mother, Lucia Stout Huebner, who began riding in front of her father's saddle at the age of four. Lucia encouraged her children to enjoy horses, and Kate started riding at age six. She joined the AVHPC to become "a good rider." According to Kate, Alex, her 9-year-old Morgan, "can be trusted; tries to listen to me; is very good at jumping; and, in general, is pretty cool!" The best things about belonging to the Pony Club, Kate says, are "getting to ride frequently, performing at shows, and having lots of friends with the same interest." At the 2001 Games Rally, Kate's team received first place in horse management and qualified to go to the Pony Club National competition. Brother Gus loved the unmounted Quiz Rally, in which his team earned second place.

Parental involvement in the Pony Club is essential—and doesn't require knowledge of horses. Parents can help in a multitude of ways, such as painting and setting up jumps, providing food and beverages at meetings or competitions, transporting riders and mounts, helping with fund-raising projects, chaperoning a team, judging or serving as a grounds person at a competition, and much more.

Parents love what the Pony Club represents and the education and happiness it brings to their children. In fact, a great number of adults have expressed the desire to belong to a Pony Club themselves—and now that's possible. Among the Pony Clubs for adults that have been springing up around the country is the Lockatong Creek Farm Adult Pony Club. Pam Johnson, who is largely responsible for establishing the club in 2001, has based it along the lines of the United States Pony Clubs, using instructional materials recommended by the organization. Activities include unmounted workshops, group riding lessons (English style), mounted games, polocrosse, drill team, combined training, camp, competitions, and social gatherings. The club has also formed a trail association in Kingwood Township. For information on membership, contact Johnson at 908-996-6955 or 908-996-9070.

Pony Clubs in New Jersey

Meetings of New Jersey's regional Pony Clubs are held in private homes. Because their locations and/or websites are subject to change, it's best to contact the United States Pony Clubs, Inc. (4041 Iron Works Parkway, Lexington, Ky. 40511; 859-264-7669; www.ponyclub.org) for further information on how to locate one in your area. Those presently in New Jersey include:

Amwell Valley Hounds Pony Club, Frenchtown; www.geocities.com/nicoslaw/.

Autumn Ridge Pony Club, Newton.

Cream Ridge Pony Club, Lakehurst.

Hunterdon Hills Pony Club, Pittstown; www.hunterdonhillspc.com.

Jockey Hollow Pony Club, Vernon; www.jockeyhollowponyclub.org.

Somerset Hills Pony Club, Bedminster; e-mail dholtaway@cs.com.

Spring Valley Hounds Pony Club, Long Valley; e-mail deromenck @sprynet.com.

For Adults

Centenary College

Centenary College offers numerous degree programs in equine studies, including: a Bachelor of Science in Equine Studies; a Bachelor of Science in Equine Studies with Concentration in Equine Business Management; a Bachelor of Science in Equine Studies with Concentration in Riding Instruction and Training; a Bachelor of Science in Equine Studies with Concentration in Communication; an Associate of

Science in Equine Studies; and a minor in Equine Studies. Among the elective courses are: Breeding and Reproduction; Teaching Therapeutic Riding I and II; Course Design and Construction; Schooling the Green and Problem Horse; Equine Videography; and Judging Seminar. Each faculty member in the equine program has an equestrian background in business, competition, or training and is active in professional organizations related to his/her specific discipline.

The college's equine facility, situated on sixty-five acres, boasts a dressage ring, indoor and outdoor arenas, a hunt course, and three barns to house horses owned by the college and by students. The indoor arena features a viewing area, classrooms, offices, and spectator seating. In September 2003 the college initiated a therapeutic riding program at its Long Valley location for handicapped individuals. (See chapter 6 for information about Therapeutic Riding at Centenary.)

Students are encouraged to join one of the Centenary riding teams. Competition is available for novice and experienced riders in intercollegiate riding, hunter/jumper, dressage, and combined training.

For more information on equine studies at Centenary College, contact the Admissions Office, 400 Jefferson Street, Hackettstown 07840; 1-800-236-8679; www.centenarycollege.edu.

Equine Science Center

Dr. Karyn Malinowski's dream "to create a first-rate facility . . . where equine science can finally and fully reach its potential" has become a reality. The Equine Science Center, part of Cook College, should be in full operation by the time you open this book. According to Malinowski, its first director, the center will be "one of the strongest equine programs on the East Coast. Horses aren't just a luxury item for hobbyists. Breeders, racing commission staff, veterinarians, and the general public have to be provided with improved research and diagnostic facilities. Horses are complex beings that require complex care. The center will serve everyone by providing distance learning technology via closed-circuit television with live animal demonstrations."

Dr. Kenneth McKeever, an associate professor at the center and one of the top animal-exercise physiologists in the nation, feels that the "basic and applied research at the center will solve problems before they occur—whether improving equine nutrition, examining the effects of growth hormones in the aging horse, or preventing some of the puzzling medical conditions that relate to the racehorse. Since equine and human physiology closely resemble one another, findings in horses can have applications for people."

Dr. Sarah Ralston, a veterinarian and associate professor with a doctorate in anatomy, initiated a unique way to raise funds for the center while, at the same time, conducting a research project. In September 1999 she traveled to North Dakota to purchase four geldings and six fillies between three and six months of age in order to study their responses to transportation stress. Back on the Cook College campus, she monitored their responses to various feeds once they had recovered from the move. The horses were then used for research and teaching, and were part of student projects. "Two-thirds of our students had never handled a horse," noted Ralston, "but these were small enough so the students were less likely to be hurt, and they got to see a change in the horses almost every day."

At the end of the year, Ralston sold the horses via a campus-held auction. The response was more enthusiastic than she had dared to hope. "Over fifty buyers showed up, some from as far away as Vermont! All the yearlings, except one, were sold to people living in New Jersey, which made both the students and staff happy because we all became attached to them." After deducting the auction expenses, Ralston reported "a large profit to benefit the Equine Science Center and the teaching program." The event has since become an annual one. By purchasing horses from North Dakota, Ralston can study various ways to minimize transport stress in young horses, conduct nutrition studies later on, and teach students how to train young horses.

When completed, the Equine Science Center will have a state-of-the-art classroom/laboratory, expanded and improved stall and pasture space, and an endowed chair for its director. Its mission is to provide academic training in equine science at the undergraduate and graduate levels, along with practical and continuous in-service training for everyone associated with the equine industry. Electronic distance learning will enable the scholars at the center to reach individuals throughout the region and to disseminate cutting-edge research on the most pressing problems facing the equine industry.

For information on the center, visit www.escrutgers.com.

Equine Science Program at Cook College,
Rutgers University

According to Dr. Karyn Malinowski, Cook College professor, state extension service equine specialist, and director of the new Equine Science Center, "The equine science program offered by Rutgers University's Cook College is one of the University's best kept secrets." Although the majority of students enrolled in this program have had little or no prior contact with horses, the hands-on training provided both in the classroom and at the on-campus farm complex gives them experience and skills in state-of-the-art techniques used in equine management. Malinowski notes that "undergraduates have the opportunity to gain firsthand research experience and learn a plethora of skills,"

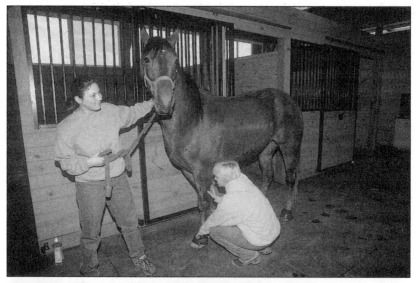

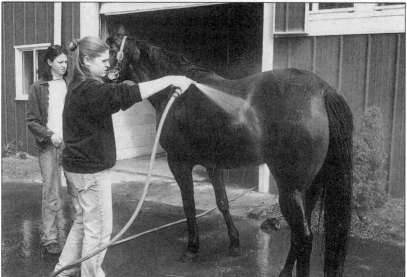

Students enrolled in the equine studies program at Cook College, Rutgers University, get hands-on training.

which will enable them to continue their education. Moreover, she adds, "a myriad of employment opportunities exist for the graduates."

The department's goal, according to Malinowski, "is to improve the quality of life for our equine athletes while helping them reach their full potential." In 1996 the New Jersey State Legislature honored the equine science program both for its support of the state's horse industry and for the excellent research by faculty in various fields. To cite just a few examples, Dr. Sarah Ralston was instrumental in developing Purina Equine Senior, a feed calibrated to meet the nutritional needs of older horses. She has also developed new techniques to study bone growth and metabolism in horses. Dr. Malinowski has proven that horses participating in strenuous equestrian events do not experience increased stress levels or altered immune function. Dr. Kenneth McKeever, along with Dr. Ralston, contributed to projects addressing the problem of thermoregulation and the prevention of heat-related injuries during the equestrian events at the 1996 Summer Olympics in Atlanta.

Because drugs can affect a horse's performance, Dr. McKeever's research on this topic involves working with the state racing commission to develop a method to detect the presence of recombinant human erythropoietin, a drug that has been tied to deaths in both human and equine athletes. Dr. Ralston is collecting the blood sera of horses that are free of drugs for use by the commission's equine drug-detection lab in its testing program. Concurrently, Dr. Malinowski is studying the effects of corticosteroid and nonsteroidal anti-inflammatory drugs on horses.

No doubt, the department's continued success in teaching and research is directly related to the caliber of its faculty. Malinowski's reputation has spread near and far since she was hired by Cook College in 1978 as the nation's first female equine extension specialist. When she began, no equine science courses were offered—nor were there any horses on campus! An accomplished rider, Malinowski was the leading force in building the college's equine science program into one of the strongest in the nation.

In her spare time—when she is not writing journal articles and book chapters or lecturing at international conferences—Dr. Malinowski has also served as chairperson of the State Horse Council Advisory Committee of the American Horse Council. In 1995, she became only the second woman in fifty years to receive the New York Farmers Club Award for her many contributions to the field of agriculture. Her achievements as a teacher were recognized in 2001 when she was named Outstanding Educator by the Equine Nutrition and Physiology Society and received the American Horse Council's Outstanding Equine Educator Award.

Dr. Sarah Ralston bought her first pony when she was eight years old. "I had no idea of what I was doing," she says, but she learned to ride. "When my pony got sick and I didn't know how to heal it, I decided I'd learn how to heal horses when I grew up." Following undergraduate work at Colorado State University, Ralston enrolled in the Veterinary Medical Scientist Training Program at the University of Pennsylvania School of Veterinary Medicine. The six-year program leads to D.V.M. and Ph.D. degrees.

A typical day for Ralston begins with an early check on the horses in the equine science program and a review of her students' work, and continues with teaching, answering e-mail, and consulting with horse persons over the phone. Her research includes a patent for the use of blood insulin to predict which foals are at risk for osteochondrosis, a condition that involves poor bone growth. In addition to holding evening continuing education classes for industry people, she lends many hours and veterinary skills to SPUR, a program for disabled riders in Monmouth County (see chapter 6), to the Gladstone Equestrian Association at the U.S. Equestrian Team headquarters, and to trail riding and endurance competitions.

To learn more about the equine science program at Cook College, contact Dr. James Wohlt, Undergraduate Director, 84 Lipman Drive, New Brunswick 08901-8525; 732-932-9454; www.cookcollege.rutgers.edu.

New Jersey Department of Agriculture Equine Programs
A prime focus of the Department of Agriculture is New Jersey's equine industry. Its equine development program offers educational and recreational opportunities to children and adults year-round (see chapter 2).

Rutgers University Board for Equine Advancement
The Rutgers University Board for Equine Advancement (RUBEA) is an advisory committee of leaders within the horse industry from both the racing and the recreational sectors. Its mission is to assist Cook College and the New Jersey Agricultural Experiment Station in decisions regarding equine teaching, research, and outreach programs, as well as to promote and support such activities through fund-raising and legislative efforts.

Each February, hundreds of individuals attend the all-day *Horse Management Seminar* sponsored by the Rutgers Cooperative Extension Service, the New Jersey Horse Council, and the New Jersey Department of Agriculture. The event offers timely information on equine topics, as well as an opportunity to meet and exchange ideas with equine professionals and other enthusiasts. For more information, contact Dr. Karyn Malinowski, Director, Equine Science Center, Department of Animal Sciences, 213 Bartlett Hall, Cook College, 84 Lipman Drive, New Brunswick 08901; 732-932-9419; www.escrutgers.com.

More Equine Educational Information for Youths and Adults

American Farriers Association School Directory, 4089 Iron Works Parkway, Lexington, Ky. 40511; 859-233-7411.

Directory of Colleges, University and Technical Schools, Box 828, Abingdon, Va. 24210.

The Equine Connection National, American Association of Equine Practitioners Locator Service, 800-438-2286; www.getadvm.com/equcon.html.

Equine School and College Directory, Harness Horse Youth Foundation, Box 266, Yellow Springs, Ohio 45387; 513-767-1975.

The Horseman's Service Directory and Desk Reference, 37550 Rogers Road, Willoughby Hills, Ohio 44094; 216-951-9693.

Manning's Guide to College (and Secondary Schools) Equestrian Programs, Manning Associates, Box 131, Taylor Road, Shelburne, Mass. 01370.

NATIONAL EQUINE-RELATED ASSOCIATIONS

American Association for Horsemanship Safety

This organization is devoted to disseminating the most recent and comprehensive information available on horsemanship safety and legal liability. It provides expert witnesses for lawsuits involving horse accidents and offers riding instructor certification clinics and seminars and workshops on horsemanship and horse safety. Contact Box 39, Fentress, Tex. 78622; 512-488-2220; www.horsemanshipsafety.com.

American Association of Equine Practitioners

This nonprofit organization's membership, which numbers more than 6,600 equine veterinarians and veterinary students throughout the

United States, Canada, and fifty-two other countries, serves more than 5.1 million horse owners worldwide. The association keeps members informed of current research, emerging diseases, ethics issues, and practice management, and it furthers professional development and equine welfare through continuing education in the veterinary profession and horse industry. Contact 410 West Vine Street, Lexington, Ky. 40507; 606-233-0147; www.aaep.org.

American Farriers Association

Because the United States has no national standards or licensing procedure for farriers, the American Farriers Association (AFA) administers a certification program that enables farriers to demonstrate their knowledge and expertise, and offers horse owners guidance in choosing a farrier. Farriers can achieve three successive levels of certification, and endorsements are granted for therapeutic and education specialties. Through an annual convention, continuing education programs, and publications, the AFA keeps its members informed of the latest techniques and research, legislation affecting farriers, and business practices. Contact 4089 Iron Works Parkway, Lexington, Ky. 40511; 859-233-7411; www.americanfarriers.org.

American Harness Drivers Club

Members conduct races at Freehold Raceway and the Meadowlands. Contact 84 Cherry Tree Farm Road, Middletown, N.J. 07748; www.jersey.net/~dekrep/ahdc.html.

American Horse Protection Association

This organization is devoted to the welfare of wild and domestic horses. Contact 1000 29th Street N.W., Washington, D.C. 20007; 202-965-0500.

American Riding Instructors Association

Established in 1984, the American Riding Instructors Association (ARIA) promotes "safe, knowledgeable riding instruction" (see chapter 3). Contact 28801 Trenton Court, Bonita Springs, Fla. 34134; 239-948-3232; www.riding-instructor.com.

Brotherhood of Working Farriers Association

This organization offers free educational clinics for the horse-owning public to emphasize the importance of proper trimming and shoeing techniques. The association also offers a certification program for farriers, as well as various publications, study guides, and videotapes. Contact 14013 East Highway 136, Lafayette, Ga. 30728; 706-397-8047; www.bwfa.net.

Carriage Operators of North America
This organization is dedicated to "promoting the humane welfare of carriage animals." Its website lists member companies in New Jersey and other states. Contact 4574 Washington Avenue, Omaha, Nebr. 68152; 651-462-4999; www.cona.org.

Eastern Competitive Trail Ride Association Inc.
The mission of this association, founded in 1970, is to encourage the growth and popularity of competitive and endurance trail riding through publications and educational programs. It maintains the rules and standards for competitions, as well as the records of all sanctioned rides. Contact Box 738, Kent, Conn. 06757; 860-927-3595; www.ectra.org.

Equestrian AIDS Foundation
According to Executive Director Janice Gray, the Equestrian AIDS Foundation was formed in 1996 "to support equestrians throughout the country who are stricken with AIDS during what is undoubtedly the most difficult period of their lives, and to let them know that their peers care about them and want to help to improve the quality of their lives." The nonprofit foundation guarantees absolute anonymity to anyone applying for and/or receiving help, which can include financial aid. According to Gray, who is also a horse trainer and instructor, the foundation's support comes from private donations as well as various fund-raising activities. Contact 203 Main Street, Suite 133, Flemington, N.J. 08822; 800-792-6068; www.equestrianaidsfoundation.org.

Equestrian Land Conservation Resource
Established by individuals concerned about the loss of equestrian land and riding areas, this organization coordinates approaches toward saving open space. Contact Box 335, Galena, Ill. 61036; www.elcr.org.

The Hambletonian Society
Formed in 1925 to sponsor the race for which it was named, the society supports and encourages the breeding of Standardbred

Humane Society disseminates information on disaster preparedness. Contact 2100 L Street, N.W., Washington, D.C. 20037; www.hsus.org.

International Side Saddle Organization
This organization promotes sidesaddle riding for personal enjoyment, competition, and showing in special events. Contact 90 Cumberland Avenue, Estell Manor, N.J. 08319; 609-476-2976; www.sidesaddle.com.

National Intercollegiate Rodeo Association
The association was created in 1949 to develop guidelines for "eligibility, scholastic standards, and rodeo structure." Its theme is "Preserving Western heritage through collegiate rodeo." Contact 1815 Portland Avenue, #3, Walla Walla, Washington 99362; 509-529-4402; www.collegerodeo.com.

National Reining Horse Association
Founded in 1966, the association is dedicated to the promotion of the reining horse and is responsible for running the annual Futurity and Championship Show, an event for young horses, plus reining shows around the world. Contact 3000 N.W. 10th Street, Oklahoma City, Okla. 73107; 405-946-7400; www.nrha.

North American Riding for the Handicapped Association
See chapter 6 for more information about this organization, which brings individuals with disabilities into beneficial relationships with horses. Contact Box 33150, Denver, Colo. 80233; 800-369-7433; www.narha.org.

North American Trail Ride Conference
This competitive trail ride organization judges the condition, soundness, and trail ability of horses on a course of natural trail obstacles. Horse and rider are evaluated on presentation rather than show-

manship. Contact Box 224, Sedalia, Colo. 80135; 303-688-1677; www.natrc.org.

United States Dressage Federation

The federation's purpose is to "promote and encourage a high standard of accomplishment in dressage throughout the United States." Contact 220 Lexington Green Circle, Suite 510, Lexington, Ky. 40503; 859-971-2277; www.usdf.org.

United States Equestrian Team

See chapter 9 for more information about the nonprofit organization that officially represents the United States in international equestrian competitions. Contact the USET at Box 355, Pottersville Road, Gladstone, N.J. 07934; 908-234-1251; www.uset.org.

United States Equine Trails Coalition

This nonprofit corporation, dedicated to the conservation, expansion, preservation, and promotion of equestrian trails throughout the United States, serves as a resource to equestrian trail users; educates the public, private land managers, and others; cooperates with other equestrian and non-equestrian organizations; supports research on related issues; and defends equine trail uses. It divides its efforts among the eight U.S. Forest Service regions in the forty-eight contiguous states. New Jersey belongs to Region 8, along with Minnesota, Wisconsin, Michigan, Iowa, Missouri, Illinois, Indiana, Ohio, Maryland, Pennsylvania, West Virginia, New York, Delaware, and the New England states. Contact 816 East Franklin Street, Evansville, Ind. 47711; 812-428-6600; www.us-etc.org.

United States Pony Clubs, Inc.

Among the leading junior equestrian organizations, Pony Clubs are represented in thirty countries worldwide. The more than 600 clubs in the United States and the Virgin Islands provide instruction and competition in English riding, horse sports, and horse management for children and young adults up to twenty-one years of age. The term *pony* refers to the age of the members rather than the size of the mounts. Pony Clubbers work through nine stages of progressive standards of proficiency, which test knowledge and riding ability. Contact 4071 Iron Works Parkway, Lexington, Ky. 40511; 859-254-7669; www.ponyclub.org.

USA Equestrian Inc. (formerly American
Horse Shows Association)

The country's largest multibreed equestrian organization offers automatic insurance coverage; a subscription to *Horse Show*; eligibility to compete in sanctioned competitions; eligibility to become a judge; an awards program; scholarships; and more. Contact 4047 Iron Works Parkway, Lexington, Ky. 40511; 859-258-2472; www.ahsa.org.

11

Riding a horse is not a gentle hobby,
to be picked up and laid down like a
game of solitaire. It is a grand passion.

Ralph Waldo Emerson

Giving Horses a Second Chance

There are many ways in which you can prolong your horse's life and keep it healthy and happy, even in its twilight years. These include frequent checks for changes in temperament and body condition; consultation with your veterinarian for a proper diet; frequent exercise; daily grooming; and conscientious hoof care. *Remember:* Your horse has given you years of devotion, service, and happiness. It deserves the same from you for as long as possible.

However, should you find yourself unable to continue to care for your horse owing to financial setbacks or serious injury to the animal, the good news is that it can now have a chance at a second life, thanks to the dedicated individuals and organizations listed below.

Because giving up your horse usually means giving up all rights permanently, it's wise to visit prospective placement centers yourself before signing an agreement. Is the facility clean and safe? Can references be supplied? What is the center's mission and goal? If you're donating your horse to a therapeutic riding center, find out if it's accredited by the North American Riding for the Handicapped Association. How often will it be ridden? If you're planning to take an income tax deduction for donating your horse, the recipient must be an approved nonprofit 501(c)(3) center/organization. Get everything you've discussed and want in a written contract. Ask if visiting your horse is permissible. Most important, determine that the center can provide the necessary care and will keep the horse until it dies a natural death; euthanization should be an alternative only when medical care is no longer practical or affordable, or when the horse has become dangerous.

The other side of the coin is adoption. If you have the means and desire, you can give that second chance to a former racehorse, wild horse, or other homeless horse. Adoption is not a simple matter, however, and may even require some extra skills to handle a horse that has been trained for a specialized discipline, mistreated, or not trained at all. Can you provide proper living quarters and the necessary level of care and training? Ethical and responsible adoption organizations will require that you and your facility meet certain standards, and they will normally conduct a later inspection. Even if adoption is not possible for your circumstances, there are organizations that encourage sponsorship of horses and will allow you to visit your special friend.

RESCUE ORGANIZATIONS AND REFUGES

Crossbridge Stables

Air Force Reserve Master Sergeant Robert Barrett and his wife, Mary-Lou, established their refuge in 1999 for formerly abused and neglected horses and those scheduled for slaughter. Their teenaged children are also involved; in fact, the idea for the refuge resulted from a 4-H project. Once the Barretts realized the need for foster homes for neglected horses, they moved from a huge Victorian house to a smaller one situated on a thirty-acre farm in Southampton, where they have added an eight-stall stable to an existing barn. Here they have several horses that were saved from the auction block and possible slaughter, along with others that were given up by owners who could no longer afford to keep them.

The cost of caring for these animals and the time needed to maintain them is quite an investment, but the Barretts aren't complaining. They love the horses, and the entire family pitches in to help. The horses have also encouraged the girls to pursue equine careers. Malynda, who qualified to participate in the Eastern National 4-H Roundup in Kentucky in 2001 at age sixteen, wants to be an equine attorney. Her younger sister, Amanda, represented her county in dressage at the state horse show and is interested in horse training and breeding.

The Barretts accept any breed, pay for all expenses themselves, and retrain the horses. All rescue work is done on a volunteer basis. Although the horses are not available for adoption, any child who is enrolled in 4-H and doesn't own a horse is welcome to ride one here.

For more information, contact the Barretts at 439 Retreat Road, Southampton 08088; 609-859-3919.

Enchanted Acres Rescue

The primary focus at this rescue organization is on Arabians and Appaloosas, but no horse that has been abused or neglected or is unwanted will be turned away.

For more information, contact Enchanted Acres Rescue, 716 Hulses Corner Road, Howell 07731; 732-730-1670.

Horse Helpers R & R Organization

Founded to help save abused horses in New Jersey and surrounding states, Horse Helpers R & R Organization (HHRRO) will rescue a horse from undesirable circumstances and, when funds allow, rehabilitate and retrain it, place it in an approved home, and give a lifetime commitment to it. Through HHRRO's quarterly newsletter, *Hero News*, all members and former owners are kept informed about the well-being of horses in the program and learn about the people involved in the organization. Membership dues enable HHRRO to accept horses that otherwise could not be saved. Wondering about the Rs in the group's name? They stands for many parts of who and what the organization means—Resource, Rescue, Revise, Rally, Regenerate, Refine, and Remedy.

For more information, contact HHRRO, Box 814, Holmdel 07733; 732-888-6096.

Mylestone Equine Rescue

When Susankelly Thompson first looked into Myles's big brown eyes, she saw "a half-starved horse who was suffering from navicular disease." It was obvious he needed immediate help, so she purchased him from a dealer who had been shuffling him around. For the next five months, while Thompson devoted herself to improving the horse's health, a special relationship developed between them. Myles blossomed, but within a year fell very ill with equine protozoal myeloencephalitis. As he lay dying, Thompson vowed to do whatever she could to "ensure that more horses would end their lives as loving pets rather than hungry, suffering, or slaughtered animals." Thus, Mylestone Equine Rescue (MER) was born in 1993, named for Myles.

Run by Susankelly and Bruce Thompson, MER is devoted to providing "shelter, care, rehabilitation, adoption, and retirement homes for horses that are at high risk for neglect and abuse." Since 1994, MER—a nonprofit 501(c)(3) organization—has been true to that mission.

Thanks to MER, horses like Linus—a feisty, twenty-year-old who is now MER's mascot—have been successful in fighting their way back to good health. At first, because the Thompsons didn't own a farm, they had to pay board for rescued horses at five different locations. On top of this financial burden, Susankelly drove approximately 600 miles a week to check on the horses at each farm. In 1999 the Thompsons purchased a farm in Pohatcong Township and, with the help of ten volunteers, have given discarded horses the opportunity to live out the rest of their days with lots of love and attention. They provide twenty-four-hour care, frequently spending long nights at the barn with a horse that needs special treatment. Their young son, Samuel, not only helps out, but knows a lot about each horse.

MER promotes public education about good horsemanship and is dedicated to teaching individuals how to recognize inhumane conditions. By instilling awareness, MER hopes to put an end to places like the "low-budget summer camps, rental barns, and theme parks" from which the organization has had to rescue animals. MER works with humane officials to reduce abuse and neglect and to encourage regulatory action to ensure humane treatment.

Although the horses at MER cannot be ridden, several have a job at the Stepping Stone School, a local educational facility. How do these horses help? Each week, the emotionally disabled children enrolled in the school are brought to Mylestone for interaction with the horses. They slowly learn to escape from their inner troubles and bond with the horses through petting and brushing them. It's a win-win situation for everyone.

If you'd like to help MER, there are several possibilities. Volunteers, eighteen years of age and older, are needed throughout the year for the organization's various activities: the annual open house in the fall; tour days, held once a month; and the necessary daily barn work. For a minimal fee, you can also sponsor a horse. Each month, you'll receive a letter and current picture so you can follow the horse's progress. Or, inquire about adopting a horse; the majority make wonderful companions.

For more information, contact Mylestone Equine Rescue, 227 Still Valley Road, Phillipsburg 08865; 908-995-9300; http://www.mylestone.org.

ReRun Inc.

Founded in Kentucky in 1996 by two horse lovers, Lori Neagle and Shon Wylie, ReRun Inc. acts as an adoption agency for former race-horses. After first evaluating the temperament, talent, and physical capability of a horse off the track, the nonprofit organization will attempt to place it with an approved owner, who may use the horse for trail riding, jumping, or simply as a companion. Although ReRun does not accept horses with severe injuries or those that do not have the temperament to adapt to a new lifestyle, the organization will try to place such horses in another program or facilitate transfer from one owner to the next.

Laurie Condurso-Lane discovered ReRun in 1999. As director of the New Jersey chapter she established, she has saved many retired Thoroughbreds from the slaughterhouse. Because the program requires adopters to have one acre per horse, making it sometimes difficult to place a horse in New Jersey, she's found adoptive owners as far away as Indiana, North Carolina, and Arkansas. Until she finds suitable homes, the horses are boarded in Allentown and Monroe Township. Condurso-Lane admits that she's very particular when it comes to finding the right person to match a horse's personality and that she'll "keep a horse as long as necessary" until she does.

Condurso-Lane agrees with ReRun's strict placement policy of assessing the soundness and temperament of each horse to determine its potential usefulness or limitations. The next step is to seek the "perfect match." Potential adopters must fill out an application form, supply two personal references, plus references from a farrier and from a veterinarian, and pay an adoption fee of several hundred dollars, which goes toward the care and feeding of other horses that ReRun acquires. A contract must be signed, giving ReRun the right to monitor the horse's care for two years. If the new owner successfully meets the care obligations during this period, the organization will sign over title to the horse; if not, it is taken back immediately.

To continue its work, ReRun needs donations of money, goods, and services. Consider offering a parcel of unused land, contributing building supplies and skills, or supporting a ReRun fund-raiser, such as the annual gala dinner, dance, and silent auction.

For information on adopting a horse, contact Laurie Lane at llane@rerun.org or 732-521-4752. For further information, contact the national headquarters at Box 96, Carlisle, Ky. 40311; 859-484-2003; www.rerun.org.

Second Chance Ranch Horse Rescue

New on the scene in April 2000 is the nonprofit rescue operation set up by the Pleis family on thirty-three acres of land owned by Cape May County as part of the Farmland Preservation Program. The facility boasts a seventeen-stall main barn, indoor and outdoor riding rings, and many paddocks and pastures. Rescued horses are treated to a second chance to live amid luxuries they've probably never seen. To support their rescue work, the Pleises offer boarding and riding lessons. The staff consists entirely of volunteers, and all donations are tax deductible.

For more information, contact Kelley Pleis, 418 State Highway 47 North, Goshen 08218; 609-463-4901.

Thoroughbred Retirement Foundation

When racehorses can no longer run or be cared for by their owners, the Thoroughbred Retirement Foundation (TRF) can ensure that they'll be safe and comfortable for the rest of their lives. Placement is offered on principal retirement farms or at smaller, "satellite" farms in fourteen states, including New Jersey. In fact, the New Jersey Sports and Exposition Authority supports TRF by sponsoring special donation programs at the Meadowlands and Monmouth Park Racetracks.

TRF, which accepts only registered Thoroughbreds with a racing record, reaches out to people as well as horses. Horse retirement programs at correctional facilities in four states offer inmates an opportunity to learn marketable skills in the horse industry while developing responsibility and self-esteem. Since 1996, TRF has also offered an adoption program from its retraining and rehabilitation facility in New York State.

For information on the Clarksburg, New Jersey, satellite farm, contact TRF at Suite 351, 450 Shrewsbury Plaza, Shrewsbury 07702. For more information about TRF, visit www.trfinc.org.

HORSE ADOPTIONS

Adopt a Wild Horse!

For years, ranchers, hunters, and other unscrupulous people roamed the western ranges, killing wild horses and burros or rounding them up for commercial purposes, usually for sale to slaughterhouses. In the early 1950s, when Velma B. Johnston discovered the brutal ways they

Each year, the Bureau of Land Management offers between 6,000 and 8,000 wild horses and about 500 to 1,000 burros for adoption through auctions across the country and on the Internet. In 2002, an auction was held in New Jersey.

treated these animals, she began a campaign to stop them. At first, most of her supporters were schoolchildren; but as news of her efforts spread, people all over the country joined "Wild Horse Annie" in trying to stop this senseless and inhumane slaughter.

In 1959 Nevada Congressman Walter Baring introduced a bill prohibiting the use of motorized vehicles to hunt wild horses and burros on all public lands. Approved unanimously in the House of Representatives that year, the "Wild Horse Annie Act" nevertheless failed to include Annie's recommendation that Congress initiate a program to protect, manage, and control wild horses and burros. After a public outcry, when it became obvious that the population of wild horses and burros was diminishing drastically for lack of oversight, Congress passed the Wild Free-Roaming Horses and Burros Act in 1971. In passing this act, Congress declared that "wild free-roaming horses and burros are living symbols of the historic and pioneer spirit of the West; [and] that they contribute to the diversity of life forms within the Nation and enrich the lives of the American people." The legislation also paved the way for individuals ultimately to own a wild horse or burro.

Today, the Bureau of Land Management (BLM, an agency of the Department of the Interior) and the U.S. Forest Service (Department of Agriculture) are responsible for the management and protection of wild horses and burros on public lands. Because federal protection and a scarcity of natural predators have allowed these herds to thrive, the number of animals must be controlled to protect range resources and to maintain the health of the herds. In accordance with management plans, excess wild horses and burros are rounded up and offered to qualified individuals through the BLM's adoption program. Originating in 1973, this program has so far placed more than 200,000 wild horses and burros in new homes all over the country, including more than 200 in New Jersey.

Each year, 6,000–8,000 horses and 500–1,000 burros—descendants of those released by or escaped from explorers, ranchers, miners, soldiers, or Native Americans—are offered for adoption. They do not belong to a particular breed, but a few exhibit the characteristics associated with specific breeds. Typical wild horses stand about 14–15 hands, weigh approximately 900–1,100 pounds, and are normally solid in color, mostly sorrel, bay, and brown. Those offered for adoption range in age from several months to nine years, although the majority are five years or younger. Mares with unweaned foals are adopted together.

Those gathered for adoption generally have not been out of the wild for more than ninety days and are not used to people. The BLM cooperates with a few state prison programs to gentle wild horses to accept halter and saddle before adoption. There are also a few programs to introduce approved adopters to the techniques of training a wild horse. With kindness and patience, they can adapt to many uses and have gone on to earn championships in dressage, barrel racing, jumping, endurance racing, and pleasure riding. These wonderful animals are known for their intelligence, surefootedness, endurance, and strength.

How can you adopt one? First, you and your home facility must meet strict requirements for horse care. Once you are approved as an adopter, you are eligible to participate in competitive bidding at adoption sites across the country (some temporary, some permanent) or on the Internet. The minimum adoption fee as of this writing is $125; mares with unweaned foals start at $250. The fees help to defray the costs of round-ups, medical treatment, transportation, and adoption.

Wild horses remain under federal protection even when removed from public lands. If you adopt a wild horse, you will begin a one-year trial period, during which time a BLM representative has the right to visit you to inspect the animal(s), to make certain the conditions of the adoption agreement are met, and to answer any questions you may have. After successfully completing the trial period, you will be eligible to apply for title to your wild horse.

Adoptions are held in New Jersey in certain years. Exact places, dates, and times are available from the Milwaukee District Office, 310 West Wisconsin Avenue, Suite 450, Milwaukee, Wis. 53203; 1-800-293-1781; www.wildhorseandburro.blm.gov.

Standardbred Retirement Foundation

Since 1990, the nonprofit Standardbred Retirement Foundation (SRF) has successfully placed more than 1,000 Standardbred horses with loving people across the country. As part of its award-winning program, SRF's ongoing follow-up ensures good care and prevents neglect or abuse of adopted horses.

One alternative to adopting a Standardbred is to open your heart and land to these horses by volunteering to become part of SRF's foster care program. SRF does not own its own land and so always needs good boarding facilities where these wonderful animals can be rehabilitated and become more desirable as adoption candidates for pleasure riding or driving purposes.

You can also opt for SRF's sponsorship program. Many of the Standardbreds SRF saves are unlikely to be adopted because of age, health, or handicap. By sponsoring one of these horses, you will help to offset the costs involved in SRF's guarantee of lifetime care for it.

In addition to saving horses from slaughter and giving them a second chance, SRF helps troubled children through its special therapeutic equine program. SRF has been recognized nationally for its efforts, receiving awards from the American Association of Equine Practitioners, the Association of Racing Commissioners International, and the U.S. Harness Writer's Association.

For more information, contact the Standardbred Retirement Foundation, Box 763, Freehold 07728; 732-462-8773; www.adopta-horse.org.

12

> *The labor of women in the house, certainly,*
> *enables men to produce more wealth than they*
> *otherwise could, and in this way women are*
> *economic factors in society. But so are horses.*
>
> Charlotte Perkins Gilman

Employment Opportunities within the Horse Industry

Myriad careers exist for anyone who has an interest in the equine industry. For example, *veterinarians* undergo the longest training period, while salespersons who sell horse-related jewelry and gift items can set up shop quickly after familiarizing themselves with their merchandise.

The role of the *horse trainer* begins shortly after a horse is born, and the job requires knowledge of every aspect of the horse's health and psyche. At the age of sixteen, New Jerseyan Francine Faraci-Walcei chose to become a horse trainer when her father let her decide between getting a horse or a brand-new car. She's happy with her decision, because she's been very successful as a trainer. "I love horses, rode in college, and enjoy training them for racing. I give them the proper food and vitamin shots, but you have to know the animal you're working with as to whether they can be trained harder or not as hard. You also have to work on their mental and physical condition, and the horse has to be happy." Faraci-Walcei's typical day begins at 4:30 a.m., except on Sundays, when she and her horses get the day off. "Trainers have to pass a test to get a license to practice," she says. "They also have to remember this is a dangerous profession. I've been kicked, and even bitten in my arm and butt, but I have several horses, have a 40 percent win average, and it's a great feeling."

Does this rhyme sound familiar: "The smith a mighty man is he, with large and sinewy hands; and the muscles of his brawny arms are strong as iron bands"? That's the blacksmith, better known today as the *farrier*, another vital link in your horse's well-being. As a tribute to

*Farrier Charlie Smith expertly prepares new shoes
for the horses at Desperado Acres. His job is one of the
dozens of careers available within the horse industry.*

their dedication and hard work, National Farriers Week is celebrated each July. Today, approximately 125 farriers serve the thousands of horses in New Jersey. "This career definitely takes a strong back," notes farrier Charles Smith. "It isn't easy filing the front of a hoof on a horse weighing over a thousand pounds." New Jersey does not have a school for farriers, nor does the state have a licensing procedure. The necessary knowledge and skills are handed down from generation to generation or learned at one of the nation's few farrier schools. Many of New Jersey's farriers are accredited by national organizations that have established rigorous testing procedures. Smith makes barn calls about every four to eight weeks, dons a leather apron, and brings along everything he needs in his truck, including hammers, nails, sharp knives, and even his anvil and the portable propane forge on which he crafts a new horseshoe to fit or reshapes an old one. A farrier has enormous responsibilities, for horse's hooves are complex, and extreme care must be taken when choosing the proper shoe and fitting it.

Not everyone is cut out to be a veterinarian, horse trainer, or farrier, but there are dozens of careers in the horse industry that will allow you to tap your talents and give you the opportunity to work with horses and horse people. Listed below are some of the choices.

JOBS BY EMPLOYMENT SECTOR
Accounting

Accountant: Specializes in the tax codes regarding farm businesses and
    prize winnings.
Auditor: Checks books of equestrian organizations.

Alternative Medicine and Training

Equine massage therapist: Uses hands-on massage to relax muscles and
    increase range of motion.
Equine veterinarian acupuncturist: Heals horses through the ancient
    art of needles placed at designated points for pain management
    and problems that do not respond to traditional treatments. In
    addition to a veterinarian's license, the training program requires
    120 hours of course work and hands-on learning.
Equine veterinarian chiropractor: Manipulates the spinal vertebrae of a
    horse to cure various ailments.
Herbalist: Sells herbal remedies as a natural alternative for horse health
    and care.

Holistic trainer: Uses a patented system of teaching and training designed to maximize understanding, communication, and trust between a horse and its rider.

Horse whisperer: Possesses a natural talent for understanding horses and talking to them for training purposes or solving behavior problems.

Reiki animal care specialist: Uses Reiki, a form of natural-energy healing, to facilitate communication of an animal's unconscious feelings and needs.

Construction

Architect: Designs barns and other equine-related structures.

Barn builder: Specializes in the construction of barns according to horses' and owners' needs.

Fence manufacturer/builder: Manufacturers and erects fences.

Equestrian Events

Announcer: Broadcasts happenings at horse shows, races, and other events.

Course designer: Determines the type, order, and spacing of obstacles on a contest course. Requires a license at higher levels of competition.

Event manager/secretary: Arranges for and keeps track of shows.

Judge: Determines the outcome of competitive classes based on thorough knowledge of breed and discipline rules and requirements. Must have accreditation to officiate at events recognized by USA Equitation Inc. Must be unbiased and able to deal with confrontation.

Jump crew: Sets up the courses precisely as the designers direct, and maintains the courses to those standards as the contest proceeds.

Ring crew: Helps set up necessary items for show events.

Ringmaster: Serves as the judge's aid; helps to avoid accidents in the ring; works with the ring crew. Cannot officiate in any class of a competition in which family members are involved.

Rodeo rider: Performs feats of cowboy skill.

Scribe: Records judges' comments, enabling judges to keep their eyes constantly on the competition.

Stewards: Calls riders into the arena for judging.

Stock handler: Takes care of the animals at rodeos and other events.

Technical delegate: Makes certain all aspects of a competition are within the regulations of the sanctioning organization.

Timers: Time various competitive events.

Ringmaster, Alan Keeley, starts events at the Bayer/USET Festival of Champions annual competition.

Feed and Supplement Industry

Equine nutritionist/feed consultant: Suggests proper feed and vitamins for raising and maintaining a healthy horse.

Grain and hay wholesaler/retailer: Sells grain and hay for horse feed.

Horse Industry Association Positions

There are a vast number of job opportunities in every breed, rider, and event association and at racetracks. Local and national organizations need executive directors, marketing and sales personnel, and financial development officers. The U.S. Equestrian Team, for example, employs department advisers for different breeds, youth advisers, people with computer skills, and public relations people.

Horse Maintenance

Boarding stable owner/operator: Manages care of privately owned horses.

Body clipper and braider: Grooms the horse and braids its tail.

Estate manager: Arranges help for fencing, barn renovations, grading rings and arenas, landscape lighting, and various other jobs that have to be done around extensive horse operations.

Exerciser: Walks or rides horses at racetracks or farms.

Farrier assistant: Apprentices to the farrier.

Groom: Brushs and feeds horses, and handles other aspects of care.

Humane official: Monitors treatment of horses and responds to reports of abuse or poor conditions.

Laundry operator: Takes care of the cleaning of horse blankets, leg wraps, and related items.

Pest control technician: Provides safe pest control, such as fly treatments for stables.

Stable hand: Duties include cleaning stalls, feeding and watering horses, and general maintenance.

Stable manager: Oversees all aspects of stable management and care of horses.

Walker: Exercises the horses outdoors for about twenty minutes so they do not get bored.

Legal

Lawyer: Works on equine legal issues, such as liability.

Mounted police: Patrol on horseback (see below).

Media

Ad designer: Designs advertisements for horse-related publications or electronic media.

Advertising copywriter: Creates text for advertisements that appear in horse-related magazines, newspapers, and other media.

Caricature artist: Entertains at parties and events, formal and informal, for adults and children by making fun drawings of horses and horse owners.

Editor: Prepares horse-related stories for publication in books, periodicals, and newspapers, or for presentation on television or radio.

Horse/rider association staff: Disseminates important materials and answers questions.

Illustrator: Draws or paints pictures for horse-related books.

Photographer: Takes photos of people, horses, and events for souvenirs at horse shows or for publications.

Portrait artist: Draws, paints, or photographs horses and their owners.

Publisher: Producer of books, magazines, and/or newspapers relating to the equine industry.

Videographer: Films and produces professionally edited tapes for races, horse farms, or individuals.

Website designer: Designs online personal and/or business information.

Writer: Develops stories about all aspects of the horse, whether fiction or nonfiction, for newspapers, magazines, videos, movies, and so on.

Medical

Artificial insemination technician: Helps insert stallion's semen into mare.

Dermatologist: Researches or treats equine skin disorders.

Equine dentist: Maintains horses' teeth and takes care of other mouth problems. Requires a two-year degree.

Equine pharmacist: Compounds medications for horses.

Equine psychotherapist: Examines the horse for clues to unusual behavior and therapies to address it.

Pharmaceutical employee: Works on production of horse-related medications.

Physical therapist: Uses various techniques, such as myofascial restructuring and energy work, to help ailing horses.

Sports therapist: Uses trigger point myotherapy, muscle therapy, and Reiki to help an ailing horse.

Veterinarian assistant: Assists veterinarian in maintaining horses' health.

Racing

Apprentice: A jockey just beginning his/her career in racing.

Jockey: A professional rider in Thoroughbred horse racing. Average weight is about 100 pounds; height is generally under 5'9".

Outrider: (1) Accompanies jockeys and horses to the starting line. (2) Aids the teamsters of wagon trains or serves in parades, circuses, and similar activities.

Recreation and Tourism

Camp counselor: Teaches riding skills to children.

Carriage driver: Offers rides as a form of entertainment.

Dude ranch owner: Operates vacation spot for persons interested in horseback riding.

Horse park staff: Personnel who direct people to proper areas, collect tickets, and perform other duties.

Huntsman: Cares for the hounds in the kennel.

Master of hounds: Sounds the horn at the start of a fox hunt and maintains order.

Pony ride operator: Offers rides to children at private parties or public events.

Singing cowboy: Entertains at various shows, including the rodeo.

Trick rider: Performs on a specially trained horse in the rodeo, movies, circus, and horse-related shows and attractions.

Trick roper: Performs on or off the horse in the rodeo, cowboy attractions, and movies.

Trail guide: Takes people out on the trail for rides that may last an hour or days or weeks.

Wrangler: Oversees the horses and tack used in television and movie productions.

Research and Education

Backcountry horsemanship instructor: Teaches park rangers, guides, and others good riding techniques and conduct for backcountry expeditions.

Extension service equine specialist: Disseminates information via teaching and publications. Requires a B.A. or M.A. degree, good people and organizational skills, and a willingness to work with youth and adults.

Hippotherapist: Uses therapeutic riding to assist challenged individuals. Requires training and accreditation.

Living history interpreter: Researches historical horse-related practices and presents them to the public.

Rescue worker: Tends to horses that have been retired, abandoned, or given up for adoption.

Tack and Clothing

Backcountry outfitter: Advises on clothing and tack necessary for back-country trail rides.

Boot maker: Makes custom-fitted riding boots.

Clothing designer: Designs riding clothing or reproduction clothing for museums, reenactment groups, and movies.

Harness maker: Makes leather harnesses.

Mail order entrepreneur: Assembles a selection of horse-related items for sale via mail or online catalog.

Saddle maker: Makes saddles by hand.

Tack maker: Custom fits saddles and equine-related items.

Tack shop owner: Organizes, gathers, and sells tack supplies.

Transportation

Air transporter: Accompanies horses on intra- and international flights.

Trailer manufacturers: Make, sell, and repair horse trailers.

Transporter: Arranges for local or long-distance moves for one or more horses.

Additional Employment Opportunities

Animal psychic: Helps discover an animal's problem.

Antiques dealer: Buys and sells rare and old equine-related items.

Auctioneer: Solicits bids during a horse auction/sale.

Blanket repairer: Repairs horse blankets.

Breeder: A person who selects certain horses to breed with others.

Butcher: Slaughters horses for market.

Equine appraiser: Determines the value of a horse.

Funeral carriage driver: Guides horse-drawn carriage carrying casket.

Horse auction organizer: Prepares and carries out sales of horses.

Insurance agent: Sells a variety of insurance related to owning, keeping, and transporting horses.

Jewelry maker: Creates jewelry in various equine-related shapes.
Manure collector: Removes manure from farms and stables.
Pet sitter: Cares for animals when owners are away.
Seamstress: Makes and repairs riding apparel.

MOUNTED POLICE UNITS

Did you know that some horses wear badges? They do—when they're assigned to a mounted police unit. Mounted police, as well as the horses they ride, perform such valuable services as patrolling parks and various sections of their communities, ensuring the public's safety during special events, and supervising and controlling crowds. A police officer sits about ten feet off the ground when mounted, affording a commanding view of a large area and would-be mischief makers.

The Mounted Park Police of Morris County, one of several units throughout the state, has conducted search-and-rescue operations to find lost persons and even rounded up animals that have escaped from local farms and businesses. Because people of all ages love to talk to the mounted police and touch their horses, the officers also serve as public relations ambassadors. In Morris County, the mounted police have been involved in novel educational programs offered to schoolchildren on safety and drugs. For fourth graders, distributing pencils inscribed "Say Nay to Drugs" was a big hit, as was a horse-naming contest. Awarding passes for a free swim in a park lake to kids wearing safety helmets while riding their bicycles proved to be another good idea. According to Sergeant Mike Puccetti, who has been a member of the Mounted Park Police of Morris County for more than fifteen years, "These rewards are a great way to encourage the children to spread the message of safety among their friends."

The horses used by Puccetti's unit, which must be geldings, are donated or purchased by the county. The costs of feeding and housing a police horse are minimal, Puccetti notes, in return for the services performed and the amount of goodwill generated. "A police car that costs $24,000 lasts only a few years, whereas I've had the same horse for fourteen years, and I don't have to change tires, change the oil, or buy gasoline. The cost difference between having a car or maintaining a horse is tremendous. Most important, you can't bring a car into the middle of crowds or onto the trails, and, because Morris County is the largest county in the state as far as the trails system goes, with parks comprising approximately 17,000 acres, this is where our horses are used extensively. Thanks to the horses, we can get to every location, as

Sergeant Mike Puccetti and Officer Chris Boyko of the Morris County Mounted Police Unit stand tall in their saddles on their highly trained, rock-steady mounts.

well as make friends with lots of kids by going to the schools, bringing our horses into the parking lots, and the kids love it. They remember we've visited them and what we've talked about. Kids respond to the horses because they're living animals, not like a bike or a car. They hesitate talking to someone in a car because they feel intimidated, but when an officer is on a horse, they come right over."

The Mounted Park Police of Morris County can do everything the road patrol does—from stopping cars for speeding to administering first aid to people hurt on the trails. It's not an easy job, however. It calls for knowledge, strength, a love for horses, respect for the outdoors, and absolute dedication.

To join a mounted unit, you must first be a police officer. Puccetti, who is certified by the American Riding Instructors Association, often gets requests from patrolmen who want to join, but he knows that not everyone is cut out to be a mounted officer. For one thing, a mounted officer must accept that he or she will fall off occasionally. There's also a tremendous amount of physical work. At the end of the day, unlike officers who work from a patrol car, on a bicycle, or on an ATV that can be parked and forgotten, a mounted officer has stalls to muck, horses to groom and feed, and tack to clean.

All candidates for Puccetti's unit are put through a series of difficult tests. Although new candidates do not have to know how to ride, the first prerequisite is falling from a horse. If they can do this, and then produce an acceptable research paper on a horse-related topic, they can begin an eight-week training program to learn the basics: the parts of the horse, grooming and tacking up, control at the walk, trot, and canter, and safe trailering. Police work atop a horse follows: how to stop a car, how to keep the horse still while interviewing someone, and how to perform defensive maneuvers, including the emergency dismount, that is, jumping off the horse at a walk, trot, or canter.

Each officer accepted into the unit is responsible for training his/her mount to overcome its natural instinct to flee when frightened. Through repetitive training, the horse is taught to go fearlessly through smoke, carefully step over obstacles, and calmly enter tunnels and strange places. It must become accustomed to waving flags, flying balls, spouting water, honking horns, bursting balloons, booming fireworks, and blaring band music. During this sensory training, the horse is gradually introduced to louder and louder sounds related to parades and other events. Members of Puccetti's unit toss firecrackers from a distance until the horse gets used to the surprise and noise; slowly, the officers toss the firecrackers closer and closer, until they land at the horse's feet. To accustom the horse to traffic emergencies, the police car siren and lights are turned on until the horse can tolerate the noise and blinking, startling lights. Not all horses will accept these conditions, and training of the select few horses to make them "bomb proof" can take up to a year.

A mounted officer's typical work day, according to Chris Boyko, a member of the Mounted Park Police of Morris County, is approximately eleven hours. He arrives early in the morning, grooms his assigned horse, gets it ready for the trail, and then repeats the morning chores after being in the saddle for about seven to eight hours. Boyko loves his work. At the time he transferred to the unit, he had never ridden before. With the excellent training, he's now a pro, and his partner, Blue Moon, has also come a long way—he had never been ridden full-time before.

Each year, mounted police units have an opportunity to show what they know, how well they've trained their horses, and how intelligently their horses react to real-life encounters at the National Mounted Police Equestrian Competition, which was initiated in 1984 by the National Park Service and the U.S. Park Police. Demonstrations of innovative tactics and equipment also benefit the officers.

In October 2000, this event was held in New Jersey for the first time, hosted by the Mounted Park Police of Morris County. Among the 102 entries from around the nation were five mounted police units from New Jersey: the Bergen County Police Department; the Lambertville Police Department; the Morris County Park Police Department; the New Jersey State Police; and the Passaic County Sheriff's Office. The three phases of the competition gave spectators an appreciation of how difficult the role of a mounted police officer actually is:

- *Uniform and Mount:* Appearance is not only an indicator of pride and professionalism, but also an important requirement of police work.

- *Equitation:* In this segment, officers are judged at the walk, trot, and canter for seat, control, and flexibility.

- *Obstacle Course:* Officers and their mounts must maneuver over and through ten obstacles that simulate the kinds of noisy and threatening situations they might encounter during their daily tour of duty. If the horse balks at any time, points are lost. If it stays still when a chain saw is suddenly turned on, points are gained.

When Officer Puccetti won the ride and shoot class at the 2000 national competition, his fellow officers were not surprised. Puccetti holds a training session each week to reinforce everything learned by Morris County's police horses, including the seventeen-year-old Padre, Puccetti's partner since the Quarter horse joined the unit in 1988.

Mounted police units can be found throughout New Jersey. At this writing, the following agencies maintain units: Bergen County Police Department; Camden City Police; Camden County Park Police; Carlstadt Police Department; Edison Police Department; Hoboken Police Department; Lambertville Police Department; New Jersey State Police; Newark Police Department; Passaic County Sheriff's Office; Union County Police Department. Recently, a ranger's mounted horse program was reactivated in Morristown National Historical Park to patrol the park's trail system.

For more information on the Morris County program, contact the Mounted Park Police, c/o Morris County Park Commission, Box 1295, Morristown 07962; www.morrisparkpolice.org/mounted.htm.

Appendixes

A

COMMON TERMS AND PHRASES
IN THE HORSE INDUSTRY

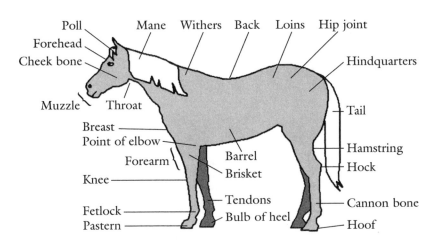

Parts of the horse.

Above the bit: When the horse carries its mouth above the level of the rider's hand, which reduces the rider's control.

Action: Elevation of the horse's legs, particularly its feet and knees.

Against the clock: A term used in show jumping, where the winner will have the least number of errors in the fastest time.

Aged: A horse fifteen years of age or older.

Aging: Determining a horse's age by the size, shape, and markings of its teeth.

Aids: Signals made by the rider or driver, using the legs, hands, body weight, and/or voice, to communicate to the horse what is expected; also known as "natural" aids. Artificial communication aids are the whip and spur.

Airs: The movements, other than the normal walk, trot, and canter, found in formal dressage events, when two or more feet leave the ground (as in the piaffe).

All-rounder: A horse or pony that excels at everything.

Back at the knee: A conformation fault, in which forelegs are curved back below the knee.

Balk: To stop short or to refuse to obey.

Barrel: The horse's body between the forearms and loins.

Bars of the mouth: Area between the molars and incisors of the lower jaw on which the bit rests.

Bit: A piece of metal that fits inside a horse's mouth and is attached to the bridle; used to control the horse's pace and direction.

Blaze: A large white streak down a horse's face.

Blinkers: Square pieces attached to the bridle next to the horse's eye, which prevent it from seeing to the right or left; also known as blinders or winkers.

Blood horse: Thoroughbred horse.

Blood weed: Lightly built Thoroughbred horse lacking the necessary bone and substance.

Bloodline: The sequence of direct ancestors.

Bloodstock: Thoroughbred horses that are bred to race.

Blue feet: Dense, blue-black coloring of the horn.

Bone: Measurements taken around the leg immediately below the knee or hock, which serve to determine the horse's ability to carry weight.

Boots: Protective coverings for the fetlock joints.

Bosal: A bitless bridle.

Bosomy: A wide and heavy chest.

Bow-hocks: A conformation fault, where the back joints are turned outward.

Boxy hoof: Narrow, upright hoof with a small frog and a closed heel.

Breastplate: A device, usually leather, worn over the horse's chest and attached to the saddle to prevent it from slipping back.

Breed: Equine group that has been bred selectively for consistent characteristics over an extended period.

Bridle: The leather straps that fit over the horse's head and hold the bit, which attaches to the reins.

Broken colored: A coat of two colors.

Bronco: A wild, unbroken horse.

Brood mare: A female horse used for breeding.

Buck: An action whereby the horse leaps up with its back arched.

Cannon bone: The bone of the foreleg situated between the knee and fetlock.

Canter: A three-beat gait a little slower than the gallop.

Cantle: The rear part of the saddle that projects upward.

Carriage: A vehicle with four wheels.

Carriage horse: Relatively light, elegant horse.

Carry a good flag: When a horse extends its tail in a high-spirited manner.

Cart: A vehicle with two wheels.

Cart horse: Heavy draft-type horse.

Carty: A horse of common appearance.

Cavalletti: A series of wooden poles, adjustable in height, used to teach horses balance.

Cavalry remount: Horse used for service in an army unit.

Charley horse: A cramp or muscle spasm, usually caused by overexertion.

Chestnut: (1) Small, horny excrescence on the inside of all four legs. (2) A coat color of pure or reddish brown, with mane and tail of the same or a lighter color.

Cinch: (1) The circumference of the horse or pony, as measured from behind the withers at the deepest part of the body. (2) A band made from leather, nylon, or webbing placed beneath the horse's belly and attached to the saddle to hold it in place; also known as a *girth.*

Coach horse: A powerfully built horse capable of drawing a heavy coach.

Coarse in the jowl: Fleshiness in the jowl area, restricting the flexion of the head.

Coffin head: Plain, ugly face with no prominence of the jowl.

Coldblood: A calm horse, usually a draft breed.

Colic: A dangerous condition in which the horse suffers acute pain in the stomach or intestines.

Colt: A young, uncastrated male horse, usually under four years of age.

Common: Horse of course appearance, usually the progeny of coldblood, mixed, or nonpedigree parents.

Conformation: The proportions and features of the horse that enable it to move correctly and perform well, sometimes as prescribed by a breed association.

Corn: Bruising of the sole between the wall of the hoof and heel.

Cow horse: A horse trained for traditional cattle-herding tasks.

Cow-hocks: A conformation fault, where the hocks turn inward like those of a cow; the opposite to *bow-hocks.*

Cow kick: A kick forward and sideways with a hind leg.

Crop: A short riding whip with a leather loop at one end, used to urge a horse forward.

Crossbreeding: Mating of purebred individuals of different breeds, resulting in a *crossbred*.

Crossing over: Faulty and dangerous action in which the feet cross each other in movement.

Curb: (1) Thickening of the tendon or ligament below the point of the hock as a result of strain. (2) A type of bit.

Currycomb: A round or oblong comb with hard teeth, used in a circular motion to remove dry mud and dirt from a horse's coat.

Cutting horse: A horse trained to separate individual cattle from the herd.

Daisy-cutting: Low foot action at the walk or trot.

Dam: A mother horse; a horse's female parent.

Deep going: Wet or soft ground.

Deep seat: A good position in the saddle.

Depth of girth: Measurement from the withers to elbow.

Dipped back: An unusually concave back between the withers and croup; a condition also known as *swayback*.

Dirt track: A racetrack with a surface of sand and soil.

Dished face: Concave head profile, characteristic of Arabians.

Dishing: Action of the foreleg when the toe is thrown outward in a circular movement; considered a fault.

Dock: The part of the tail the hair grows on and also the hairless underside.

Docking: Amputation of most of the tail and the resetting of the remainder to achieve a permanent high carriage.

Double muscling: Pronounced muscling at the croup in some heavy horse breeds.

Draft: A horse that pulls a vehicle of any type.

Elk lip: Wide, overhanging upper lip.

Entire: Uncastrated male horse, a stallion.

Ergot: Horny growth on the back of the fetlock joint, above the hoof.

Extension: Reaching forward with the legs at various gaits.

Feather: Long hair on the lower legs and fetlocks, usually abundant on draft breeds.

Fender: An adjustable strap that attaches the stirrup to a Western saddle; known as *stirrup leathers* on English saddles.

Fetlock A projection behind and above the hoof that is susceptible to horny growths.

Filly: A female horse under four years of age.

Five-gaited: Saddlebred horse trained to perform the slow gait and rack in addition to the normal walk, trot, and canter.

Flattens out: When a horse fails to respond to the rider.

Flexion: When the horse yields its lower jaw to the pressure of the bit.

Foal: A baby horse—colt, gelding, or filly—up to the age of twelve months.

Forehand: The horse's head, neck, shoulder, withers, and forelegs.

Forelock: An extension of the mane lying between the ears and over the forehead.

Fox trot: A gait where the horse walks with the front feet and trots with the hind, and the hind legs step into the foreprints and slide forward.

Free-going: A horse that willingly moves.

Frog: The elastic, rubbery, horny middle part of a horse's foot, which is shaped like a V and acts as a shock absorber.

Front runner: A horse that usually tries to take the lead from the beginning of a race.

Full mouth: A complete set of permanent teeth, usually by age six.

Gentling: The process of teaching a horse to accept a saddle and rider.

Gait: The pace at which a horse moves. Natural gaits are the walk, trot, canter, and gallop. Some breeds select for additional natural gaits, such as the running walk, fox trot, and tolt (Icelandic). Other horses are trained to perform artificial gaits, including the slow gait and rack.

Gaited horse: A horse bred to have an additional natural gait, usually a running walk, or a horse trained to perform artificial as well as natural gaits.

Gallop: A controlled run; during one segment of this movement, all four feet are off the ground at the same time.

Gelding: A male horse that has been neutered.

Girth: (1) The circumference of the body that is measured from behind the withers around the barrel. (2) The strip of leather that goes under the horse just behind its forelegs and attaches to both sides of the saddle to hold it in place.

Goes short: When a horse indicates lameness by shaking its head up and down.

Good clean bone: When the cannon bone (situated between the knee and the fetlock) is free of splints, and no puffiness exists between the cannon and the tendon.

Grass cutter: A horse that barely lifts its feet off the ground.

Grullo: A smoky or mouse-colored body color with black mane and tail; most often with a black dorsal stripe and black on lower legs.

Gymkhana: A series of mounted games.

Hack: (1) A light riding horse. (2) To go for a ride outdoors.

Half halt: A combined leg and hand aid to encourage the horse to round its spine and be supple.

Half pass: A dressage movement in which the horse goes both forward and sideways in the direction of travel, crossing front and hind legs; also known as a *leg yield.*

Halter: The headgear used for leading and tying up.

Hand: A unit of measurement used to describe a horse's height from the ground to the withers; one hand equals 4 inches.

Handicap: The weight to be carried by a racehorse, estimated so that each horse has an equal opportunity of winning.

Hard hat: An English-style riding helmet.

Hard horse: A tough, enduring horse not susceptible to unsoundness or injury.

Harness: Collective term for the equipment that attaches a horse to a vehicle to be pulled.

Harness horse: Horse used in harness racing; or a horse having the conformation of a harness-racing horse, that is, straighter shoulders.

Head shy: When a horse pulls away from anything that approaches its head.

Headstall: Part of the bridle that goes behind the horse's ears.

Heavy headed: A horse that shows very little response to the bit.

Heavy horse: Any large draft horse; one of muscular build.

Herd bound: A horse unwilling to go out alone or to leave the stable; sometimes also referred to as *stable bound.*

Hindquarters: The body from the flank to the tail and including the hind legs.

Hock: The pointed, backward-bending joint on the horse's hind legs.

Hot: A horse that becomes excited.

Hotblood: A description for Arabians, Barbs, and Thoroughbreds.

Hunt: A sport in which hounds track the scent of a fox, hare, or artificial prey, followed by horses and riders.

Hunter: A horse specifically chosen and trained for the qualities needed to follow a pack of hounds for hours over varying terrain.

Hybrid: Cross between a horse and an ass, zebra, or similar species.

In foal: Description of a pregnant mare.

In front of the bit: When a horse pulls or hangs heavily on the rider's hands with its head outstretched.

Independent seat: Maintaining a firm, balanced position in the saddle without relying on the hands.

In-hand: Not ridden, as in show classes where horses are paraded around the arena in halters.

Irons: Stirrups on English-style saddles; the supports for the rider's feet while in the saddle.

Jog: A slow trot.

Jumping clean: When a show jumper clears an obstacle without touching it.

Knee roll: Padding beneath English saddles to support the rider's leg when jumping.

Leaning on the bit: When a horse attempts to use the rider's hands to support the weight of its forward motion.

Leg up: A boost into the saddle from a pair of helping hands.

Light hands: A delicate use of the reins to control the horse.

Light horse: As opposed to a draft horse or a pony, one that is suitable for pleasure riding.

Light mouth: A horse responsive to the slightest pressure of the reins.

Line breeding: Mating of individual horses with a common ancestor a few generations removed to produce particular features.

Livery: Where privately owned horses are boarded, exercised, and fed.

Loins: Area on either side of the spinal vertebrae, immediately behind the saddle.

Longe (lunge) line: A long rope or tape attached to a mounted or unmounted horse working in a circle around the trainer.

Long reining: A method of training a young, unmounted horse to respond correctly to rein aids.

Lope: In Western riding, a slow canter.

Making a noise: A horse that is not sound.

Mane: Long hair that grows in a line from the top of the horse's head down to its withers.

Mare: A mature female horse over age four.

Milk molars: A foal's baby teeth.

Morning glory: A horse that seems very good during morning workouts, but does not perform well in actual races.

Muck out: Remove droppings and soiled bedding from a horse's stall.

Muzzle: The mouth, nose, and jaws of a horse or pony.

Near side: The left side of the horse.

Off side: The horse's right side.

On the bit: A horse that accepts a constant delicate contact from the rider's hands, is relaxed and supple, and carries its head in a neat vertical plane.

On the flat: Riding in an arena at the walk, trot, and canter, without jumping.

On the leg: A horse that is longer legged than desirable for good conformation.

Outcross: The mating of two horses of different bloodlines.

Over the knee: A conformation fault, where the horse stands with its foreleg bent slightly forward at the knee.

Overhorsed: A rider who is not experienced enough or too small to control a particular horse.

Pacer: A horse that trots with the hind leg and foreleg on the same side moving forward together rather than with a diagonal movement.

Paddle: A conformation fault, where the horse throws its feet out to the side as it trots.

Pedigree: The details of a horse's ancestry, recorded in a studbook.

Pirouette: At a walk or canter, the horse's front legs make a wide circle while the hind legs circle in place (a complete turn on the haunches).

Plenty of bone: Ideally, a measurement of 8½ to 9 inches in circumference around the cannon bone between the knee and pastern.

Plenty of bottom: A horse with stamina and ruggedness.

Points: The external features of the horse, which make up its conformation.

Poll: The area between the horse's ears.

Pony: Any full-grown horse not more than 14.2 hands tall at the withers.

Puller: A horse that responds to the rider's hands by pulling on the reins.

Purebred: A horse of any breed that has no nonpedigree ancestors in its bloodline.

Put to a drive: When a jockey asks a racehorse to give its best speed.

Quarters: The hindquarters of the horse.

Rack: The fast, even gait of the five-gaited American Saddlebred horse; each foot strikes the ground separately in quick succession.

Rank: A horse that refuses to respond to its rider and behaves in an unruly manner.

Rear: To rise up on the hind legs.

Rein back: A command to the horse from a rider or driver to step backward.

Reins: Long leather straps attached to a horse's bridle and used to guide and control the horse.

Roadster: A light, open racing cart with two wheels and a seat.

Roan: A base coat of red, black, or brown that is sprinkled with white hairs or other colors.

School: (1) Train a horse or rider. (2) An enclosed area in which a horse is trained or exercised.

Seat: The position of the rider in the saddle while communicating with the horse.

Shy: When a horse suddenly moves sideways or forward due to fright.

Silks: The cap and blouse worn by a jockey or driver, with colors identifying the mount's owner.

Sire: The male father of a foal.

Sloping shoulder: When the wither is well back to allow maximum length to the shoulder blade.

Socks: The white leg markings on a horse.

Stallion: A mature male horse used for breeding; sometimes referred to as a *stud*.

Stamp his get: When the offspring of a stallion consistently inherit his characteristics.

Stand: When a stallion is made available to mate with mares.

Steeplechase: A horserace with obstacles to be jumped.

Studbook: The registry of the pedigrees of individuals of a particular breed.

Sulky: A light, two-wheeled vehicle used in harness racing.

Sure with his mares: Said of a stallion that successfully impregnates mares in one breeding session.

Tack: Equipment, such as the saddle and bridle, used in riding a horse.

Tack up: Putting the saddle and bridle on the horse.

Touched by the wind: A horse that is not sound.

Trap: A four-wheeled carriage with seats back to back.

Trot: A two-beat gait where the opposite front and back legs move forward at the same time.

Trotter: A horse used in harness racing, usually a Standardbred; see also *pacer*.

True action: When a horse moves its legs in a straight line at all times.

Underhorsed: A rider place on a horse too small for the rider's size or weight.

Wagonette: A carriage with seats facing each other.

Warmblood: A crossbred horse with Thoroughbred or Arabian blood.

Well-set: When the head and neck are in good relation to a sloping shoulder and the head is carried well.

Well-sprung ribs: A large-diameter barrel when the horse is viewed from the front.

Withers: The highest point on the horse's back, located between the shoulder blades near the last hairs of the mane.

Yearling: An immature horse between one and two years of age.

Zebra marks: Stripes on various parts of a horse's coat, indicating ancient breeding.

B

SOURCES FOR EQUINE EQUIPMENT AND SALES

Below is a sampling of available suppliers. Stores open and close frequently, so be sure to consult your Yellow Pages before visiting.

Equine Equipment in New Jersey

BERGEN COUNTY

Ramapo Saddlery & Tack, 135 West Ramapo Avenue, Mahwah; 201-512-1418.

Sport Horse Saddlery, 525 Cedar Hill Avenue, Wyckoff; 201-445-1614.

BURLINGTON COUNTY

Toll Booth Saddle Shop, 2441 Route 206, Eastampton; 888-615-3473; www.tollboothsaddle.com.

CAPE MAY COUNTY

Boot & Bridle, 149 Landing Road, Clermont; 609-624-3054.

CUMBERLAND COUNTY

Bo's Tack, 331 Morton Avenue, Rosenhayn; 856-451-2830.

K-C Stables Tack & Supply, 18 Lawrence Road #1, RR1, Bridgeton; 856-455-5342.

GLOUCESTER COUNTY

Harmony Acres Hoofbeats, 66 Harmony Road, Mickleton; 856-423-4325.

Horse'n Around Tack Shop, 236 Mt. Pleasant Road, Sewell; 856-227-6080 or 856-227-9292.

Sparkle Horse Supplies, Route 45 & K-Mart Plaza, Mantua; 856-468-0304.

Williams Horseman's Supply, 858 Whitehall Road, Williamstown;
856-875-6666.

HUNTERDON COUNTY
Euro-American Saddlery, 176 Highway 202, Ringoes; 908-788-7789;
www.eurosaddlery.com.
Horsemen's Outlet, 37 Molasses Hill Road, Lebanon; 908-238-1200.
Lazy K Distributors, 725 County Road 579, Flemington;
908-782-2293.

MIDDLESEX COUNTY
Roosevelt Sales, 32 Cinder Road, Edison; 732-321-9709.
Stitching Horse Leathers, 4422 Route 27, Box 623, Kingston;
609-921-6854; www.stitching-horse.com.

MONMOUTH COUNTY
Agway, 29 Park Avenue, Englishtown; 732-446-7632.
Al's Tack Supply, 355 Route 33, Englishtown; 800-733-8225.
Gaitway Farm, State Highway 33, Englishtown; 732-446-7100.
Kislins, 8 East Front Street, Red Bank; 732-741-2088.
Rick's Saddle Shop, 40 Main Street, Englishtown; 732-446-4330;
www.saddlesource.com.
Tack Shelter, 41 Highway 34S, Colts Neck; 732-303-0055.

MORRIS COUNTY
Snow Bird Horse Cents, Snowbird Acres Farm, 204 Schooley's
Mountain Road, Long Valley; 908-876-4200;
www.snowbirdacresfarm.com.
Stephan Farm Supplies, 28 Schooley's Mountain Road, Long Valley;
908-876-3580.

OCEAN COUNTY
Hall N' Tack & Hillbilly Haven, 1101 West Cross Street, Lakewood;
732-901-7010.
Horse Tracs, 1561 Route 9, Toms River; 732-557-0900.
Lakewood Riding Center, 406 Cross Street, Lakewood; 732-367-6222.

PASSAIC COUNTY
Barnard's Saddlery, 3209 Route 23 South, Oak Ridge; 800-571-8255;
www.barnardssaddlery.com.

SALEM COUNTY
Cowtown Cowboy Outfitters, 761 Route 40, Woodstown;
888-761-4246 or 856-769-1761; www.cowtowncowboy.com.
Lisa's Tack Shack, 237 Avis Mill Road, Pilesgrove; 856-769-0111.

SOMERSET COUNTY

Beval Saddlery, 10 Park Avenue, Gladstone; 908-234-2828; www.beva.com.

Coach Stop Saddlery, 244 Lamington Road, Bedminster; 908-234-2640.

J & W Custom Stable Supply, 2271 South Branch Road, Neshanic Station; 908-369-6204.

Pets Mart, 145 Pronenda Boulevard, Bridgewater; 732-748-7266.

SUSSEX COUNTY

Spring Valley Tack and Togs, 56 Paulinskill Lake Road, Newton; 973-383-3766.

WARREN COUNTY

Village Saddlery & Harness, 115 Highway 46, Hackettstown; 908-684-3012.

Online Catalogs and Shopping Sources

Back in the Saddle, 570 Turner Drive, Durango, Colo. 81303; 970-385-4575; www.backinthesaddle.com (tack, clothing).

Blue Ribbon Leather Company, 737 Madison Street, Shelbyville, Tenn. 37160; 931-684-8799 (saddle seat tack and clothing).

BMB, 3100 South Meridian Avenue, Wichita, Kans. 67217; 888-262-8225; www.bmbtack.com (mostly western tack supplies).

Chamisa Ridge, 3212-A Richards Lane, Santa Fe, N.M. 87507; 800-743-3188; www.chamisaridge.com (dressage and various New Age products).

Dover Saddlery, 525 Great Road, Littleton, Mass. 01460; 800-989-1500; www.doversaddlery.com (tack and clothing for hunter/jumper, dressage, and combined training).

Horse Country, 60 Alexandria Pike, Warrenton, Va. 20186; 800-882-4868; www.horsecountrylife.com (hunt racing and fox hunting tack and clothing).

Libertyville Saddle Shop, 2121 Temple Drive, Libertyville, Ill, 60048; 800-872-3353; www.saddleshop.com (English and western tack and clothing).

Nasco, 901 Jamesville Avenue, Fort Atkinson, Wis. 53538; 800-558-9595 or 920-563-2446; www.enasco.com (riding, breeding, stable, and farrier equipment).

Pard's Western Shop, 306 North Maple Street, Urbana, Ill. 61802; 800-334-5726; www.pards.com (western tack and apparel).

Riding Right, 7301 S.W. Kable Lane, Portland, Ore. 97224; 800-545-7444; www.ridingright.com (dressage tack and clothing).

Shepler's, 6501 West Kellogg, Wichita, Kans. 67277; 800-835-4004; www.sheplers.com (western tack and apparel).

State Line Tack, Brockport, N.Y. 14420, 800-228-9208; www.statelinetack.com (English and western tack and clothing).

Wiese Equine Supply, 1989 Transit Way, Brockport, N.Y. 14420; 800-869-4373; www.wiese.com (veterinary items and riding supplies).

Horse Auctions in New Jersey

Camelot Auction Company, Cranbury; 609-448-5225; e-mail: camelotauctioncompany@comcat.

Hacker's Auction, Tabernacle; 609-268-0396

C

EQUINE PUBLICATIONS
AND OTHER RESOURCES

Periodicals

All About Horses, 1400 Washington Street, Hoboken, N.J. 07030; 201-798-7800; www.allabouthorsesonline.com. An annual free directory about the New Jersey equine industry.

American Quarter Horse Journal, 1600 Quarter Horse Drive, Amarillo, Tex. 79120; www.aqha.com.

Dressage Today, 656 Quince Orchard Road, Gaithersburg, Md. 20878; 1-800-877-5396; www.primemediamags.com. An excellent magazine filled with information about dressage.

Equine Journal, 103 Roxbury Street, Keene, N.H. 03431; 800-742-9171; www.equinejournal.com. Up-to-date news, in-depth interviews, and features about equestrian activities in New Jersey, New York, Pennsylvania, and surrounding states.

Equus, 656 Quince Orchard Road, Suite 600, Gaithersburg, Md. 20878. A magazine filled with heart-warming stories and good advice on a variety of horse-related topics.

Horse & Rider, 1597 Cole Boulevard, Golden, Colo. 80401. Magazine devoted to Western riding, with discussions on a variety of horse-related topics.

Horse Illustrated, Box 6050, Mission Viejo, Calif. 92690; www.animal-network.com/horses. A magazine filled with training tips on all styles of riding; features on horse behavior, nutritional needs, new products, books, and more.

Horse News, Box 32, Flemington, N.J. 08822; 908-782-4747 ext. 689; www.horsenews-online.com. Monthly news, features, photos, and competition results from major equestrian events in New Jersey, Pennsylvania, Delaware, Maryland, and New York.

Horses U.S.A., Box 6050, Mission Viejo, Calif. 92690; www.animalnet-work.com/usa/horse.

NRHA Reiner, 3000 N.W. 10th Street, Oklahoma City, Okla. 73107; www.nrha.com. The official publication of the National Reining Horse Association.

Practical Horseman, 6405 Flank Drive, Harrisburg, Pa. 17112.

Ride with Bob Avila Magazine, 12 Roszel Road, Suite C-205, Princeton, NJ 08540; www.ridewithbob.com.

Recommended Books

Anderson, C. W. *Book of Horses and Horsemanship*. New York: Macmillan Company, 1963. Great information on equipment, care, training, horsemen's talk, famous horses, riding skills, breeds, and breeding.

Davis, F. W. *Horse Packing in Pictures*. New York: Charles Scribner's Sons, 1975. The best diagrams on knot and hitch tying.

Draper, J., et al. *Horse and Rider*. New York: Barnes and Noble, 1999. A complete encyclopedia of horse breeds, with step-by-step photographs on how to ride, riding equipment, and much more.

Hatley, G. *Horse Camping*. New York: Dial Press, 1981. Expert advice by the founder of the Appaloosa Horse Club.

Hill, C. *Stablekeeping and Trailering Your Horse*. Pownal, Vt.: Storey Books, 1997. Everything a horse owner needs to know about selecting, maintaining, and operating trailers and transporting horses.

Holderness-Roddam, J. *The Horse Companion*. New York: Barrons, 1997. A comprehensive guide to horses, riding skills, equipment, health, grooming, and diet.

Irwin, C. *Horses Don't Lie: The Magic of Horsewhispering*. Saskatchewan, Canada: Horsepower Productions Inc., 1998. The author points out that honesty is important in building a relationship with your horse.

Kellon, E., V.M.D. *Keeping the Older Horse*. Holmes, Pa: Breakthrough Publications, 2000. Using the latest scientific research in wellness and recent developments in nutritional supplements, scientific conditioning, and therapies for chronic ailments, Dr. Kellon describes ways to roll back the clock for your horse.

LaBonte, G. *The Miniature Horse*. Minneapolis: Dillion Press, 1990. Interesting facts about this wonderful, easy-to-care-for breed.

McBane, S., et al. *Horse Facts*. New York: Barnes and Noble, 1994. From the origin of the horse to its uses and breeds, you'll find the information you seek in this well-written, easy-to-understand book.

Price, S. D. *The Horseman's Illustrated Dictionary*. New York: Lyons Press, 2001. With full explanations of more than 1,000 terms and phrases used by horse people past and present, this book is a winner for its clear language and informative illustrations. Horse associations, tack retailers, and Internet resources are also included.

Useful Websites

American Association of Equine Practitioners Online at www.aaep.org/ownereducation. Articles on numerous medical conditions and horse husbandry.

CyberSteed at www.cybersteed.com. Home of the World Equine Health Network.

Equine Info at www.equineinfo.com. Offers links for various horse topics.

HayNet at www.haynet.net. Provides a list of equine resources.

The Horse at www.thehorse.com. Guide to equine health care.

Horseman's Radio Weekly at www.hrwnet.com. Information on the equine industry. Check here for a current radio list or call 800-523-1560.

HorseSafe at www.horsesafe.com (Box 99, Loxahatchee, Fla. 33470; 877-828-4677 or 561-333-0217). A place for horse owners to turn for help in recovering their stolen and missing horses, equipment, and trailers. It also can store in its nationwide database a horse owner's equine-related data, including DNA results and photographs.

Horse Web at www.horseweb.com. Numerous pages of horses, horse products, and related services.

The National Sporting Library at www.nsl.org. Research center and information about equine and related sports.

New Jersey Horse at www.newjerseyhorse.com. Features classifieds, events, news, a directory of farms and businesses throughout the state, equine health issues, quizzes and games, and more.

Ride with Bob at www.ridewithbob.com. Weekly updates on equestrian news.

Index

Page numbers in *italics* indicate images.

About the Author

Arline Zatz is an award-winning travel writer whose thousands of features and photographs have appeared in magazines and newspapers nationally, including *The New York Post, The New York Daily News, The Star-Ledger, New Jersey Outdoors Magazine, Trailer Life Magazine, Sports Illustrated,* and numerous other publications. She is also the author of *New Jersey's Special Places, 30 Bicycle Tours in New Jersey, Best Hikes with Children in New Jersey, New Jersey's Great Gardens,* and *100 Years of Volunteer Wildlife Law Enforcement.* In addition, she is a columnist for the *Becoming an Outdoors-Woman International* newsletter and *Travel World International* magazine.